RECIPES OF BOULESTIN

Selected from
THE BEST OF BOULESTIN, SIMPLE FRENCH
COOKING FOR ENGLISH HOMES, THE EVENING
STANDARD BOOK OF MENUS, WHAT SHALL WE
HAVE TODAY? *and* A SECOND HELPING

Boulestin used to complain, in his early prefaces, that the English took no interest in food and never talked about it: 'Do not be afraid to talk about food. Food which is worth eating is worth discussing. And there is the occult power of words which somehow will develop its qualities. Good food is more important than many so-called "important things of life".' And at the turn of the century in one of his characteristic asides he was castigating the English guest who, after a glorious meal (accompanied by hysteria in the kitchen), 'says not one word, not one about the whole affair. Dish after dish is carelessly eaten as if the performance was rather a bore, the *mot d'ordre* being: not to pay any attention to anything so gross as food.'

Today much of what Boulestin said no longer applies. And this is because of the revolution in English cooking which was largely brought about – certainly started – by Boulestin himself. Far from its being impolite to talk about food, it is the favourite topic of conversation; it is now regarded as almost impolite *not* to comment on one's host's food. As Anne Scott-James has amusingly pointed out: 'At parties, guzzling conversations about the dish one is eating are enjoyed by all; indeed, for there to be no mention of a dish disconcerts the hostess, who assumes it is a failure.'

Boulestin's remarks about the English have been overtaken by events. He need no longer complain of soggy cabbage or indiscriminate white sauce on the Anglo-Saxon table. Moreover, he need no longer warn us against the wrath of our cooks. *We* are our cooks. Most people now do their own cooking – and most people enjoy it. Foreign foods are now obtainable in Britain and every town has its Chinese restaurant and its delicatessen; yams can be bought at Shepherd's Bush and squid in Islington. And English people enjoy doing foreign cooking, above all French cooking, which still produces the best dishes of all.

And so, with all these changes in the British attitudes to food, it is time for a reissue of some of those classic French recipes for the English kitchen which helped to start them off.

Recipes of BOULESTIN

Selected from
THE BEST OF BOULESTIN, SIMPLE FRENCH
COOKING FOR ENGLISH HOMES, THE EVENING
STANDARD BOOK OF MENUS, WHAT SHALL WE
HAVE TODAY? *and* A SECOND HELPING

by X. MARCEL BOULESTIN

ST. MARTIN'S PRESS
NEW YORK

Copyright © 1971 X Marcel Boulestin
All rights reserved. For information, write:
St. Martin's Press, Inc., 175 Fifth Ave., New York, N.Y. 10010
Printed in Great Britain
Library of Congress Catalog Card Number: 76-132188
First published in the United States of America in 1971

AFFILIATED PUBLISHERS: Macmillan & Company, Limited, London —
also at Bombay, Calcutta, Madras and Melbourne — The Macmillan
Company of Canada, Limited, Toronto

'The invitation of a guest implies responsibility for his whole contentment while he is under our roof.' – BRILLAT-SAVARIN.

'If Medicine be ranked among those Arts which dignify their Professors . . . Cookery may lay claim to an equal, if not a superior, distinction; to prevent disease, is surely a more advantageous Art to Mankind, than to cure them.

'Those in whom the Organ of Taste is obtuse, or who have been brought up in the happy habit of being content with humble fare, whose health is so firm that it needs no artificial adjustment; who with the appetite of a Cormorant, have the digestion of an Ostrich, and eagerly devour whatever is set before them without asking questions about what it is or how it has been prepared, may perhaps imagine that the Editor has sometimes been rather overmuch refining the business of the Kitchen.' – MEREDITH, *The Art and Science of Cookery*, unpublished manuscript, *circa* 1849–50.

'Pour manger une dinde truffée il convient d'être deux, je n'en use jamais autrement, ainsi j'en ai aujourd'hui. Nous serons deux, la dinde et moi.'
ABBÉ MORELET

Contents

	Page
Preface	ix
Glossary	xi
CULINARY PROCESSES AND BASIC PREPARATIONS	1
SAUCES AND COMPOUNDED BUTTERS	14
HORS D'ŒUVRES AND LIGHT ENTRÉES	26
SOUPS	34
EGG DISHES	49
FISH	60
MEAT	81
POULTRY AND GAME	110
PICKLED MEATS AND PÂTÉS	135
VEGETABLES	140
SALADS	185
SWEETS	195
SAVOURIES AND CHEESE DISHES	219
CAKES AND JAMS	223
SUNDRIES	228
Descriptive Index	235
Alphabetical Index	244

Preface[*]

FRENCH cooking is not, as some English people seem to think, complicated, rich and expensive. They must not judge it by the *table d'hôte* dinners they may have eaten, either in France or in England, where nondescript dishes boast of pretentious names, and where there is always a white sauce for the fish and a brown one for the meat. This represents only hotel cooking at its worst. Chemistry should be avoided in the home kitchen. In any case, hotel food, even when good, does not represent French cooking.

You may have tasted the cuisine I mean at some wayside inn during the summer months in Touraine or Brittany, or in Perigord, where truffles grow; or even in some of the smaller Paris restaurants, if you knew how to find them. It is the cooking of the French *bourgeois* family, whose favourite proverb is, '*on ne mange bien que chez soi*', and its great merits are excellence, simplicity and cheapness.

I am told that English cooks always tell their mistresses that French cooking is so extravagant because 'everything is cooked in pounds of butter'. This, to begin with, is only partly true. Also they forget, or rather they do not know – how could they, traditionally convinced as they are that a 'joint' must appear on the table at least once a day? – that every scrap is used up; that some of our best dishes are made up of 'remnants'; in fact, that there is no waste whatever in a French kitchen.

I am also assured that many English cooks find cooking a tedious drudgery; perhaps that is because they have no imagination, or are not given a chance of showing any initiative. It certainly must be extraordinarily dull to send up boiled potatoes and boiled cabbage meal after meal. No one could take an interest in work of that kind. They should try experiments with new dishes, they should be encouraged to do so, and neither mistresses nor cooks should despise or fear food of foreign origin, however simple or complicated. They are not afraid of it abroad; in fact, they always remember it pleasantly. Why should not they try to have those same nice dishes in their own houses? It would make their menus more varied and their household bills infinitely lighter.

[*] From *Simple French Cooking for English Homes,* first published in 1923.

Recipes of Boulestin

Such is the simple aim of this little guide. It has no pretensions of being a complete cookery book; indeed, more advice about steak and kidney pie or jam roll pudding would savour of impertinence.

Most of the recipes it contains are simple and the dishes easy to make. I had ample proof of this during the war, when I was mess president of a divisional headquarters mess. We had in succession two soldiers who had never been professional cooks (or even company cooks): one was a bricklayer, the other a greengrocer; they could do nothing except burn their ration of bacon in the lid of a biscuit tin. When on a rest I told them to watch the Frenchwoman who cooked for us; then they tried a few plain things, and in a week or two they were able to make some of the simpler dishes quite well. And luck would have it that the fellow used to bricks and mortar turned out to have a very light hand. Anyhow, a real cook, either amateur or professional, will have no trouble whatever in doing what they did.

I hope that these recipes will not be received by the public at large in the true Forsyte spirit,* but that they will be conducive to what Henry James calls 'the larger latitude'.

I trust that the cook, however temporary, and also the mistress, will take this book to bed at night. The latter will find it better reading even than the Continental Bradshaw: the one shows you all the wonderful places to which you can never afford to go; the other tells you of all the delicious dishes you can all afford to enjoy and give your friends.

It also contains some more elaborate recipes – recipes of quite remarkable local dishes, handed down, like Homer's verses, from generation to generation, which have not found their way yet even into French cookery books, and are entirely ignored by the chefs of international hotels. These, indeed, have been trained to cater for an 'exclusive' cosmopolitan crowd with exclusively cosmopolitan tastes; the result being that you get precisely and hopelessly the same cooking in Paris, London, Monte Carlo, Biarritz or Cairo – good of its kind, good enough in any case for diners who dance between courses and want to be seen rather than eat well. So that it is hoped that this guide will be equally useful to people who have a good cook, to those who only have a plain one, and to those who have not got one at all.

MARCEL BOULESTIN

* 'No Forsyte has given a dinner without providing a saddle of mutton.'—JOHN GALSWORTHY, *The Man of Property*.

Glossary

BOUQUET: *A few sprigs of parsley, one bay leaf and a little thyme; used to flavour soups, sauces, etc. When additional ingredients such as cloves, celery or rosemary are also required for flavouring they will be given in the recipes as, 'a bouquet with . . .'*
JUS: *A sauce obtained by melting and stewing together, very slowly, vegetables, bones, etc. (See p. 7.)*
CONSOMMÉ: *The ordinary clear soup made with beef and vegetables which is used in making other soups and many dishes. (See p. 7.) If necessary, stock or* bouillon *can usually be used instead of consommé, though they will not of course give quite the same flavour or body to a dish.*
ROUX: *Flour cooked with butter. There are two kinds, the brown and the white, and they are the basis of most dishes. (See p. 9.)*
FINES HERBES: *Parsley, chervil and tarragon, finely chopped together.*
COURT-BOUILLON: *Water flavoured with wine, onions, carrots, salt and pepper and a* bouquet, *in which fish is boiled. It is essential to boil all the ingredients together for at least half an hour before putting in the fish, so that the water is saturated with these ingredients and ready to receive it. (See p. 8.)*
JULIENNE: *vegetables cut in very small, thin strips are said to be en julienne.*
FUMET: *Concentrated fish, meat or game stock. (See pp. 8 and 9.)*
BAIN-MARIE: *This corresponds to a double boiler. The simplest way to cook* au bain-marie *is to stand the saucepan containing the ingredients to be cooked in a larger one full of boiling water.*
GRATINER: *To brown in the oven with breadcrumbs and butter.*
CROÛTONS: *Small cubes or triangles of bread fried in butter.*
PURÉE: *Any vegetable mashed to a smooth consistency, with the addition of butter, seasoning, and sometimes milk or jus.*

NOTE

Where Boulestin gives oil or vinegar in a recipe he intends olive oil, and wine or herb vinegar.
Though of course, given in the recipes, salt and pepper are not included in the lists of ingredients, except in the case of (a) salads, and (b) sweets needing salt. Where peppercorns are specified they are listed.

Culinary Processes and Basic Preparations

Here is a story, straight from the Press, crisply encapsulated in an eloquent headline: 'EX-WIFE RETURNS AS COOK'.

'A Curious settlement of a matrimonial tangle is reported from Bellinzona. About a year ago the wife of a wealthy tradesman, named Pulchello, eloped with another man and a divorce followed in due course.

'Mme Pulchello was recently deserted by her lover and left penniless, so she went back to her former husband and asked to be taken back, stating that she had made a great mistake and would do anything to please him.

'Mme Pulchello is an excellent cook, and her ex-husband, who is something of a gourmet, had not forgotten this fact. He had suffered much, gastronomically, since her departure.

'"I am engaged to be married next month," he said to her, "so I cannot take you back as my wife, but you can come back as cook. If you accept I will pay your debts and give you good wages, but there must be no attempts at love-making because you killed my former love for you long ago."

'The divorced wife accepted the offer, taking up her duties the next day.'

*

The whole of cooking can be reduced to two processes: either you want to extract the juice and the goodness out of something, whatever it is, or you want to keep them in that something. Roasting, frying, grilling, braising are all but different examples of the latter process, soup-making and boiling examples of the former one.

[1]

ROASTING

To roast is to cook, say, a piece of meat either by utilizing the direct heat from the fire, that is roasting on a spit, or the indirect heat reflected by the sides of the oven, of a *cocotte* or of a pan. Needless to say, the perfect *rôti* is done on a spit in front of an open fire. It corresponds more or less to grilling, only the piece is always considerably larger, and that is why it must be arranged so that it is revolving continuously, so that it is evenly cooked not only outside, but inside. The chemical reactions otherwise are exactly the same; the fat melts, the albumen and the glucose become carbonized and form a coating which prevents the essential juices from oozing out. In fact, the outside of the meat would become entirely charred if constant basting did not prevent it. And that is the thing to remember, that basting is not only done to prevent the meat from becoming too dry, but it is necessary for the inside of the meat to cook without the outside being entirely carbonized.

This applies to all manner of roasting. The spit is, unfortunately, not much used nowadays in towns for many obvious reasons (I must point out, though, that in many quite big houses of the south-west parts of France there is no oven and all roasting is done in the large open fireplace of the kitchen), so we are reduced to roasting in the oven, where again the regulating of the fire and the basting are necessary to ultimate success. Should the meat be too dry, it must be wrapped up in fat bacon or painted with butter.

Another form of roasting is to cook the meat in a cast-iron *cocotte* or saucepan in which you put a little butter to melt. The meat cooks in this and the roasting is done naturally by the heat radiating from the sides (it should be, again, occasionally turned and basted) of the pan which acts like an oven. Needless to say, the lid should not be used, for if you use it, the steam will condense on it and rain back on the meat, which will be cooked, of course, but steamed and not roasted – which is another story altogether.

According to the piece of meat and to personal taste, meat should cook from seven to ten minutes to the pound for beef, mutton and lamb, and ten to twenty for veal and pork. Experience in this will serve more than rules, but these figures anyhow can be used as a basis.

Should you be in doubt about it the following tests will be found extremely useful:

Beef, Mutton, Game: Prick with a skewer or the point of a sharp knife. If a few drops of pale pink juice come out, the meat is just right.

Veal, Pork, Fowls: The juice should come out quite white. The part to prick in the case of fowls is in the thick part of the leg, which takes longer to cook (the same rule applies to a boiled or steamed fowl). The flesh of veal, pork and fowl must be really cooked, that is, white. Undercooking, which is a matter of taste for other meats, is entirely out of the question.

GRILLING

As for grilling, nothing is more easy, and nothing is more pleasant than a good *grillade*. Of course meat, to be perfect, ought to be grilled on glowing charcoals (which give the meat a special taste and perfume it with the burning essences from the wood), but it is not always easy to arrange a charcoal grill in a modern house; still, you can get quite good results by grilling on coals or gas. Even quite small ranges have a grill, which, in most houses, is usually used only for making toast.

First of all you must get the right piece of meat and it must be fresh meat. Warm the grill and put, say, your steak on it exposed to the full heat of the gas, leave it two or three seconds then paint it over with butter, put it under the gas again, see that the meat is right in the flames where it sizzles and gets crisp and slightly burnt all over for a little while, after which you put the grill back to its normal position and season the meat, then repeat these operations for the other side. Should you think that the inside is not quite cooked enough leave it a little longer but with less gas. By doing this you will have a steak which will compare favourably with one done on charcoals, that is, pleasantly charred on the outsides, red in the middle and with all the essential juices kept in. It is necessary to add that you must not use a fork when turning it over, as if you prick it, the juices will ooze out and get wasted in the pan.

Salmon, sole, lobster and cod are extremely good grilled: in fact, grilling gives your material a chance of being tasted at its best.

FRYING

Frying is, as everybody knows, cooking in boiling fat, this fat being, according to taste, traditions and circumstances, beef fat, lard or oil. Butter is no use for frying, as it burns before it reaches the high temperature required for good frying. Also, the thing you want to fry must contain a great deal of starch, potatoes being the perfect example of an aliment which fries well naturally. It therefore stands to reason that, if you wish to fry something which is not of a starchy nature, you have to prepare it, either by painting it with beaten egg and breadcrumbs (*Escalopes viennoise*, fish) or dipping it in a special batter (apples, salsify, etc.), in the shape of fritters.

In this last case it may be said that the aliment itself is not actually fried, but just cooked, and, so to speak, steamed inside the batter, which itself is really fried. For instance, in a perfect apple fritter the apple is soft and reduced to a pulp, while the outside batter is browned and crisp.

The fat must be really boiling, otherwise the *friture* will be a failure; this point is reached when a little blue smoke appears out of the pan. Also the things you wish to fry must not be too large, and you must not put in too many at the same time, otherwise the drop in the temperature of the fat, caused by their sudden immersion, will prevent their frying as they should.

All things, like potatoes, fritters, etc., should be fried in deep fat in an iron pan with a wire basket. The fat can easily be clarified from time to time, and the best to use for general purposes is a mixture in equal parts, easy to make at home, of pork fat and beef fat, the part round the kidney being the most satisfactory.

When your potatoes or your fish are fried, they must be drained properly (which can be easily done, first with the wire basket, then by putting them on a piece of white paper, which will absorb the fat); then sprinkled with salt and served at once.

BRAISING

In braising, that principle of keeping the essential juices is more important than ever. The meat, trimmed and prepared, must be treated as if for frying or roasting, and it is only when it is well browned all over that you submit it to the process of braising, which is cooking in steam in a closed vessel, on a bed of vegetables, bacon rind, calf's-foot, etc. The steam coming out of all these and the little gravy they have produced at the bottom of the saucepan condenses on the lid and drops back on the meat, giving it at the same time all the pleasing perfumes of the vegetables and of the seasoning you have put in. At a later stage of the process you will then, and only then, add the stock, or the glass of wine, or even the water necessary, so that the whole thing does not become dry, which is the reason why, once you have brought it to a boil, the cooking must go on slowly and on a very low fire. On all these conditions depend the flavour and the goodness of your dish.

BOILING

The boiling of the meat is done with two entirely different aims in view: either you want the goodness, the flavour, to remain in your meat, or you want to extract these from it and impart them to the liquid, which means that either your aim is to eat that piece of meat at its best, or, in the second case, you want to make a soup.

In either case the first thing to do is to add salt to the water, as it prevents certain substances (which become fixed by the salt) from coming out of the meat and disturbing the clearness of the bouillon.

1. When you are preparing a dish which requires the boiling of meat, *blanquette* of veal or *Gigot à l'anglaise,* you must, acting on the principles I have stated above, put the meat in boiling water: the heat closes the meat, and prevents all the nutritive, the sapid, the essential juices from escaping into the water. As the immersion of a large piece of meat brings down the temperature of the water, bring it to a boil again and let it boil just gently so that the meat is not too much disturbed. This is the time, also, to put into the water onions, herbs, spices and pepper, which slowly penetrate the meat and add to its delicate flavour.

(Here I ought to remark on the process known as *court-bouillon,** which is water flavoured with wine, salt and pepper, onion, carrot, and a *bouquet,* in which you boil fish. It is essential to boil all these together quite half an hour before you put in the fish, so that the water is saturated with these ingredients and ready to receive it. If you put the fish in at the same time, as fish does not take so long to cook, it will be ready before the herbs have time to exude their flavour; in fact, you might just as well boil it in plain water.)

2. For soup making you put, of course, the meat in cold water, so that all the goodness it contains oozes out little by little; this takes place during the process of slow boiling, which is a phenomenon more or less similar to the one of digestion in the stomach. At the end of the six or seven hours which are required for a really good *bouillon,* the meat is just a mass of tasteless, fibrous material, out of which all flavour has gone (although it is used sometimes for the making of dishes, with the addition of seasoning, sauces, etc.).

An example of a perfect type of boiled meat is a leg of mutton cooked as we say in France, *à l'anglaise.* Carefully done, this dish is delicious, and the meat far more flavoured and tender than that of roast mutton.

* See p. 8.

LIAISONS

A liaison or 'binding' is an operation which consists in thickening a liquid by means of flour, butter, cream or yolk of egg, and in binding together during this process and by the addition of this new medium all sorts of elements contained in the liquid. It is a very complex chemical operation; it is also, especially in the form of the *roux*, one of the simplest and most necessary culinary operations.

There is no need to insist on the mechanism of these phenomena or to explain the chemical reactions which take place, and I shall just explain their interest and their usefulness from the cook's point of view.

The well-known *roux*, either brown or white, is easy enough to make. You melt some butter in a saucepan, and add, when it is melted, about the same quantity of flour, stirring all the time; the flour begins to cook and you add hot milk, chicken stock or veal stock, according to your requirements, the results being *Béchamel, Veloutè* or sauce for *blanquette*; or you let the flour get brown and you obtain a brown *roux*, your basis for other sauces of a darker colour.

The other liaisons are, on the other hand, usually done at the end of the cooking of the soup or the sauce. In the liaison with flour the thickening is due to the fact that the flour is thoroughly well mixed with a little water; when you drop the mixture into the boiling soup, of course, the starch swells and the soup thickens.

The liaison with cream is based on a slightly different principle. In the case of a soup, it simply thickens and also adds its own pleasing rich taste to a liquid which, by itself, would probably be a little thin. In the case of a sauce, the thickening is due to the cream being allowed to boil and reduce.

The liaison with yolk of egg thickens even more, also colours and gives taste. The yolk of egg is diluted with a little of the liquid, soup or sauce, and put into it while it is at the boiling-point. But it must not be allowed to boil after that or the yolk would coagulate, and, instead of being 'bound', the mixture, owing to the yolk getting hard, would be curdled.

In all these liaisons it is, of course, essential to stir and whip well, so that the mixing is absolutely smooth and homogeneous. They all have the same object, and perform, as I have said, a dual operation: they fix an unstable mixture, thicken a liquid: also they add to the richness and the smoothness of the finished article. This is, of course, the only part of the operation in which the cook is interested, but if she knows the prin-

CULINARY PROCESSES AND BASIC PREPARATIONS

ciples of a liaison and the chemical reactions they involve, it will no doubt be more easy for her to get them right.

CONSOMMÉ *Clear Soup*

For making a really good (good from all points of view) clear soup you must follow some important rules. Slow and long cooking is absolutely necessary, and the secret is in the skimming.

You put your beef (four pounds or so of brisket of beef will make eight portions of soup, or a little more) in cold salted water (allowing for reduction), and this must be brought up *very slowly* to the boil; this slow process helps the forming of the scum, which must be frequently removed; indeed, it is advisable when the water is near the boiling-point to retard it by adding a tablespoonful of cold water.

The more scum you produce and get rid of, the clearer and the better your soup will be; but if you do not take this little trouble at the beginning, nothing later will clarify it properly; also the soup will not be well flavoured, as the essential juices kept in by the matter which ought to have come out as scum will remain in the meat – which will also, as a result, be tougher when you want to use it for a dish. All this cannot be emphasized too much.

Having skimmed well, you add the vegetables; two or three carrots, two turnips, one tomato, a little celery, two onions stuck with a clove, one or two leeks and the classical *bouquet* and pepper. (Should you have by you bones or carcase of fowl, put them in now.) Bring to the boil and let it simmer *slowly* and *regularly* for about five hours. Pass through a strainer and remove the fat.

(Cooks in a hurry can often use stock or *bouillon* cubes instead of consommé, though these will not of course give the same flavour or body to a dish.)

§ *Beef; chicken; carrots; turnips; celery; tomato; onions; leeks; thyme; bayleaf; parsley; cloves.*

JUS *Gravy*

Put in a saucepan carrots and onions cut in slices, enough to cover the bottom of the saucepan; then put in any odd bones and skins of any meat you may have, legs of chicken, one calf's foot, salt and pepper. Cover the saucepan and put it over a moderate fire. When all the ingredients have started melting, add a good deal of water and let it simmer for quite eight or ten hours till it is very much reduced. Skim off the fat and pass through a sieve. It must have the consistency of good milk.

§ *Carrots; onions; leftovers of meat and poultry; calf's foot.*

COURT-BOUILLON *Court-Bouillon*

Fish should always be cooked in what is called a *court-bouillon*.

Court-bouillon is water to which are added carrots and onions cut finely, a *bouquet*, salt and pepper (trimmings of mushrooms if you have some by you), and either white wine or vinegar.

There should be enough liquid to cover the fish, and the proportion should be a tablespoonful of vinegar or a port-glassful of dry white wine to two pints of water. Perfectly good results are obtained with vinegar, which, of course, hardly adds to the expense, and wine need only be used if there is any left in the house.

As fish cooks very quickly, you must begin by cooking the *court-bouillon* by itself. Bring it to the boil and cook for half an hour, for if you do not take that precaution, and put the fish in from the beginning, it will be cooked before the stock itself has had time to be perfumed by the ingredients you have put in and the fish will not have the desired added flavour.

Have the *court-bouillon* at the boiling-point, put in your fish, bring to the boil again, and the moment it boils decrease the fire, so that it just simmers. The slow cooking will prevent the fish from breaking into pieces.

The time depends very much on the size of the fish; you must allow about ten minutes to a pound for a large fish, while small things like fillets of sole only take five minutes. Do not take the fish out of the stock till you are ready to serve it, and if some of the *court-bouillon* is required as basis for the sauce to go with the fish, leave enough with the fish so that it does not become dry while the sauce is being prepared.

The *court-bouillon* is useful for all sorts of delicious sauces. They are all quite easy to make once you have the starting point right.

§ *Carrots; onions;* bouquet; *mushrooms; white wine or vinegar; the fish to be cooked in it.*

FUMET *Concentrated stock*

Fumets, which are extremely useful in the kitchen, can be made easily with either meat or fish. They help a great deal in the preparation of all sorts of sauces, and as they are made mostly with bones and trimmings, they can be prepared whenever there is an opportunity.

The liquid, such as it is, is in these cases reduced by three-quarters to a well-flavoured essence which can be used when wanted. Strained through a muslin, it will keep in a cool place for several days.

CULINARY PROCESSES AND BASIC PREPARATIONS

FUMET DE POISSON *Fumet of Fish*

We can do exactly the same preparation for essence of fish, taking as a starting point the *court-bouillon,* already explained, in which we have cooked our fish.

If, for instance, we have a dish of fillets of sole, we cook, we 'poach' our fillets in a *court-bouillon,* but we add to the strength of this by adding the bone, head and trimming of the fish. When the fillets are cooked we keep them hot in some of the *court-bouillon,* and we reduce the rest by three-quarters; strain this liquor and use it when wanted.

§ Court-bouillon; *bone; head and trimmings of fish.*

FUMET DE GIBIER *Fumet of Game*

Take carcase and bones of birds, put them in a saucepan with just enough water to cover them, salt, pepper, one carrot and one onion cut in slices, a bouquet with a clove. Bring to the boil, skim, and cook on a slow fire, skimming again if necessary, till it has reduced by three-quarters, and strain. It is used for the making of game dishes.

§ *Carcase and bones of game; carrot; onion;* bouquet; *clove.*

ROUX *Flour and Butter, White or Brown*

There is in French cooking one preparation which is the basis of many dishes and of practically all sauces, that is the *roux.*

Take a certain quantity of butter and melt it in a saucepan; when it is at the foaming stage put in with a wooden spoon the same quantity of flour and cook, stirring a few seconds over the fire.

This preliminary cooking is very important, as it transforms the flour, cooks the starch, and begins the good work for the sauce to be made.

There are two *roux;* the white, which is used for making white sauces, and the brown (obtained by cooking the flour a few seconds more, when it becomes coloured), used for brown sauces.

With the white *roux* we make the two great basic sauces, the *Béchamel* and the *Velouté,* which comes in constantly in the making of sauces and dishes.

§ *Butter; flour.*

SAUCE BÉCHAMEL *Béchamel Sauce*

Having prepared the white *roux,* add, little by little, hot milk. The first tablespoonful put in will transform the *roux* into a kind of paste. Add more milk, whipping well till it is quite smooth and thin. Add salt and pepper and a flavouring of grated nutmeg, bring to the boil, and let it simmer.

In about a quarter of an hour it will be thick again. Add more milk and go on cooking, and so on till you have the quantity required. It should cook altogether for about twenty-five minutes.

About quantities: to a piece of butter the size of a small egg and the same amount of flour you can add little by little about a pint of milk. Increase seasoning as you increase the quantity of liquid.

A *Béchamel* properly whipped should not be in the least lumpy; anyhow, it is easy enough to be quite certain that the sauce is perfectly smooth. Pass it through a fine strainer before using.

Some people recommend putting in pieces of onions, of carrots, a *bouquet*, but this is not at all necessary. On the other hand, a little grated nutmeg is indispensable.

§ Roux; *milk; nutmeg.*

VELOUTÉ *Velouté*

The other main basic sauce, the *Velouté,* is prepared in the same way as the *Béchamel* sauce.

Having your white *roux* ready you add to it, little by little, instead of milk, stock, whipping well. Bring to the boil, let it thicken, thin it with more stock, and cook more till you have the right quantity. Finish by passing through a strainer.

The stock used is according to the dish, chicken stock for a chicken dish, veal stock for a veal dish, fish stock for a fish dish.

§ Roux; *stock.*

SAUCES BRUNES *Brown Sauces*

A very good foundation for brown sauces is a *roux* to which you add at the beginning a little chopped onion; while the flour gets cooked the onion becomes browned, and you add a tablespoonful or two of meat stock.

You have then your basis ready for the addition of tomato sauce, vinegar and gherkins, or Madeira, according to the recipe of whatever dish (with a brown sauce) you have to make.

§ Roux; *onion; stock.*

Sauces like Hollandaise, Mouselline, Béarnaise, *and White Butter, whose basis is butter or butter and yolk of egg, must never reach boiling-point. Otherwise they will melt or curdle.*

BATTER FOR FRYING

The following is a very simple and good recipe for a frying batter which can be used for all sorts of things.

CULINARY PROCESSES AND BASIC PREPARATIONS

Take half a pound of sifted flour, put it in a basin, make a hole in the middle, and put in it, in succession, one egg, a pinch of salt, and one ounce of melted butter. Mix well, add tepid water, little by little, till the batter has the consistency of thin cream. See that it is very smooth. This should be prepared at least one hour before using.

If this batter is wanted for fruit fritters, add a pudding-spoonful of sugar and a drop of rum or brandy. Some people put in the yolk of egg first and add later the white whipped to a stiff froth.

It can even be used for making pancakes, in which case a tablespoonful of milk or cream can be added.

§ *Flour; egg; butter. For fruit fritters, add sugar and rum or brandy; for pancakes add milk or cream.*

PATISSERIE CROQUANTE *Shortcrust Pastry*

Rub with the fingers 2 oz of lard and 2 oz of butter (or a fraction more) into half a pound of flour. When the result has the appearance of breadcrumbs, add a small cup of cold water, or less, to make a manageable dough when mixed with a wooden spoon. Place the dough on a floured pastry-board and roll out to the required shape and thickness with a floured rolling-pin. To preserve lightness, try to roll only once. If a flan-case is being prepared, put in a greased shallow round tin and prick with a fork all over the bottom to prevent rising. Then bake in a hot oven for about twenty minutes or until very pale brown.

§ *Lard; butter; flour.*

PÂTÉ FEUILLETÉE *Puff Pastry*

Take a quarter of a pound of flour, a quarter of a pound of fresh butter, half a tumblerful of water, a liqueur glass of rum, and a pinch of salt.

Put the flour on the board, make a hole in the middle, put in salt, rum, and a piece of butter the size of a walnut. Add the water little by little. Work it well with your hand quickly. Make a ball of the batter, roll it in flour, make a few cuts with a knife, wrap it in a cloth, and let it rest a quarter of an hour.

After which you roll the batter with the rolling-pin, put in the middle the rest of the butter and cover it with the batter.

Put it on the board and roll it lightly; fold it again and roll. Cover with a cloth and let it rest a quarter of an hour. Do this operation twice more with an interval of fifteen minutes. It is ready for use.

§ *Flour; butter; rum.*

BOUQUET

A *bouquet* is composed of a few sprigs of parsley, one bay leaf and a little thyme; it is constantly used for soups, dishes and sauces. When additional ingredients such as cloves, celery or rosemary are also required for flavouring, these will be given in the recipes as, 'a *bouquet* with...'

§ *Parsley; bay leaf; thyme.*

FINES HERBES

These are, chopped finely together, parsley, chervil and tarragon; they are used mostly in salads. Spring onions chopped are often added to them for lettuce salad, and a little garlic (rubbed on the bowl or on a piece of breadcrust) for chicory.

§ *Parsley; chervil; tarragon. Spring onions or garlic can be added.*

MIXED SPICE

Mixed spice can easily be prepared at home without expense or trouble and kept in a tin box or a jar with a really tight cork. The point about mixed spice is the happy balance of flavours. The following mixture will serve practically all purposes:

Pound together finely in a mortar, three parts of peppercorns (half white, half black) and one part composed of cloves, nutmeg, cinnamon, dry thyme and bay leaf; add a very small amount of mace, mix well, and keep in a dry place.

§ *Peppercorns; cloves; nutmeg; cinnamon; dried thyme; bay leaf; mace.*

HERB VINEGAR

Put in a glazed earthenware jar two handfuls of tarragon, one of chervil and mustard and cress mixed, one clove of garlic, one small green (or red) pepper. Pour over this three bottles of wine vinegar (either white or red), cover the pot and let the mixture infuse for ten days. Decant it and put into bottles.

§ *Tarragon; chervil; mustard and cress; garlic; green pepper; wine vinegar.*

*

PITFALLS

The dangerous person in the kitchen is the one who goes rigidly by weights, measurements, thermometers and scales.

I would say once more that all these scientific implements are not of much use, the only exception being for making pastry and jams, where exact weights are important. The only other general rule – and a rather vague one – is that one roasts about, 'twenty minutes to the pound', as the saying goes. Beyond that – well, beyond that there is nothing certain, and the possibilities are infinite, since so many things have to be considered.

The truth is that one cannot possibly give an exact recipe; it is the part of the cook to take it in and work on it in an intelligent way. Having first tasted what she is doing, she must adapt the recipe to the strength of the gas, the acidity of her vinegar, the size of her vegetables, the quality and the freshness of her meat. If she does this, she is safe, safe even from an exact (and bad) recipe, such as the one I saw once, which said, 'put in the tournedos and cook for hal an hour', for, if she watches, she will see that after ten minutes the tournedos is ready and she certainly will not give it the generous extra twenty minutes, which would reduce it to the consistency of burnt indiarubber.

*

Sauces and Compounded Butters

LITERATURE AND COOKING

It is interesting to see in André Gide's journal the genesis of the elements in his famous novels, the incidents in his own life, the dramas in his soul, the thoughts in his mind which, rearranged, queried, explored, discussed, submitted to the indispensable and unavoidable literary transposition, boiled down, mixed, reduced, seasoned with invented details, make an harmonious and homogeneous work.

Exactly the same thing happens in cooking. The process is the same, the result similar. Every day the cook composes, creates, makes chemical reactions; the raw materials are transformed, flavours are blended, smells altered, miracles performed – for a delicate sauce, the smoothness of which is due only to an unstable liaison subject to rigid rules, is nothing short of a miracle.

It is very wonderful to see (and to taste) a perfect chicken poêle à la crème, but it is more wonderful still to see on a kitchen table a raw chicken, a pint of wine, a bowl of cream, and a bunch of herbs – the unadorned facts of the novelist – and to realize how it is done, to be able to do it. That is where the cook is an artist, interesting and interested. And if not, the novel, the poem, is but a pot-boiler and of no value to the cook or to the world, of no consequence to us, well summated by the sweeping French expression, Ça n'existe pas.

*

BEURRE FONDU *Melted Butter*

Melted Butter sauce, which seems simple enough, can easily be a failure.

The ordinary way is to melt the butter, divided in small pieces, slowly and stop it the moment it has melted – that is while it is still creamy and cloudy.

The other way is to put in a small saucepan the whole amount of butter you require in one piece and to melt it quickly on a fierce fire, stirring all the time.

In either case the result ought to be the same – that is, a luscious, creamy and cloudy melted butter. Needless to say, the butter must not reach the boiling point, or, indeed, get too hot. This cannot be emphasized too much.

§ *Butter.*

BEURRE NOIR *Black Butter*

Melt butter on a quick fire till it gets black without getting burnt. Add a few capers.

§ *Butter; capers.*

SAUCE AU BEURRE NOIR *Black Butter Sauce*

Melt an ounce of butter in a pan. When it is becoming brown add a little vinegar and chopped parsley. Pour over the eggs or the fish in the serving-dish. Some people add a few capers.

§ *Butter; vinegar; parsley; capers.*

BEURRE MAÎTRE D'HÔTEL *Maître d'Hôtel Butter*

Pound a piece of butter the size of an egg till it is like soft ointment, add a pudding-spoonful of chopped parsley and a drop of lemon juice. Spread over the steak when in the serving-dish.

§ *Butter; parsley; lemon juice.*

SAUCE MAÎTRE D'HÔTEL *Maître d'Hôtel Sauce*

Put a good piece of butter in a small saucepan with a drop of water and the juice of a lemon; cook one minute and add chopped parsley and a little salt.

§ *Butter; parsley; lemon juice.*

BEURRE MEUNIÈRE *Meunière Butter*

It is always advisable when cooking anything (fish, vegetables, etc.) which is to be served *Meunière* not to put in the serving dish the butter which has been used for the cooking, as it will be found too oily and black by the time the things are properly cooked.

So we throw away that butter and replace it by a small piece of fresh butter (with the addition of a little lemon juice), to be poured over the fish or vegetables in the serving dish when it has just reached the foaming stage.

In a good dish of something *Meunière* the butter must be still foaming when it arrives on the table.

§ *Butter; lemon juice.*

SAUCE AU BEURRE BLANC   *White Butter Sauce*

It requires about one ounce of butter for each person, and for some reason is better if made with butter slightly salt. First reduce in a small saucepan a tablespoonful of vinegar in which you put two shallots finely chopped. Then add the butter (in pieces or whole), and melt it (slowly or quickly), stirring with a wooden spoon, exactly as for ordinary melted butter. Stop and remove it when it is melted but still creamy and whitish. Serve either over the fish or in a sauceboat.

You can increase the quantity of vinegar if you like the sauce fairly sharp, but, in any case, it must be reduced almost to nothing.

§ *Butter; vinegar; shallots.*

*

THE IMPORTANCE OF TASTING

However good the cook may be, the dish she sends may be all wrong if she has neglected to fulfil one of her most important duties – tasting; tasting at the beginning, as she goes along, at the end.

It is absolutely indispensable and far more reliable – that is, if she has any palate at all – than measures and weights. Then she will avoid these dreary dishes – sauces with too little salt, soups hot with pepper. She must especially remember that a good dish, otherwise well prepared, may be spoilt if the right quantity of salt is not there at the time she cooks, to bring out the flavour properly. No amount of salt added on the dinner table will correct it.

The dish must be rather under-seasoned to begin with, and she can correct it at a later stage, but if there is too much seasoning it is almost impossible to put it right. The cook must not forget that, in reducing, a liquid reduces but not the amount of salt and pepper put into that liquid, so that the finished dish properly reduced is bound to be more seasoned than when it started.

And perhaps it would be better if the habit of tasting were also observed by the diners; this practice of adding salt and pepper at the table before tasting is rather dangerous. If the dish is correctly seasoned it certainly spoils it.

*

SAUCE MORNAY   *Mornay Sauce*

Add to hot *Béchamel** a yolk of egg and grated cheese (the best

* See p. 9.

is Parmesan and Gruyère in equal parts). Pour this over whatever you want to serve, fillets of sole, turbot, endives, boiled potatoes, poached eggs. Brown under a grill or in the oven, and serve in the same dish.

§ Béchamel *sauce* (roux, *milk, nutmeg*); *yolk of egg; cheese.*

SAUCE POULETTE   *Poulette Sauce*

Add to a *Béchamel* a yolk of egg diluted in a little vinegar; serve with French beans, new potatoes, mussels, seakale, etc. It must not boil after the addition of the yolk of egg.

§ Béchamel *sauce* (roux, *milk, nutmeg*); *yolk of egg, vinegar.*

SAUCE À L'INDIENNE   *Curry Sauce*

This is a *Béchamel* to which you add a flavouring of curry powder. Cook for ten minutes more and serve. The quantity of curry powder is according to personal taste.

§ Béchamel *sauce* (roux, *milk, nutmeg*); *curry powder.*

SAUCE HOLLANDAISE   *Hollandaise Sauce*

Put in a small saucepan a few peppercorns coarsely broken, a pinch of salt and two tablespoonfuls of vinegar. Bring to the boil, reduce by three-quarters and let it get cool. Add then the yolks of two eggs, a few small pieces of butter and a teaspoonful of cold water.

Cook on a slow fire (or, better still, standing in hot water), whipping well till it begins to thicken; after that add little pieces of butter, one by one, still whipping well, till you have the required quantity of sauce. Should it become too thick or show a tendency to curdling add also a little more cold water. Pass the sauce through a strainer or squeeze through a muslin.

§ *Vinegar; peppercorns; yolks of egg; butter.*

SAUCE BÉARNAISE   *Béarnaise Sauce*

This sauce goes admirably with grilled fish, steaks and such like. It is not difficult to make but requires attention, as it will curdle if allowed to become too hot.

Put in a small saucepan two tablespoonfuls of wine vinegar, two chopped shallots and a sprig of tarragon. Bring to the boil and reduce it almost to nothing. Let it get cool. Add then two yolks of eggs, a drop of cold water, and little by little small pieces of butter. Do this whipping and, with the small saucepan standing in another one with boiling water, add butter till you have enough sauce, then add salt and pepper and pass through a fine strainer into a bowl. Stand the bowl in boiling water, add a last piece of butter, chopped tarragon and parsley and serve.

§ *Wine vinegar; shallots; tarragon; yolks of egg; butter; parsley.*

SAUCE MOUSSELINE *Mousseline Sauce*

A delicious sauce to serve with boiled fish, simpler than *Hollandaise*, better than white sauce. Put in a small pudding bowl two yolks of egg, a little lemon juice and a drop of cold water; add two ounces of butter in small pieces. Stand the bowl in a saucepan full of boiling water and stir quickly with a wooden spoon; in a minute or two the sauce will be like a soft cream, as it should be.

First the yolks thicken, then the butter melts, binding it all; it is essential that this sauce should not be more than warm, otherwise it will curdle; if it just curdles you can still save it by adding two or three drops of cold water and stirring quickly. Should you want more sauce, stir in little pieces of butter one by one. The quantity of lemon juice is a question of taste; for seasoning, salt only; can be made very successfully with salt butter.

§ *Yolks of egg; lemon juice; butter.*

SAUCE DE MOUTARDE *Mustard Sauce*

Make first a *Mousseline* sauce and stir in lightly mustard, either English or French, according to taste.

§ *Mousseline sauce (egg yolks, lemon juice, butter); mustard.*

SAUCE MAYONNAISE *Mayonnaise*

About the Mayonnaise, which is often half a failure, several important things should be remembered. It should be made in a bowl previously washed with warm water, and very carefully; the yolks, one, two or three, according to the quantity of sauce wanted, well broken first with a wooden spoon, and salt, pepper, and a few drops of vinegar added. Then the oil should be put in, drop by drop and very slowly at first.

When after a time the sauce begins to thicken too much, this is the moment to add the proper quantity of vinegar, after which you go on adding oil till it is finished. For two yolks you must reckon about a pint of oil and not more than a tablespoonful of vinegar.

§ *Egg yolks; vinegar; oil.*

SAUCES AND COMPOUNDED BUTTERS

SAUCE TARTARE *Tartare Sauce*

This is a mayonnaise to which are added, finely chopped, gherkins, capers, parsley (sometimes shallots) and a little mustard.

§ *Mayonnaise (egg yolks, vinegar, oil); gherkins; capers; parsley; mustard, shallots can be added.*

SAUCE VERTE *Green Sauce*

Have a handful of spinach leaves, one of watercress, a little parsley and tarragon. Wash these, drain them well and pound them through a fine sieve. Add the purée thus obtained to a mayonnaise, well seasoned, and mix well.

These proportions of herbs would give enough colour and taste to the quantity of mayonnaise required for four people.

Some people boil the herbs for five minutes, refresh them under the cold tap, pound them and squeeze them through a cloth. It makes an even smoother sauce, but it is not necessary. On the other hand, simply chopping them would not be enough; you do not want any pieces in the sauce.

§ *Mayonnaise (eggs, vinegar, oil); spinach; watercress; parsley; tarragon.*

SAUCE DE RAIFORT *Horseradish Sauce*

Put in a small saucepan a tablespoonful of vinegar and two chopped shallots. Reduce by half, add finely-grated horseradish and a small cup of cream. Bring to the boil, and let it simmer for a quarter of an hour, at the end of which the sauce has thickened properly. It should be quite thick. It can be passed through a strainer or not, according to taste, and served hot or cold.

§ *Vinegar; shallots; horseradish; cream.*

SAUCE DE CÉLERI *Celery Sauce*

Use for this the celery leaves which are not quite good enough to be eaten raw, wash them well, remove the stringy parts and chop finely, add one small onion, also finely chopped, and cook these in a small saucepan with just enough butter to melt the mixture slowly and without getting browned. When it is quite soft add the same quantity of flour as you had of butter, stir in well and cook one minute; then thin it to the proper consistency of a sauce by adding hot milk and cook slowly for about twenty minutes. See that it is well seasoned and rub through a sieve. Serve in a sauceboat.

§ *Celery; onion; butter; flour; milk.*

SAUCE DE FENOUIL *Fennel Sauce*

Blanch a head of fennel for a few minutes in hot salted water, drain it well, chop it finely and mix it with either a *Béchamel* or a *Mousseline* sauce. Serve with fish. It goes particularly well with salmon and mackerel. The fish can be either boiled in the ordinary way in a *court-bouillon*, or grilled; in this case it should be grilled resting on a few leaves of fennel, which will flavour the fish when grilling.

§ Béchamel *sauce (roux, milk, nutmeg)* or Mousseline *sauce (eggs, lemon juice, butter); fennel.*

SAUCE LANDAISE *Landaise Sauce*

A sauce from the south-west of France to serve with cold meat or boiled fish. Take two sweet peppers or pimentos, cut them in small dice and cook them in pork fat or oil for a few minutes; add two or three tomatoes (skin and pips removed), also cut in small pieces, and a *bouquet* with a little rosemary; cook slowly till reduced almost to a pulp, add then two gherkins chopped finely, a tablespoonful of vinegar; remove the *bouquet* and cook for two minutes more. See that it is well seasoned and serve hot in a sauceboat.

§ *Pimentos; tomatoes;* bouquet *with rosemary; gherkins; vinegar; pork fat or oil.*

SAUCE DIABLE, I *Devil Sauce, I*

Cook in a little butter one small onion, two shallots and a rasher of bacon chopped together, add a *bouquet* and a tablespoonful of vinegar. Reduce by a quarter and add a tablespoonful of tomato purée, one of meat stock, salt and pepper. Bring to the boil, cook for five minutes and squeeze through muslin or a strainer into a hot sauceboat. Should be highly spiced.

§ *Butter; onion; shallots; bacon;* bouquet; *vinegar; tomato purée; meat stock.*

SAUCE DIABLE II *Devil Sauce, II*

Cook in a little butter one small onion, two shallots and a little bacon chopped together; add a glass of white wine and a little wine vinegar, also a *bouquet;* let it reduce by a quarter, after which you add a small quantity of veal stock, a little tomato purée, salt and pepper, and a sprinkling of Cayenne pepper; bring to the boil and cook for about five minutes; see that it is highly seasoned and squeeze through muslin into a hot sauceboat.

§ *Butter; onion; shallots; bacon; white wine; wine vinegar;* bouquet; *veal stock; tomato purée; Cayenne.*

SAUCES AND COMPOUNDED BUTTERS

SUGO *Meat Sauce*

Is the jus or sauce often served with paste or rice. Cook together a marrow-bone, a few chicken livers, a little veal, all finely chopped; add parsley, celery, carrots, onion, tomato, dried mushrooms, salt and pepper, also a little flour. Cook about a quarter of an hour, then add half a glass of dry white wine and the same quantity of stock. Let the sauce simmer till it has thickened and the pieces of meat and liver have almost melted. Pass through a fine hair sieve or a muslin.

§ *Marrow bone; chicken livers; veal; parsley; celery; carrots; onion; tomato; dried mushrooms; flour; dry white wine.*

SAUCE AUX NOIX *Italian Sauce with Crushed Walnuts*

This is a very pleasant sauce to serve with spaghetti; it has a delicious and unusual flavour. Peel a handful of walnuts and pound them well in a mortar. Fry in oil a very small quantity of garlic and parsley finely chopped together; add the pounded walnuts, cook a little, but do not brown, moisten with a little olive oil and very little boiling water. Mix well with the hot spaghetti and serve immediately.

§ *Walnuts; garlic; parsley; olive oil.*

SAUCE TOMATE, I *Tomato Sauce, I*

Cut four tomatoes in quarters, remove the seeds, put the quarters in a small saucepan with one carrot and one onion finely chopped, salt and pepper; cover with water and bring to the boil; cook it well, then squeeze through a muslin. Add a brown *roux* – a little stock, a drop of wine vinegar and cook again, whipping well, to proper consistency. Add a few small pieces of butter at the last minute. Should be fairly thick.

§ *Tomatoes; carrot; onion; brown* roux; *stock; wine vinegar; butter.*

SAUCE TOMATE, II *Tomato Sauce, II*

Add to a little brown *roux* some tinned *purée* of tomatoes, a tablespoonful of *bouillon*, salt, pepper, very little grated nutmeg, a piece of butter the size of a walnut, and let it simmer for ten minutes.

§ *Brown* roux; *tinned tomato purée;* bouillon; *nutmeg; butter.*

SAUCE AUX CAPRES *Caper Sauce*

Put in a saucepan a good piece of butter, a puddingspoonful of flour, add salt and water and stir with a wooden spoon over a slow fire till nearly boiling; then add a few small pieces of butter and mix well. The sauce should have the consistency of cream. Add capers.

§ *Butter; flour; capers.*

SAUCE PIQUANTE, I Piquante Sauce, I

Chop two shallots, put them in a wineglassful of vinegar, with two tablespoonfuls of consommé, let it reduce, add chopped gherkins and capers, salt and pepper.

§ *Consommé; shallots; vinegar; gherkins; capers.*

SAUCE PIQUANTE, II Piquante Sauce, II

Prepare as before, but add at the beginning (instead of gherkins later) a few heads of garlic cut in four pieces. Cook slowly for one hour with pepper and salt.

§ *Consommé; shallots; vinegar; capers; garlic.*

SAUCE SOUBISE Soubise Sauce

Cut two large onions, cook them in half water, half milk, salt, and a little nutmeg. When well cooked pass through a sieve and mix with a *Béchamel* sauce. Stir well and boil for a minute or two.

§ *Onions, milk; nutmeg;* Béchamel *sauce (roux, milk, nutmeg).*

SAUCE AU SAFRAN Saffron Sauce

Make a white *roux* and prepare like a *Béchamel* sauce, adding at the time of mixing a pinch of red saffron. Cook for twenty minutes. Add a few pieces of butter and pass through a sieve.

§ *Roux; nutmeg; milk; saffron; butter.*

SAUCE BORDELAISE Bordelaise Sauce (For hare)

Bring to the boil a quarter of a pint of wine vinegar; add a small clove or garlic finely chopped and reduce the vinegar by half. Put in the liver, also chopped, then the blood of the hare, stirring over a moderate fire. Add the gravy from the roast hare and squeeze through a strainer.

§ *Wine vinegar; garlic; hare's liver; hare's blood; gravy from hare.*

SAUCE ALSACIENNE Alsatian Sauce (For hare or venison)

Put in a small saucepan a glass of port wine with a pinch of nutmeg, salt and pepper. Reduce by one-third; add twice the quantity of redcurrant jelly, previously melted, a tablespoonful of grated horseradish, a little cream, stir well, cook for one minute more and serve.

§ *Port; nutmeg; redcurrant jelly; horseradish; cream.*

SAUCE POIVRADE Pepper Sauce (For venison)

Brown in butter the trimmings out of the venison, a small carrot, one onion and one shallot, all cut in small pieces. When brown, drain well, add two tablespoonfuls of vinegar, two tablespoonfuls of stock, and the same quantity of the liquid in which the venison has marinated. Bring to the boil, skim, and simmer till it has reduced by half.

Add then a little mustard, pepper, a little more marinade, bring to the boil once more for two minutes. Pass through a fine strainer, stir in a quarter of a pint of cream, bring to the boil and let it reduce and thicken. Finished, it should have the consistency of cream.

§ *Trimmings of venison; carrot; onion; shallot; vinegar; stock; liquid in which venison was marinated; mustard; cream.*

SAUCE GRAND VENEUR   *Grand Veneur Sauce (For venison)*

To the previous sauce add at the last minute a tablespoonful of redcurrant jelly; let it dissolve, stirring, on a slow fire, and serve at once.

The venison is either served whole, like a joint, with the chosen sauce in a sauceboat, or carved and the sauce poured over the slices in the serving dish.

§ *Poivrade sauce (trimmings of venison, carrot, onion, shallot, vinegar, stock, liquid in which venison was marinated, mustard, cream); redcurrant jelly.*

SAUCE AUX AIRELLES   *Cranberry Sauce*

Cook the berries with a little water in a covered saucepan. When cooked pound them and pass them through a hair sieve. To the purée thus obtained add soft sugar to taste, a little pepper and enough of the water in which the cranberries have cooked to obtain the consistency of a thick sauce.

§ *Cranberries; sugar.*

SAUCE VINAIGRETTE, I   *Vinaigrette Sauce, I*

Chop together the yolks of two hard-boiled eggs, a few gherkins and capers, and two shallots. Prepare an ordinary dressing of oil, vinegar, salt and pepper, to which you add a little mustard. Mix well and beat a little.

§ *Egg yolks, gherkins; capers; shallots; oil; vinegar; mustard.*

SAUCE VINAIGRETTE, II   *Vinaigrette Sauce, II*

Chop together very finely the yolks of two eggs, half a dozen gherkins, some capers, a few shallots, and a sheep's or calf's brain. Prepare in a basin your oil, vinegar, salt, pepper and mustard. Mix the whole thing and beat it well for some time. This sauce should be quite smooth in appearance and the consistency of thick cream. *It is specially good served with hot calf's head.*

§ *Yolks of egg; gherkins; capers; shallots; sheep's or calf's brain; oil; vinegar; mustard.*

SAUCE AU VIN BLANC   *White Wine Sauce*

Make a brown *roux*, add a glassful of dry white wine and boil for a few minutes.

§ *Brown* roux; *dry white wine.*

*

SAUCES FOR COLD MEATS

There are, after all, other things than mayonnaise sauce. To a mayonnaise you add mustard, parsley, gherkins, capers and tarragon chopped together and you have a Tartare sauce far less sickly and with a pleasant sharp taste. Another sauce which is very easy to prepare is the Ravigote: chop a hard-boiled egg and mix it well with salt, pepper, French mustard, parsley, chervil, oil and vinegar. The proportions should be two tablespoonfuls of vinegar to four of oil, that is, if your wine vinegar is of average strength; they vary a great deal. And a very good dressing for salads is a plain one made with wine vinegar, salt and pepper, oil, and a little mustard mixed with the crushed yolks of hard-boiled eggs; these should be well crushed and mixed in the vinegar and the oil till the dressing has the consistency of a smooth thin cream; the whites of the eggs should be finely chopped and added afterwards when dressing the salad.

*

SAUCE RÉMOULADE   *Rémoulade Sauce*

Put in a bowl two shallots, one small onion, parsley and chervil, all finely chopped. Add salt, pepper, and mustard and in turn, oil and vinegar, stirring all the time.

§ *Shallots; onion; parsley; chervil; oil; vinegar; mustard.*

SAUCE RAVIGOTE   *Ravigote Sauce*

Dissolve two teaspoonfuls of French mustard in two tablespoonfuls of wine vinegar; add salt, freshly-ground pepper, and four tablespoonfuls of olive oil. Mix with this, whipping well, chopped parsley and chervil and the crushed yolks of two hard-boiled eggs. Whatever the quantity may be, the proportions must remain the same.

§ *French mustard; wine vinegar; olive oil; parsley; chervil; eggs.*

SAUCES AND COMPOUNDED BUTTERS

BEURRE D'ANCHOIS *Anchovy Butter*

Take the fillets of four anchovies, wash them, and pound them in a mortar with a good piece of butter.

§ *Anchovies; butter.*

SAUCE SABAYON *Sabayon Sauce*

A perfect sauce for sweet fritters, or for a pudding, for a change. Put in a saucepan or a bowl four yolks of eggs and three tablespoonfuls of sugar. Cook this standing in boiling water, whipping all the time till it is smooth and thick like thick cream. Add then a flavouring of liqueurs (rum, brandy, Curaçao, according to taste) and finish whipping, off the fire, till it becomes almost frothy.

§ *Yolks of egg; sugar; rum and/or brandy/Curaçao.*

*

No one, these days, can afford to waste materials, for materials are always more or less costly. Even if money did not count waste is stupid and wicked. It is immoral. Personally, I would rather see things 'pinched' ('stolen' is rather a big word) than see them wasted; at least they profit somebody. But most people waste perfectly good things not out of wickedness but simply because they do not care; they do not realize the value and the sport of economy. For it becomes an amazing sport to make things do, to 'manage' this week on less than you did the week before.

There are many, of course, who, disappointed at seeing that many famous French dishes are simple, complicate them purposely, probably adding other flavours detrimental to the taste. That is also where 'daintiness' is to be feared; frills and arrangements, artistic effects carefully prepared (the dish meanwhile gets cold and loses freshness), colour schemes, parsley all round (and not enough in the sauce), little decorations made of gelatine, all the horrors of a third-rate table-d'hôte – such is, unfortunately, often the ideal pursued and, more unfortunately still, too often attained. Yet all that is wanted to get the better result, the finer cooking, is understanding and simplicity in the kitchen, appreciation and leisure in the dining-room.

Hors D'Œuvres and Light Entrées

Hors d'œuvres are usually connected with restaurant luncheons, yet nothing is more pleasant than to have hors d'œuvres occasionally in one's own house; or should the meal be a little short because friends arrive unexpectedly, hors d'œuvres come pleasantly to the rescue.

Indeed hors d'œuvres when good, and limited both in number and quantity, are a very good prelude to a luncheon. But the thing to avoid is a show of indifferent hors d'œuvres: inferior sardines, odd bits of fish covered with a nondescript sauce, remnants of vegetable masquerading as salade russe, and mayonnaise upholstering a multitude of sins. In fact, the value of hors d'œuvres depends on their usefulness and their quality.

For they can be useful and they can be pleasant, and that is where the danger lies; should they be very attractive we might be tempted to eat more than we ought to, to give them an importance that they never ought to have, that they are not meant to have – in which case they become as damaging as a cocktail drunk immediately before a meal instead of half an hour before, as all aperitifs should be drunk. Our appetite is spoilt instead of being sharpened, and we cannot give the luncheon the fair share of attention to which it is entitled; after all, the meal, the 'œuvre' is the thing, not the hors d'œuvres.

But they serve a double purpose: they help the guest to pass a little time while the first dish is prepared; they give the cook a chance of preparing that dish properly, knowing that, at least, everybody has arrived; and they are also useful, as I have said, for prosaic and economical reasons.

Therefore it stands to reason that hors d'œuvres should be good and simple, and, in a private house, limited to one, two or three at the most (the question of hors d'œuvres in a restaurant is another matter altogether). Of course melon, caviar, Bayonne ham, smoked salmon, olives, or radishes are perfect of their

HORS D'ŒUVRES AND LIGHT ENTRÉES

type, and so are oysters or grapefruit. None of these spoil our appetite; they have a specific taste of their own, and prepare us well for the more important things that are to follow. But we must be careful in any case and remember, when arranging the menu, what is the next dish; it would be, for instance, to say the least, careless to have fish after caviar, an omelette after a salad of eggs, or a hors d'œuvre with a very strong taste just before a very delicately flavoured dish.

Otherwise they are easy to prepare and, especially in the summer, very pleasing; the principal kinds being salads, and potted fish and meats.

*

ANCHOIADE, I *Savoury Anchovy*

For this you will need about a dozen fillets of anchovy in oil and a dozen of fillets of salt anchovy, six peeled almonds or walnuts, four dried figs, a small head of garlic, one middle-sized onion, a little lemon juice and *fines herbes*.

Pound the fillets of anchovy and keep them aside. Then chop finely the onion, the garlic, the nuts, the figs and the *fines herbes*. Add to the pounded fillets (the salt anchovy should be washed to remove the excess of salt) little by little two tablespoonfuls of olive oil, mix well and pound again till you obtain a mixture the consistency of mayonnaise. Add then all the things you have chopped finely, a little freshly ground pepper and beat well.

Prepare some crisp buttered toast and spread on each piece your *anchoiade*. Serve at once. Some people add Cayenne pepper; also some use only the fillets of anchovy in oil. Such is this savoury dish, very popular all over Provence. The garlic is really indispensable. But I understand that the walnuts and lemon juice the *anchoiade* contains remove very effectively the smell of garlic.

§ *Anchovies in oil; salt anchovies; almonds or walnuts; dried figs; garlic; onion; lemon juice;* fines herbes; *toast; butter. Cayenne pepper can be added.*

ANCHOIADE II *Grilled Anchovies*

Take some fillets of anchovy in oil, cut them in small pieces and pound them well, add parsley and a little garlic finely chopped and a little more oil (as the oil contained in the tin usually is not sufficient to moisten the mixture). Prepare some squares of stale bread and either fry them in butter or simply toast and butter them. Spread them with the pounded anchovies, put a piece of butter on each and just melt it under the grill.

§ *Anchovies in oil; parsley; garlic; oil; bread; butter.*

ROLLMOPS *Rollmops*

Take some salt herrings (not smoked), wash them well and soak them in milk for three or four hours. Drain them well, slice them in two and carefully remove the bones, dry them in a cloth, and dispose them flat on a board. Salt them, rub them with a little mustard and put over each pepper corns, coriander and thin slices of onion. Roll them and keep them rolled with either a thread or a piece of wood (like a cherry stick used for cocktails).

Put them in a dish and pour over them wine vinegar which you have boiled for five minutes with a bouquet. Leave this to get cold, then put the rolled fillets in a jar, and over each layer put salt, peppercorn, coriander, cloves, and at the top or at the bottom of the jar a clove of garlic and a bay leaf. Fill with the vinegar, cover and keep in a cool place.

We can make a little stock of these; in four days they are ready to eat, and will keep well for several weeks.

(In Flanders they are served unrolled, drained and with fresh cream poured over them.)

§ *Salt herrings; milk; mustard; peppercorns; coriander; onion; wine vinegar;* bouquet; *cloves; garlic; bay leaves. Cream can be added.*

CREVETTES EN TERRINE *Potted Shrimps*

Cook the shrimps in boiling sea water (or water with salt) with coarsely broken pepper for four minutes. Drain them well in a cloth and shell them carefully. Then sprinkle with a little salt and pepper, a pinch of Cayenne, and mix with melted butter, taking care not to crush the shrimps, as they should remain whole. Pot in jars and pour more melted butter on the top. Serve with slices of brown bread and butter. It is advisable not to keep them more than a week or two.

§ *Shrimps; peppercorns; Cayenne; butter.*

SALADE DE THON AU CÉLERI *Tuna Fish and Celery Salad*

Take some tuna fish, cut it in small pieces, season with wine vinegar and a little French mustard. Add some raw celery seasoned in the same way, and cut in very small pieces. Add chopped *fines herbes* (tarragon, parsley and chervil), also chives if obtainable, stir well and serve in a small salad bowl.

§ *Tuna; wine vinegar; French mustard; celery;* fines herbes; *chives.*

HORS D'ŒUVRES AND LIGHT ENTRÉES

HUÎTRES BORDELAISE *Oysters Bordelaise*

For some strange reason this savoury dish is not known outside the Bordeaux district. It ought to please English palates as well as the famous 'angels on horseback'. It is an ideal supper dish or a good beginning for a dinner. It consists of oysters and sausages eaten together.

The oysters should be very cold, the sausages very hot and crisp; pork sausages, of course, either the long thin ones or the small Chipolata. It seems as if the hot spicy sausage meat brings out the sea flavour of the oysters. For this dish the oysters should be served in the Continental fashion, that is, in the hollow shell and with all their water.

§ *Oysters; pork Chipolata sausages.*

BEURRE DE SARDINES *Sardine Butter*

Take one or two tins of sardines, carefully remove the skin and bones and pound in a mortar; add the same quantity of butter, a little salt and pepper and mix thoroughly so that it becomes a very smooth paste. Serve with toast. You can, if you like, add to the mixture a few cooked soft roes. The mixture will keep for several days in an ice chest, but it should always be served very cold, the consistency being that of butter on a cold day. You can either give it a shape or keep it in a terrine. It is also delicious for sandwiches.

§ *Sardines; butter. Soft roes can be added.*

MOULES AU SAFRAN *Mussels with Saffron*

Heat in a sauté pan three tablespoonfuls of olive oil, add one small onion chopped, and two leeks (white part only) cut in thin pieces; cook for a few minutes, then add two tomatoes cut in pieces, chopped garlic, a *bouquet* of thyme and bay leaves, a pinch of saffron, and two glassfuls of dry white wine, salt, and coarsely broken pepper. Let all this reduce.

Add mussels carefully cleaned, put the lid on, and toss them occasionally; they will soon open; keep them on a slow fire five minutes more, remove them, take them out of the shells and pour over them the stock through a strainer. Serve cold with chopped parsley.

§ *Mussels; onion; leeks; tomatoes; garlic; oil; thyme; bay leaves; saffron; dry white wine; peppercorns; parsley.*

PILAFF AUX MOULES *Mussel Pilaff*

Put the rice in cold salted water, cook it quickly and, when ready, drain it well and dry it. Each grain should be separate and not too cooked. Take two or three rashers of bacon, boil them, cut them in small pieces and toss them lightly in good olive oil. Keep them aside and also cut one slice of ham in small pieces.

Peel and cut two or three tomatoes (according to size) and chop one onion finely. First fry the onion in the oil you have used for frying the bacon, then add the tomatoes. When all this is melted add seasoning, a cup of *bouillon* (or of hot water), a bay leaf, a sprig of thyme, one lump of sugar and a pinch of saffron – let all this simmer on a slow fire.

Meanwhile the mussels should be cooked in the following manner: In a saucepan put a small piece of butter, two chopped shallots, parsley and a small piece of celery, half a glass of dry white wine, then the mussels carefully cleaned. Cook six minutes with the lid on, shaking the pan occasionally. Remove the mussels from the shells, pass the stock in which they have been cooked through muslin, put the mussels in it and keep hot.

Now everything is ready for the pilaff. Take a flat pan, put in it, well mixed together, the tomato sauce you have made, the sauce in which the mussels have stood, the rice, the pieces of ham and bacon, the mussels and a little grated cheese. Stir all this well over a slow fire, see that it is hot, then put the pilaff in a well-buttered mould, stand it upside down in the serving dish so that you have only to lift the mould after two or three minutes in a very hot oven. Serve at once, sprinkled with a little more grated cheese.

> § *Rice; bacon; ham; olive oil; tomatoes; onion;* bouillon; *bay leaf; thyme; sugar; saffron. Mussels; shallots; parsley; celery; dry white butter; cheese.*

PANCAKES À LA RUSSE *Russian Pancakes*

Make some small and very thin pancakes. When cold, spread each with butter in which you have worked some caviare, add a few drops of lemon juice and very little Cayenne pepper. Roll and serve cold. Pressed caviare, which is considerably cheaper than the others, can be used for this.

> § *Pancakes (see pp. 10 and 213); caviare; butter; lemon juice or Cayenne pepper.*

LAITANCES À LA GRECQUE *Roes à la Grecque*

Put your soft roes in a flat saucepan or in a fireproof dish, season them with salt, pepper, and a pinch of saffron; add one or two chopped shallots, the flesh (skin and pips should be removed) of one tomato cut in small pieces, a *bouquet*, a puddingspoonful of *fumet* of fish; add olive

HORS D'ŒUVRES AND LIGHT ENTRÉES

oil so that it comes just level with the soft roes, and cook for about four minutes. Remove the *bouquet* and serve cold.

§ *Soft roes; saffron; shallots; tomato;* bouquet; fumet *of fish; olive oil.*

SALADE DE POMMES AUX ŒUFS DURS *Egg and Potato Salad*

Boil, in their skins, about one pound of potatoes (the long yellow kind, the ordinary ones being too floury for salad). Peel them and let them get cold. Also have some hard-boiled eggs, four being a good proportion for a pound of potatoes. Make the dressing as follows: salt and pepper, two tablespoonfuls of wine vinegar, four and a half of best olive oil, chopped chervil and chives. Pound the yolks in this dressing, cut the whites in small pieces, the potatoes in thin slices and mix well. You can vary this salad by adding chopped gherkins, fillets of anchovy, or spring onion.

§ *Eggs; potatoes; wine vinegar; olive oil; chervil; chives; gherkins, anchovies or spring onions.*

FONDS D'ARTICHAUTS À L'ORIENTALE *Salad of Hearts of Artichokes*

Take some globe artichokes, remove the stalks and all the leaves, leaving only the hearts and put them at once in fresh water with the juice of one lemon.

Put in a saucepan equal quantities of olive oil and water, lemon juice, a little sugar, small onions and young carrots cut in small pieces, salt and pepper. Bring to the boil and cook a little while; add the artichokes, put the lid on (it should fit really well) and cook about three-quarters of an hour.

Meanwhile cook a handful of fresh peas, a few new potatoes as small as possible, and add them to the rest. Let the mixture get cold and sprinkle with parsley and fennel, chopped.

§ *Globe artichokes; lemon juice; olive oil; sugar; small onions; carrots; peas; potatoes; parsley; fennel.*

SALADE DE CONCOMBRE *Cucumber Salad*

In France cucumber is usually served as an hors d'œuvre salad. In this case it is peeled and cut in thin pieces, then sprinkled with salt and left for about one hour. The salt brings the water out of the vegetable, which is then well squeezed in a cloth, the seasoning being only pepper and wine vinegar.

§ *Cucumber; wine vinegar.*

CROÛTES AUX ASPERGES　　　　　　　*Asparagus on Croûtons*

Having boiled the asparagus (quite small ones will do for this), drain them well. Cut off the tips and as much as you can of the green part till it becomes stringy; do not cut any farther.

Prepare a very smooth *Béchamel* sauce, add a little cream to it and cook it till it thickens well.

Pass it through a strainer if you like to make certain that it is not at all lumpy; add to it the asparagus tips, cook a few minutes more, put on fried bread and serve.

There should be plenty of asparagus tips in the sauce, which really just binds them together.

§ *Asparagus;* Béchamel *sauce (roux, milk, nutmeg); cream.*

ŒUFS FARCIS AUX CHAMPIGNONS　　　*Eggs stuffed with Mushrooms*

Have some hard-boiled eggs; cut them in two lengthways. Cook in butter a few fresh mushrooms for about ten minutes; season them with salt, pepper, and a little lemon juice. Chop together finely the mushrooms and the yolks of eggs, mix with *Béchamel* sauce so that the stuffing is the consistency of a stiff sauce. Fill the eggs, which you put in a buttered fireproof dish, with, if you like, a little *Béchamel* sauce around the eggs. Brown and serve at once. The proportions should be about a quarter of a pound of mushrooms for six eggs.

§ *Eggs; mushrooms; lemon juice;* Béchamel *sauce (roux, milk, nutmeg).*

SALADE ALGÉRIENNE　　　　　　*Tomato and Sweet Pepper Salad*

Take some tomatoes and some sweet peppers, either green or red, cut them in two and remove the seeds; having grilled and peeled them, cut in very fine slices, add two small onions, one shallot and parsley finely chopped; season with pepper, salt, oil and vinegar.

§ *Tomatoes; sweet peppers; small onions; shallots; parsley; vinegar; oil.*

*

There is no doubt about it, bad ordering is often responsible for a bad meal, either in a house or in a restaurant, and the final impression of excellence may be spoilt by the deplorable arrangement of dishes, dishes, mark you, perfectly good each of them taken separately.

Yet the rules are easy to remember, just as they are easily forgotten, so the whole matter is not really as simple as it seems. Indeed, it all comes to this; the dishes must make a contrasting effect.

*

HORS D'ŒUVRES AND LIGHT ENTRÉES

If you have a cream soup, do not have afterwards a fish with a white sauce; do not make two dishes with a sharp taste to follow each other; arrange your menu in a way which means the maximum of effect on the dinner table, and the minimum of work in the kitchen.

And you must, of course, think about the economical side of your menus, combining cleverly economy with enjoyment. For instance, suppose for a dinner party you want to serve the Suprêmes de volaille à l'Alsacienne, *which is a delicious and elaborate dish. You must think of a good way of utilizing the legs which have been left over; in which the* Cuisses de poulet à la Moutarde *or the* Crêpes de volaille *come in pleasantly useful for luncheon the following day.*

[33]

Soups

As the Mock-Turtle used to sing:

> 'Who would not give all else for two p
> 'Ennyworth only of beautiful soup?'

The poor peasant of the Centre and the South has his rich soups and his bottle of wine.

There is great charm as well as great nutritive value in these soups, of which the farmers and the labourers make their evening meal – soups made of cabbage or of onions, or of mixed vegetables and salt pork, or of sorrel – though I doubt if we should like them as they do, so thick with slices of bread that the ladle stands upright in the middle of the tureen.

There it is, time-honoured leit-motiv, steaming on the long oak table. A bunch of garlic hangs from the ceiling, and a ham in the chimney; and the two candles in pewter candlesticks give less light than the big log fire. They sit down to it, farmer and stable boys, and women, heavily, solemnly. They do not talk much, they eat. Or, on a summer evening, they sit on low chairs outside the house, just by the door, holding a plateful on their knees. The day's work is over, the last lazy cow back in the stable after a last mouthful at the hedge. The twilight is blue and peaceful, only disturbed occasionally by the guttural song of some frogs in the ditch. The earth smells. But its perfume is not, to them, as sacred as that of the soup.

For these were and are still the traditional soups. Our versions have been adapted by the peasant women, who have adapted themselves, risen to the rank of cook, and left the fields for the country house or the provincial town. So that these admirable dishes, without having lost any of their primitive characteristic qualities, have become more civilized; they are no more a complete meal, but a pleasant and appetizing prelude.

*

SOUPS

CROÛTE-AU-POT   *Clear Soup with Vegetables and Toasted Bread*

Have some *consommé** ready, cut some pieces of bread crusts and dry them in the oven. Cut your vegetables in smallish pieces, put both vegetables and bread crusts in an earthenware pot with your consommé.

§ *Consommé; bread crusts; vegetables.*

CONSOMMÉ À LA CHIFFONNADE   *Consommé Chiffonade*

Take the heart of a lettuce, cut it finely, removing the hard parts and cook it slowly in a little butter; when it is nearly cooked add a handful of sorrel leaves cut in the same way; finish melting them together.

When the consommé is boiling, throw in a tablespoonful of vermicelli. Cook five or six minutes, then put in the *chiffonnade* of sorrel and lettuce, cook five minutes more and add at the last minute a little plucked chervil.

§ *Consommé; lettuce; butter; sorrel leaves; vermicelli; chervil.*

CONSOMMÉ FROID   *Cold Consommé*

Take some consommé and add to it a quarter of a pound of raw beef and a little chicken meat, if you have any, very finely chopped; then three tomatoes reduced to a pulp and the white of an egg. Mix well, add salt and pepper, bring to the boil, stirring well, then let it simmer for two hours. Pass through a sieve and pour it in cups. Serve cold.

§ *Consommé; beef; tomatoes; white of egg. Chicken meat can be added.*

SOUPE DES VENDANGES   *Soup Vendanges*

Take a piece of beef weighing about three or four pounds and insert in it two heads of garlic; put it in a large saucepan full of salted cold water, bring to the boil and skim carefully several times (in some parts of the Gironde they also put a marrow-bone and the neck of a fowl); then add carrots (sliced in two), turnips and onions cut in quarters and a small cabbage coarsely chopped. Bring to the boil again and let the soup simmer for two hours and a half.

Make a *roux* in a small saucepan and cook in it for a few minutes a head of celery and a few leeks cut in pieces about three inches long. Add this to the soup. Meanwhile boil half a dozen tomatoes with a *bouquet*, salt and pepper, and when well cooked squash them through a sieve and

* See p. 7.

add them to the soup, which must go on simmering for another hour and a half.

§ *Beef; garlic; carrots; turnips; onions; cabbage;* roux; *celery; leeks; tomatoes;* bouquet. *Marrow-bone and neck of fowl can be added.*

POTAGE À LA PURÉE DE GIBIER *Game Soup*

A very good soup can be made with remnants of roast game. Boil them for about three-quarters of an hour with carrots, onions, a head of celery, a *bouquet*, salt and pepper. When it has reduced pass the soup through a fine colander, remove the pieces of flesh which have remained on legs, carcases and bones, pound them in a mortar and pass them through a sieve. Add a very small quantity of stale breadcrumbs, mix with the stock and bind at the last minute with fresh cream. Serve little fried *croûtons* with this.

§ *Remnants of roast game; carrots; onions; celery;* bouquet; *breadcrumbs; cream;* croûtons.

SOUPE DE CONCOMBRE, I *Cucumber Soup, I*

Take an average-sized cucumber, cut it in thin slices and toss these in butter at the foaming stage for two or three minutes. Treat in the same manner two small onions cut finely. Put both vegetables in a saucepan and pour in boiling water, five cups of water which will be reduced to four at the end of the cooking. Season with salt, pepper, a little nutmeg and a pinch of Cayenne pepper.

Bring to the boil and simmer for about half an hour; at the last minute stir in a binding of two yolks of eggs diluted with a tablespoonful of cream. Serve with *croûtons*.

§ *Cucumber; butter; small onions; nutmeg; Cayenne; eggs; cream;* croûtons.

SOUPE DE CONCOMBRE, II *Cucumber Soup, II*

To vary this soup for a second time, add to it a cupful of consommé and five minutes before serving a tablespoonful of vermicelli. Finish by the binding of yolks of eggs and cream, and do not serve *croûtons*. This will look and taste entirely different.

§ *Cucumber; consommé; butter; small onions; Cayenne; eggs; cream; vermicelli.*

POTAGE GERMINY *Soup Germiny*

Have ready two tablespoonfuls of sorrel 'melted' in a little butter, and add to it about a quart of consommé; bring to the boil and simmer for eight to ten minutes. Prepare in a basin a binding of four yolks of egg, well broken, to which you add a teacupful of fresh cream. Two minutes before serving, add to this, one by one, two tablespoonfuls of the hot soup, so as to warm the mixture. Then pour it into the saucepan and put it on a very slow fire: stir well with the ladle. It soon thickens, but you must be careful that it does not reach the boiling-point. Finish, off the fire, by adding two small pieces of butter. Shake the saucepan gently till the butter has disappeared, add a little chervil, see that it is well seasoned, and serve with very small *croûtons*.

§ *Sorrel; butter; consommé; eggs; cream; chervil;* croûtons.

SOUPE POLONAISE *Polish Sorrel Soup*

This is an iced sorrel soup from Poland, perfect for a hot summer evening.

Take two handfuls of sorrel, wash well, remove the stalks and the medium fibre, chop coarsely and cook for ten minutes in one quart of boiling salted water.

Chop finely one small clove of garlic and one hard-boiled egg and throw them in the soup. Remove it from the fire and add a great deal of pepper, the juice of a lemon, a few very thin slices of cucumber and one egg well beaten. Put the soup in a bowl and let it get cold.

Just before serving add five or six pieces of ice, but it is essential to do this when the soup is really cold and at the last minute only, otherwise the ice will melt too much and the soup will be watery. It should be icy cold, acid and well spiced.

§ *Sorrel; garlic; eggs; lemon juice; cucumber; ice.*

POTAGE DE L'OSEILLE *Sorrel Soup*

Take half a pound of sorrel (it reduces even more than spinach), remove the stalks and centre rib and wash the leaves well. Melt them in a saucepan with a piece of butter the size of a small egg, add boiling water, allowing for reduction, salt and pepper. Bring to the boil and simmer for about half an hour. Beat the yolks of two eggs with a tablespoonful of milk and stir this in just before serving.

§ *Sorrel; butter; yolks of egg; milk.*

CRÈME AUX ÉPINARDS *Spinach Soup*

Prepare in exactly the same way as sorrel soup, but serve slightly thicker and add a little paprika.

§ *Spinach; butter; yolks of egg; milk; paprika.*

POTAGE PRINTANIER, I　　　　　　　　　　　　　　Soup Printanier, I

This soup, as its name implies, is at its best in the spring. Get some carrots and turnips which have, then, all the charm of youth; wash them well and scrape them lightly, their skin is very thin and will come off easily. Also get a white cabbage, remove the outside leaves and use the heart only; cut it in four quarters and the other vegetables in thin narrow slices; add the white part only of two leeks, and cook all this very slowly in butter in a saucepan, keeping the lid on all the time. When tender, add some good consommé, the heart of a lettuce cut in four, a handful of fresh peas and a little chopped chervil. You should add consommé in sufficient quantity so that there is enough for your purpose when it has been reduced by one-third, as it should do, on a slow fire. See if it is properly seasoned and, just before serving, add the yolk of one egg well beaten and mix it well with this pleasant mixture of spring vegetables.

§ *Carrots; turnips; white cabbage; leeks; lettuce; peas; consommé; butter; chervil; yolk of egg.*

POTAGE PRINTANIER, II　　　　　　　　　　　　　Soup Printanier, II

This is a cream soup made with the vegetables of early summer. Cook in salted water one quart of fresh peas, the white of two small leeks (cut in small pieces) and two small lettuces.

When all these are cooked drain them well and keep the stock in a bowl; pound the vegetables in a mortar and add to this purée, stirring well, the stock little by little till you have a mixture the consistency of thick cream. Put it in a saucepan and add chicken stock till you have the required quantity. Bring to the boil and simmer it two or three minutes; finish by a liaison of two yolks of egg diluted in two tablespoonfuls of cream. Serve with *croûtons*, or with fine macaroni.

§ *Peas; leeks; lettuces; chicken stock; yolks of egg; cream;* croûtons *or macaroni.*

PURÉE DE CIBOURE　　　　　　　　　　　　　　　　Bean Soup

This soup, which is of the 'rustic' kind, is much appreciated by the inhabitants of the Basque country; it is seldom made in the other parts of France. Soak some haricot beans for twelve hours (if they are dry ones) and put them in salted water with equal quantity of potatoes. Chop together finely two shallots, two heads of garlic, olives and two leeks. Bring to the boil and cook for at least three hours on a moderate fire. Pass through a sieve, add a little beef stock, a good deal of freshly ground pepper, and just before serving, if you like, the yolk of one egg. This soup should be neither too thick nor too clear. It has a pleasant taste.

§ *Haricot beans; potatoes; shallots; garlic; olives; leeks; beef stock; peppercorns. Yolk of egg can be added.*

POTAGE AUX CAROTTES   *Carrot Soup*

Take one pound of small carrots, scrape and wash them well and put them into a saucepan with two pints and a half of cold water, salt, pepper, one or two onions, and a few bay leaves. If you have a ham bone to put in, it will give a good flavour to the soup. Bring the soup to the boil and let it simmer for three or four hours. Then remove the carrots and pass them through a sieve into a clean saucepan. Pour the soup over them through a strainer, add a cup of consommé or meat stock, cook a few minutes more, and just before serving 'bind' the soup with the beaten yolk of an egg.

§ *Carrots; onions; bay leaves; consommé or meat stock; yolk of egg.*

POTAGE À LA PURÉE DE MARRONS   *Chestnut Soup*

This is an old provincial recipe for chestnut soup; it is rather out of the ordinary and a pleasant change from the better-known kind of soups. Take a pound of chestnuts (for five or six people), remove the outer skin and put them in a narrow and deep saucepan in salted water till the water begins to boil, after which you can easily remove the thin skin; then put at the bottom of a saucepan a clove, a bay leaf, a few small pieces of bacon, one large potato and a carrot cut in slices, salt and pepper; over this the chestnuts and water, and cook them till they are soft. Drain them and pound them well, add a sufficient quantity of good stock, breadcrumbs (one slice of stale bread will do), the potato which has boiled with the chestnuts, and pass the whole thing through a sieve, so that it is as smooth as cream. Bring to the boil and let it simmer a little while. Just before serving you can, if you like, 'bind' it with either cream or the yolk of an egg. It should be served with *croûtons* crisply fried in butter, and the consistency should be that of an ordinary thick soup. The old recipe goes on giving a variation on the same theme, in which vegetable stock is used instead of meat stock – for Fridays and other *jours maigres*.

§ *Chestnuts; clove; bay leaf; bacon; meat or vegetable stock; potato; carrot; breadcrumbs; croûtons. Cream or yolk of egg can be added.*

POTAGE AUX HERBES MAIGRES   *Herb Soup Without Meat*

Take a handful of sorrel, remove the stalks, and cut it very thin. Do the same to two lettuces and to a handful of chervil, and cook all these in butter till thoroughly soft and almost 'melted'; then add hot water, salt and pepper, bring to the boil, and let it simmer for half an hour or so. Just before serving 'bind' it by adding the yolks of two eggs, stirring them in quickly. If both sorrel and chervil are unobtainable, use instead spinach and parsley treated in the same fashion, but it should be remembered that spinach takes a little longer to cook than sorrel.

§ *Sorrel; lettuce; chervil; egg yolks. (Spinach and parsley can be used instead of sorrel or chervil.)*

POTAGE SAINT-GERMAIN *Pea Soup*

Cook fresh peas in water with salt and one onion. When cooked pass through a sieve. Add some consommé to proper consistency (fairly thick), boil for a few minutes, then add just before serving a pinch of sugar; also a few leaves of sorrel, lettuce and chervil finely chopped, warmed in butter for a few minutes.

§ *Peas; consommé; sugar; sorrel; lettuce; chervil.*

POTAGE AUX LENTILLES *Lentil Soup*

Same preparation as before; but before serving add, instead of lettuce, sorrel and chervil, a piece of butter the size of a walnut, and the yolk of an egg beaten up with a little gravy.

§ *Peas; consommé; sugar; butter; egg yolk; gravy.*

CRÈME DE POIS VERTS *Pea Soup*

Put in a saucepan, about a quarter full of water, the bones and carcase of a chicken together with two slices of very lean bacon, one onion, and a little mint. Add salt, bring to the boil, and keep simmering for about two hours and a half. Allow this to cool, and carefully remove the fat. In another saucepan boil one pound of fresh peas. When these are cooked pass them through a sieve. Stir in about half a pint of milk, mixing the peas and milk well; add to it the yolk of one egg, well beaten.

Pass through a strainer the stock first prepared, put it into a clean saucepan, and bring nearly to the boil; then very slowly stir in the milk and peas and bring to the boiling-point once. Just before serving add a good tablespoonful of cream.

§ *Bones and carcase of chicken; lean bacon; onion; mint; peas; milk; yolk of egg; cream.*

GARBURE *Garbure*

The *Garbure* is the traditional soup of the South, and it appears day after day on the tables of the Béarn and of the Landes district. It can be made in many different ways, according to the part of the country or the time of the year, but it always contains certain principal ingredients, which are: cabbage, beans or potatoes, and pork in some form or other.

Cook the haricot beans in salt water (about half a pound to one large cabbage), having previously soaked them if they are not fresh ones, then add the cabbage cut in small pieces, a few carrots, and boil on a quick fire. About one hour before serving add either a tablespoonful of bacon fat or a piece of bacon or pickled pork, salt, pepper, a *bouquet* of parsley, thyme and bay leaf (it should be removed with the meat before serving): add more boiling water if necessary. You can put in peas instead of haricots if you like, or broad beans when in season, and turnips. In fact, the cabbage is the foundation of the *Garbure,* the pork gives it a special flavour, and the beans or potatoes, which should be reduced to a pulp, give it the necessary consistency.

§ *Cabbage; haricot beans (or peas or broad beans); carrots; bacon fat (or bacon or pickled pork);* bouquet. *Turnips can be added.*

SOUPE AUX CHOUX *Cabbage Soup*

Take a good-sized cabbage, break off the leaves and wash them well, cut them in pieces about three inches long. Prepare the following vegetables: three or four carrots and two turnips, sliced lengthways in four pieces, one leek, one clove. Throw all this in an iron saucepan when the water is boiling. Add salt about three quarters of an hour afterwards. Cook about two to three hours, according to what kind of cabbage you have been using.

Half an hour before serving put in the following seasoning: one slice of bacon, parsley, two heads of garlic, all chopped very fine and mixed together, salt and pepper. The soup should be boiling when you add the mixture. Stir it occasionally.

§ *Cabbage; carrots; turnips; leek; clove; bacon; parsley; garlic.*

POTAGE PARMENTIER *Potato Soup*

Cook in salted water four or five potatoes of the white floury kind. Drain them and pass them through a sieve; put this purée in a saucepan with a little butter, a tablespoonful of milk, salt, pepper and chopped chervil. Add your consommé in sufficient quantity, bring to the boil and let it simmer and reduce (it should not be too thick, about half-way between a clear and real thick soup) and serve with *croûtons.*

§ *Potatoes; milk; chervil; consommé;* croûtons.

CRÈME AUX TOMATES   *Cream of Tomato Soup*

Fry in butter for a few minutes four leeks and eight tomatoes, let them simmer for five minutes; then add the required quantity of water (about two pints), about six medium-sized potatoes, salt and butter, and bring to the boil. Cook for about three-quarters of an hour; pass them through a sieve, bring to the boil again and add two tablespoonfuls of cream or milk.

§ *Leeks; tomatoes; potatoes; butter; cream or milk.*

TOURAIN AUX TOMATES   *Clear Tomato Soup*

Cut in quarters eight tomatoes, one onion in thin slices, fry these in pork fat for a few minutes; add a pint and a half of hot water, salt and pepper (a good deal of pepper); bring to the boil and keep simmering till the tomatoes are well cooked. Pass through a sieve, throw in some vermicelli and cook again for five or six minutes.

This is the traditional soup which, even now in all the Périgord, is offered to husband and wife on their wedding night. A large tureenful is brought to them in great state (and with a good deal of noise) by the neighbouring peasants, usually a few hours after the bride and bridegroom have retired. They eat it in bed; the guests watch them and finish the rest. It seems more sensible than many other old customs, such as for instance throwing rice (uncooked) at them in the street.

§ *Tomatoes; onion; vermicelli; pork fat.*

CRÈME D'ASPERGES   *Cream of Asparagus*

Cook for five minutes in salted water half a bundle of asparagus, two onions and two or three floury potatoes. Drain them well and put them in a saucepan with a piece of butter the size of a small egg, and two lumps of sugar; cover with a buttered paper and cook very slowly for a few minutes, being careful that these vegetables do not brown. Remove the paper, put in half water, half clear soup (preferably made with chicken or veal), allowing for reduction.

Bring to the boil and simmer for about half an hour. Meanwhile, make a little white *roux* in another saucepan.

Remove the vegetables, mash them through a sieve; add to the purée you obtain enough of the stock to make the soup fairly liquid. Pour it over the *roux*, bring to the boil and cook for five minutes more till it thickens. Finish by a yolk of egg diluted in a little cream, and put in a handful of asparagus tips previously cooked.

§ *Asparagus; onions; potatoes; butter; sugar; clear soup;* roux; *yolk of egg; cream.*

SOUPS

POTAGE JULIENNE *Julienne Soup*

Cut in very thin slices carrots, turnips, potatoes, leeks, cabbage, onions; put them in a saucepan with three or four lumps of sugar, cover the saucepan and cook very slowly, stirring occasionally. When nearly cooked add consommé and finish cooking.

§ *Carrots; turnips; potatoes; leeks; cabbage; onions; sugar; consommé.*

POTAGE AU CRESSON *Watercress Soup*

Take one pound of floury potatoes and cook them in salt water, also take a bundle of watercress, clean it, remove the stalks, chop the leaves and add them to the potatoes when these are about three-quarters cooked. Squeeze through a wire sieve and put back in the saucepan with a certain quantity of water: cook a few minutes more without bringing to the boil; then add a little cream, see that it is well seasoned, bind with the yolk of an egg in which you have stirred a little lemon juice, and add just before serving a few leaves of watercress and chervil cut fine. This refreshing soup, which must be the consistency of rather thin thick soup, is served with small *croûtons* of bread, fried perfectly crisp.

§ *Potatoes; watercress; yolk of egg; lemon juice; cream; chervil; croûtons.*

POTAGE AUX POIREAUX *Leek Soup*

Melt in butter (as described in *Potage à l'oseille* see p. 37) a handful of sorrel. Also cook slowly in a covered saucepan four leeks, four potatoes, and a good piece of butter, stirring occasionally. When cooked add water, salt, pepper, and a tablespoonful of cream. This soup can be made either rather thick, and served as it is, or rather thin – in which case you bring to the boil again ten minutes before serving and throw in a little vermicelli.

§ *Sorrel; leeks; potatoes; butter; cream. Vermicelli can be added.*

MINESTRONE *Minestrone*

This can be made with all sorts of vegetables, the usual mixture being tomatoes, celery, carrots and onions, thinly sliced and first cooked slowly in just enough butter to cook them, for a quarter of an hour. Add a *bouquet*, a handful of macaroni or spaghetti broken in small pieces, water (allowing for reduction), salt and pepper, bring to the boil and simmer for half an hour. Serve with it grated Parmesan cheese.

§ *Tomatoes; celery; carrots; onions; butter; bouquet; macaroni or spaghetti; Parmesan cheese.*

SOUPE À L'OIGNON *Onion Soup*

Take two medium-sized onions, cut them in very fine slices and fry these brown in butter. Add enough hot water, allowing for reduction, salt and pepper. Cook for half an hour. Have ready a few thin slices of French roll dried in the oven, pour your soup over these in the soup tureen, sprinkle with grated cheese and brown quickly. Serve in the tureen.

§ *Onions; butter; French bread; cheese.*

SOUPE D'HARICOTS ROUGES *Red Bean Soup*

Allow a handful of beans for each person. Put them in a saucepan full of cold water, with salt, pepper and a *bouquet*. Bring them to the boil and cook for at least one hour. Then put on the lid of the saucepan, and let the beans simmer, adding more water if necessary till they are quite soft. Drain them and mash them through a sieve.

To the purée thus obtained add hot milk, so that the mixture has the consistency of an ordinary thick soup. Take one small thin slice of cooked tongue and the bottoms (also cooked) of two artichokes. Cut them in very small pieces, like matches, and add them to the soup. See that it is well seasoned and really hot, and serve. You can finish, if you like, by stirring in, off the fire, a piece of fresh butter which will act as a binding.

§ *Red beans;* bouquet; *milk; tongue; artichoke bottoms.*

SOUPE VELOURS *Soup Velours*

Make a stock with the bones and carcase of a fowl, one onion stuck with a clove, one carrot, and a *bouquet*. Bring to the boil and let it simmer for half an hour, till it has reduced to the right amount wanted. Pass through a strainer and mash the carrot through a sieve. Put back on the fire, bring to the boil, throw in a tablespoonful of refined tapioca and the mashed carrot, cook for six minutes and serve.

§ *Bones and carcase of poultry; onion; clove; carrot;* bouquet; *tapioca.*

BOUILLABAISSE *Bouillabaisse*

This is the world-famous fish soup of the Mediterranean. There does not seem to be an exact and unique recipe for it; each person seems to think his the best and only recipe. We cannot all live at Marseilles or Toulon, and have exactly the right kind of fish, but we can hope to achieve with the resources at our disposal a fish soup which can be a perfectly good substitute for *Bouillabaisse*.

SOUPS

Put in a large saucepan three chopped onions, four pieces of garlic, three tomatoes, peeled and pips removed, a *bouquet* with fennel, and a piece of orange peel. On this bed put pieces of fish with firm flesh, like conger eel, turbot, crab or lobster, half a glass of good olive oil, and hot water just enough to cover the fish; season with salt, pepper, a little nutmeg and saffron; bring to the boil and cook on a fierce fire for five minutes.

Put in then the smaller or softer-fleshed fish such as red mullet, whiting, or smelts, cook five minutes more on a quick fire. Remove the odd things, the fennel, parsley, bay leaf, etc., pour the liquid over slices of bread fried in oil and rubbed with garlic and serve the pieces of fish, sprinkled all over with chopped parsley in another dish. Serve at once. It is the quick cooking which is the secret of *Bouillabaisse* and to which is due the smooth mixture of oil and stock.

§ *Firm-fleshed fish (conger eel, turbot, crab, lobster); softer-fleshed fish (red mullet, whiting, smelts); onions; garlic; tomatoes; bouquet with fennel; orange peel; olive oil; nutmeg; saffron; fried bread.*

SOUPE DE POISSON À LA BRETONNE *Breton Fish Soup*
Most people usually associate fish soup either with Marseilles or with America; indeed, both the Bouillabaisse *and the chowder are well known and remarkably good when well prepared. But I came across some quite good fish soup at Boulogne last autumn during the famous 'fish week', and I tasted a very pleasant one once in a small village near Dinard. Needless to say, these dishes never appear on the menu of even the smallest hotel, probably because the patron thinks, rightly or wrongly, that they are not civilized enough for visitors; as a matter of fact, the food the patron and his wife have on the kitchen table is often better than the more elaborate dishes which are sent to the table d'hôte.*

A fish soup, which is very popular with Breton fishermen, is simple to make and very pleasant. It is very different from the Provençal dish of the same type, as no oil is used for the cooking, and it does not contain crab, saffron, tomato or any of the ingredients which give the Bouillabaisse *its special flavour:*

You simply chop very fine and brown in a good piece of the best butter what the Bretons call *des herbes* that is, spring onions and sorrel (about a handful), one carrot, one potato, a little parsley, chives and (unexpectedly) mint; add salt and pepper, boiling water, bring to the boil, put in some fish (it does not matter very much which as long as it is not a flat fish) and cook about twenty minutes. They eat it with bread and boiled potatoes, and as the man said all too modestly '*Ça aide à faire passer le pain.*'

For a more civilized table, it will of course be better to strain the liquid, and remove the skin and bones of the fish before serving, but *les herbes* should be served with the pieces of fish.

§ *Fish (any except flat fish); spring onions; sorrel; carrot; potato; parsley; chives; mint; butter.*

POTAGE À LA BISQUE *Crayfish Soup*

Put in a saucepan one onion, one carrot cut in slices, a little parsley and thyme (all previously browned in butter), two pints of water, a glass of white wine, a tablespoonful of wine vinegar, a little brandy, and seasoning. Throw in your crayfish, about one dozen for five people (or small crabs if crayfish are not available, or a smallish lobster). Remove them when cooked, take all the edible parts and pound them well. Meanwhile, cook a handful of rice in the stock; when cooked pound it and add it to the flesh of the shellfish. Pass this mixture through a fine sieve and add it to the stock which must be also carefully strained. Cook slowly for half an hour, add a little more white wine, a small piece of butter and cook, stirring occasionally till reduced to the required quantity. Just before serving bind it with cream and the yolks of two eggs. See that it is highly seasoned, and do not keep it waiting. It should have the consistency of fresh cream.

§ *Crayfish (or small crabs or lobster); onion; carrot; parsley; thyme; white wine; wine vinegar; brandy; rice; butter; yolks of egg; cream.*

SOUPE MARINIÈRE *Mussel Soup*

Take some fine mussels and clean them well. Put them in a saucepan with a pint of water, a glassful of dry white wine, one onion, a *bouquet* with a clove, salt and pepper. Cook about a quarter of an hour on a quick fire, after which the mussels are opened and cooked. Remove them, take them out of the shells and keep them hot. Let the stock reduce by a quarter or so, add a glass of fresh cream, a little chopped parsley and pour over the mussels in the soup tureen. This soup should be highly seasoned.

§ *Mussels; dry white wine; onion; parsley;* bouquet *with clove; cream.*

BOURRIDE ARCACHONNAISE *Bourride Arcachonnaise*

This is a fish soup from Arcachon. Any fish will do for this soup, and two pounds will do for six or seven people. Cut it in several pieces and cook in a *court-bouillon* for one hour.

There should be enough left of it at the end to make soup for the required number of people, so allow for reduction. Strain well, mashing the fish against the side of strainer, and let this stock get tepid.

Make some mayonnaise, about a bowlful, starting with the yolks of four eggs and two or three cloves of garlic well pounded; add to it little by little, mixing well, the fish stock, and cook very slowly, whipping well till the consistency of the soup is that of cream. Fry some *croûtons* in olive oil and pour the soup over them in the soup tureen just before serving.

§ *Fish;* court-bouillon; *mayonnaise (eggs, vinegar, oil); garlic; olive oil;* croûtons.

BOUILLON DE POISSON *Fish Bouillon*

This is a clear fish soup for which any fish can be used. You want about one pound of it, also a few shrimps or mussels, to make enough soup for four people.

Melt a small piece of butter in a saucepan, and fry in this for two or three minutes one leek, one carrot, one onion, two tomatoes, a piece of celery, all cut in pieces. Add a *bouquet*, a good pinch of mixed spice, the fish cut in pieces, boiling water, allowing for reduction – say, five and a half bowls of water, which at the end will make four – salt and pepper. Bring to the boil and simmer for at least three-quarters of an hour.

Meanwhile cut some thin slices of French roll, butter them, and spread over a mixture of grated cheese and saffron. Put these to dry and brown in the oven. Allow two or three for each person. Strain the soup before serving, and serve with it, separately, the *croûtons* to be put into the plates after the soup has been served.

(The saffron required for this dish is to be found in shops in two forms – ready to use and ground in little packets or bottles, or shredded, in which case it must be dried in the oven and pounded.)

§ *Fish; shrimps (or mussels); leek; carrot; onion; tomatoes; celery;* bouquet; *mixed spice; butter; French bread; cheese; saffron.*

SOUPE DE CRABE *Crab Soup*

Take one leek, one onion and three medium-sized potatoes, fry these in butter for a few minutes, then add half a pound of any fish (even a piece of conger eel near the head would do, if really fresh), and a small crab broken in pieces (if at the seaside you can use those small crabs one can catch on the beach or in rocks), salt, pepper, and a *bouquet*. Cook these for five minutes, then add a sprinkling of curry powder, and paprika and hot water, allowing for reduction. Bring to the boil again and simmer for three-quarters of an hour. Pass through a strainer, squashing the fish and vegetables well. You can serve this in two ways:

1. As a clear soup with very thin pieces of French roll dried in the oven.

2. As a thick soup, with a binding of two yolks of egg and a tablespoonful of cream added at the last minute. Serve *croûtons* with this if you like.

> § 1. *Crab; fish; bouquet; leek; onion; potatoes; butter; curry powder; paprika; French roll.*
>
> 2. *As above, with the addition of yolks of egg; cream;* croûtons *instead of French roll.*

CONSOMMÉ AUX HUÎTRES *Oyster Soup*

Take a good-sized piece of beef, some bones with a marrow bone as well, and put them in a saucepan with salted water. Bring to the boil and skim carefully, after which add the following vegetables: three carrots, two onions, one leek, one turnip, and some parsley. This *consommé* should then simmer for five or six hours. Then skim it again very thoroughly and pass it through a fine sieve.

Poach the oysters for a few minutes in white wine, place them in the soup tureen and pour the *consommé* over them.

> § *Oysters; beef; bones (including marrow-bone); carrots; onions; leek; turnip; parsley; white wine.*

*

Pink-coloured soup was the opening note of a dinner given by a famous hostess. It was followed by an Oriental dish of rice and chicken, and an Eastern curry served on crisp wafers. Fruit came next, followed by celery and specially prepared Turkish coffee, which was drunk while burning incense gave an Eastern aroma to the room (and no doubt to the coffee).

'We have so much colour in our rooms,' said the hostess, 'that we must plan meals highly spiced and original. The ordinary meal would be entirely out of place in a room decorated, for instance, with Chinese lacquer and silken hangings.'

*

Egg Dishes

The omelette! There they err, the writers of letters, and their ideas of how to make an omelette belong, unlike Madame Poulard's, to legend. Ah, they say, the place had charm, atmosphere. Now, the cooking is done, more or less, by a ruthless limited company; but her omelette, her secret...

It must have been the moonlight, for she had no secret, except that she was an extremely good cook. Yet reminiscent visitors will have none of this unromantic truth. She did this or that; she put cream in it, she put water. (Putting water in the eggs is one of the superstitions current in England about French omelettes. What about the effect of the water on the hot iron? But that is a detail.)

She shook it in a special way.... She used plenty of butter. Yet we know she did not, as you cannot make an omelette if you put too much butter in the frying-pan.

Even those who talk intelligently about her gifts seem to think that she had, if not a secret, at least special implements and unusual habits. She had, we read, 'a frying-pan with a handle about a yard and a half long', which she used dexterously on an enormous open fire.

Quite so. But this pan is the traditional pan even now of every country cook in that part of France and in the South-West, where two things only are used for cooking, an open fire for frying and roasting, charcoals for the rest, flames and glowing embers. When baking is required a Dutch oven is used or the things are sent to the local baker, who puts them in the large brick oven when he has finished baking the bread.

We read also the surprising statement that 'might not please the enthusiasts quite so much; the pan was never washed; it was wiped, for to introduce water to a frying-pan was anathema to the old-fashioned French country cook.' 'Was', indeed! And since when was an omelette pan ever washed, either by the illiterate peasant, or the most fastidious chef? This would be simply asking for disaster.

However, it is pleasing to see so many people bothering at all about Madame Poulard's marvellous omelette, and it is amusing to hear that for the first time in history, it is claimed, a monument is to be erected to an omelette.

It will be at the Mont St Michel, on the Breton coast, where the late Madame Poulard's famed omelette is to be immortalized in granite or marble.

We should have thought that marble or granite was the most unsuitable material for the representation of an omelette which was always so light and soft. This well-meant compliment would, no doubt, have shocked the nice and simple Madame Poulard from all points of view, as a cook and as a woman.

*

OMELETTE *Omelette*

It is not particularly easy to describe in a clear and concise way how to make an omelette. But we can, to begin with, dismiss a few legends; the whites and the yolks are not beaten separately, there never is any water or milk added to the beaten eggs, it is never cooked, as I have seen it stated, for ten to fifteen minutes. Indeed, once the eggs are in the pan it is not a question of minutes but of seconds.

You want a good, fairly thick iron pan, which should be kept well greased, never washed and never used for anything but frying. This pan must be left on the fire empty for a good quarter of an hour so that it is really hot when you make the omelette.

It must be so hot that the small piece of butter you put in smokes at once and almost catches fire.

Having put in the fat, such as it is (butter, pork fat, goose fat, lard), swirl it round quickly, and put in at once your beaten eggs. Remember also that the moment the eggs are in they begin to cook, so do not wait a second.

Shaking the pan vigorously with the left hand, stir the eggs with the right hand, with a fork you are keeping flat; pass it under the eggs, lifting them and stirring them, and around the edge of the pan, gathering them, so to speak, to allow them to cook evenly.

You now have your eggs cooked (and looking rather like underdone scrambled eggs) flat in the pan. Fold the omelette away from you with the fork.

Still holding the pan with the left hand bang the handle hard with your right fist, this will make the omelette slide to the end of the pan; improve the shape if necessary.

The omelette being now at the edge of the pan, take the pan with the right hand and with the left, hold a hot dish vertically and close to the pan, which you turn over. The omelette is ready and, we hope, perfect.

As I have said, all this only takes a few seconds, and that is why speed is necessary; this can only be acquired by practice. If time is wasted the omelette will probably be leathery, flat, browned outside like a pancake and inside like scrambled eggs. An omelette must be the same consistency all through.

The secrets are:
1. The pan (in a perfect state) must be really hot.
2. The moment you have put in the fat, swirl and put in the eggs.
3. Start shaking and stirring at once.

Other rules to be observed: the eggs, seasoned, should be beaten at the last minute and not too much, just enough to mix the whites and the yolks well.

Do not use too much butter. For an omelette of four to six eggs (that is, for two or three people) a piece of butter the size of a walnut is quite enough.

If the pan catches (it is probably because it is damp, or there may have been a drop of water or condensed steam touching it) boil a tablespoonful of oil in it for a quarter of an hour and wipe it well with a dry cloth. A new pan should be treated in the same way.

Above all, do not be discouraged if you fail; some people are born omelette-makers, some are not.

To the unsuccessful ones I give this tip: Try lard or pork fat instead of butter. Butter always contains a certain amount of moisture which fat does not, and the taste of goose fat or bacon fat, for instance, is delicious.

§ *Eggs; butter (or lard or pork fat).*

OMELETTE AUX FINES HERBES   *Omelette with Mixed Herbs*
Prepare as described above, adding into the mixture chopped parsley and chives. Cook in the usual way.

§ *Eggs; butter (or lard or pork fat); parsley; chives.*

OMELETTE AU JAMBON   *Ham Omelette*
Cut some ham in very thin pieces and add to the mixture.

§ *Eggs; butter (or lard or pork fat); ham.*

OMELETTE À L'OIGNON   *Onion Omelette*
Cut an onion in thin slices, brown it in butter, adding it then to the mixture.

§ *Eggs; butter; onion.*

OMELETTE AUX CHAMPIGNONS					*Mushroom Omelette*
	Cut the mushrooms in thin slices, cook them in butter, and add them to your eggs.
		§ *Eggs; butter; mushrooms.*

OMELETTE AU FROMAGE						*Cheese Omelette*
	Add grated cheese to the eggs and beat well. Some people in this case add a little milk.
		§ *Eggs; butter (or lard or pork fat); cheese; milk.*

OMELETTE AUX POMMES DE TERRE				*Potato Omelette*
	Cut two or three potatoes in little cubes, fry them in butter till cooked; add salt and pepper and a little parsley and spring onion chopped together. Put this in a dish, pour the beaten eggs (already seasoned) over the mixture and make your omelette.
		§ *Eggs; butter; parsley; spring onions.*

OMELETTE AUX LAITANCES					*Omelette with Roe*
	Cook a few soft roes in butter. Prepare your eggs and make your omelette. When almost cooked arrange the roes in the middle of it and fold over.
		§ *Eggs; butter; soft roes.*

OMELETTE À L'OSEILLE						*Sorrel Omelette*
	Prepare your eggs in a basin as usual. Get two or three handfuls of nice sorrel leaves; they should be young and fresh. Wash them well and remove the stalks and middle ribs of the larger leaves and dry them; then cut them very fine, but with a knife, not with a chopper. Mix them with your eggs, add just a little chopped garlic and chervil and make your omelette in the usual way. It should be made rather thick, so that, the inside being less cooked, the sorrel which is there remains almost raw. This gives it a peculiar acid taste, extremely pleasant and fresh.
	This is the real sorrel omelette as it is done in that southern part of France where food is of the best. No omelette made with cooked sorrel can compare with it.
		§ *Eggs; sorrel leaves; garlic; chervil; butter (or lard or pork fat).*

OMELETTE AUX FLEURS DE SALSIFIS			*Salsify Flower Omelette*
	This omelette is not easy to make, not because it is difficult to do it well, but because it is not easy to get the necessary flowers. Salsify

flowers are not usually sold in shops; in fact, they are only to be found in the vegetable garden in the late spring. The best salsify for this purpose is the one imported from Spain, which has black roots and yellow flowers.

Nip them literally in the bud, and wash them well in several waters to get rid of the kind of milk which oozes out when you break them. Then dry them in a cloth for a few minutes, after which cook them in butter till they are brown, with salt and pepper. Mix them with the beaten eggs and make your omelette in the ordinary way.

Do not be surprised to see the buds open in the hot butter. It affects them more quickly than the sun; some show a few already yellow petals. It is a pretty sight; also the taste is delicious.

§ *Eggs; butter; salsify flowers.*

OMELETTE NIÇOISE *Omelette Niçoise*

Omelette Niçoise is a flat omelette: take one aubergine, or egg plant, and one courgette, which is a kind of young vegetable marrow, peel them, cut them in pieces, and fry them in butter and oil mixed. When they are soft, chop them finely, also a little parsley and chervil.

Break the eggs (for one of each vegetable, six to eight eggs, which would do for four to six people) in a bowl, add salt, pepper, a little grated cheese, and a pinch of spices; beat well, add the mixture of aubergines and courgettes, and cook like any omelette. Do not fold it, but toss it like a Spanish omelette.

§ *Eggs; aubergine; courgette; parsley; chervil; cheese; spices; butter; oil.*

OMELETTE AUX FOIES DE VOLAILLE *Chicken Liver Omelette*

Cut some chicken livers in small pieces, cook them in butter with salt and pepper. Make your plain omelette. When it is almost cooked put the chicken livers neatly in the middle, add a few drops of *jus*, and fold your omelette over them.

§ *Eggs; chicken livers; butter;* jus.

OMELETTE AU CRABE *Crab Omelette*

As there is a certain quantity of crab flesh in this omelette, it is enough to allow one egg and a half to each person instead of the usual two.

Take a medium-sized crab. Having cooked it, empty it, separating the white flesh and the insides. Pound the insides in a bowl and season with just salt and pepper (no dressing).

Beat the eggs and season them. Mix well with the pounded insides, add the white flesh, beat again and make the omelette in the ordinary way.

It is more important than ever for this omelette, which contains a certain amount of matter besides the eggs, that the pan should be really hot before you put in the mixture.

As usual, the omelette should be cooked in an instant.

§ *Eggs; crab; butter (or lard or pork fat).*

OMELETTE À LA CRÈME   *Cream Omelette*

This is an ambitious omelette, and a delicious one. Beat the eggs and cook as usual; add to the omelette before folding a few fresh mushrooms, previously cooked in cream and butter, fold it in the usual way, pour over your omelette – which must be light, soft, and not too well cooked – a thin *Béchamel* sauce, well seasoned, and to which cream and a little grated cheese have been added, and brown lightly under a gas grill (if you have not got a salamander). Needless to say, all these operations must be done in a few minutes. You can decorate it, if you want it more elaborate, with a few slices of truffles.

§ *Eggs; mushrooms; cream; butter; cheese;* béchamel *sauce (roux, milk, nutmeg). Truffles can be added.*

OMELETTE À L'ESPAGNOLE   *Spanish Omelette*

This omelette is slightly browned, tossed like a pancake and served flat. Fry in butter one medium-sized potato cut in small cubes, half an onion cut finely and add to these when they are almost cooked half a sweet pepper and one tomato (pips and skin removed) cut finely.

Cook for one minute more, add to the beaten eggs, season and cook in the ordinary way. Let the mixture cook a little more than you would for an ordinary folded omelette, and toss. These quantities of vegetables and three eggs would make an omelette large enough for two people. It is almost a meal in itself.

§ *Eggs; potato; onion; sweet pepper; tomato; butter (or lard or pork fat).*

ŒUFS POCHÉS   *Poached Eggs*

Fill a large saucepan with salted water, add a little vinegar and bring to the boil. Break your eggs, one by one, in a bowl and drop them, also one by one, carefully into the water. Cook a few minutes only; the inside of the egg must be soft. Take them out one by one and put them

EGG DISHES

for a few seconds in tepid water; then let them dry a little at the entrance of the oven.

§ *Eggs; vinegar.*

ŒUFS POCHÉS BÉARNAISE — *Poached Eggs Béarnaise*

Poach your eggs and put them on a stiff *Béarnaise* sauce.

§ *Eggs; vinegar; Béarnaise sauce (eggs, shallots, vinegar, butter, tarragon, parsley).*

ŒUFS EN COCOTTE — *Eggs en Cocotte*

Put a little melted butter in a little fireproof dish and break your eggs over it, one in each *cocotte*. Cook *au bain-marie*, adding salt and pepper and, just before serving, a little Tomato sauce, *jus*, or cream.

§ *Eggs;* Tomato sauce *(tomatoes, carrots, onion, brown roux, stock, wine vinegar, butter) or* jus *or cream.*

FRITTATA ALLA GENOVESE — *Genoese Omelette*

Chop finely one onion and fry it in a mixture of oil and butter; boil in salt water a few leaves of spinach, beetroot greens, young tender artichokes, or any suitable vegetables of that type; when cooked chop them and add them, together with the fried onion, to the beaten eggs, with a little marjoram, salt and pepper, and grated Parmesan.

There should be a good deal of chopped vegetable, so that the finished *frittata* is more green than yellow. Cook on a moderate fire in a frying-pan till the whole thing is set. Do not fold it.

§ *Eggs; Parmesan cheese; onion; spinach (or beetroot greens, artichokes, or other similar vegetables); marjoram; oil; butter.*

ŒUFS BROUILLÉS — *Scrambled Eggs*

Scrambled eggs – or, to give the dish its French name, *œufs brouillés* – to be soft and creamy, must be cooked extremely slowly, well stirred, on a slow fire. It must be remembered that no milk should be added to the scrambled eggs, and they should not be too much cooked.

The eggs, two for each person, should be seasoned with salt and pepper, beaten with a fork lightly, fairly well, but not too much, and this should be done at the last minute only. Meanwhile, the butter is melting slowly in a thick saucepan. Put in the eggs and cook, stirring all the time. As soon as they have reached the right smooth, creamy consistency, remove them and stir in a few small pieces of butter. Slow cooking is absolutely essential. They should be served the moment they are ready.

§ *Eggs; butter.*

ŒUFS BROUILLÉS AU FROMAGE   *Scrambled Eggs with Cheese*
Prepare as before, adding some grated cheese at the beginning. Stir all the time. Add cream before serving.
§ *Eggs; butter; cheese; cream.*

ŒUFS BROUILLÉS AUX CHAMPIGNONS   *Scrambled Eggs with Mushrooms*
Peel and cut a few mushrooms. Cook them in butter, then add them to the scrambled eggs with a little cream just before serving.
§ *Eggs; butter; mushrooms; cream.*

ŒUFS BROUILLÉS AU SAFRAN   *Scrambled Eggs with Saffron*
Beat the eggs well (two for each person), add about a pudding-spoonful of milk, salt and pepper, and beat again. Mix in a pan a little butter, a teaspoonful of concentrated beef stock, a pinch of saffron, and cook it for a few minutes; then put in the eggs, stirring all the time. They should be cooked on a slow fire so that they remain light and creamy, and, of course, served the moment they are ready.
§ *Eggs; butter; milk; beef stock; saffron.*

ŒUFS BROUILLÉS AUX TRUFFES   *Scrambled Eggs with Truffles*
Peel some black truffles and cut them in small pieces. Warm them in butter. Prepare and cook your scrambled eggs, add the truffles and a little *jus*. Stir well.
§ *Eggs; butter; truffles; jus.*

ŒUFS BROUILLÉS AU HOMARD   *Scrambled Eggs with Lobster*
Take some small pieces of cooked lobster tossed in butter with paprika for two minutes. Prepare the scrambled eggs, dispose a small amount of the prepared lobster in the middle and pour all over a cream sauce made with reduced *fumet* of fish and fresh cream.
§ *Eggs; butter; lobster pieces; paprika; fumet of fish; cream.*

ŒUFS LANDAISE   *Eggs Landaise*
Take two or three pork sausages, remove the skin and break them into small pieces; chop an onion finely and remove the skin and pips of two tomatoes.
Cook the sausage-meat and onions first; when nearly done add the tomatoes, cut in small pieces, and cook one minute more. Put all this in a fireproof dish, break four eggs over it, season well, sprinkle with

grated cheese. Begin cooking on the top of the range and finish in the oven or under the grill.

§ *Eggs; pork sausages; onion; tomatoes; cheese.*

ŒUFS GRATINÉS *Eggs with Cheese*

Have the eggs soft boiled so that part of the yolk is soft and the white not yet hard (six minutes' cooking is about right). Shell them carefully (dropping them into cold water will help) and cut them in smallish pieces.

Prepare a *Béchamel* sauce to which you add small pieces of cooked mushrooms. Add the pieces of egg and put the mixture in individual ramequins or soufflé dishes, sprinkle with grated cheese, brown lightly and serve.

§ *Eggs;* Béchamel *sauce* (roux, *milk, nutmeg*); *mushrooms; cheese.*

ŒUFS À LA BELGE *Belgian Eggs*

Make about a bowlful of rather thick *Béchamel* sauce, well flavoured with salt, pepper and nutmeg. Let it cool a little, then stir in the yolks of four eggs. Beat the whites to a stiff froth and add them to the mixture.

Take a mould and butter it well; put in the preparation and cook in a moderate oven, standing in boiling water, for about a quarter of an hour.

Have half a bowlful of *Béchamel,* rather thin, add to it a little tomato purée and a little grated cheese (also chopped truffles, if you like); put the sauce on the fire so that it is really hot, and pour it all over the eggs, which you turn out in the serving dish.

§ *Eggs;* Béchamel *sauce* (roux, *milk, nutmeg); butter; tomato purée; cheese. Truffles can be added.*

PIPÉRADE *Pipérade*

A delicious dish, very popular in Béarn and in the Basque country, but not well known otherwise, is the Pipérade.

It is a kind of egg dish, and some people make it either like scrambled eggs or like an omelette. But this is not right, and when finished it should be impossible to see which is egg and which is vegetable, the aspect being that of a rather frothy purée. Take a few sweet peppers, cut them in slices, remove the seeds, and cook them slowly in pork fat or olive oil. Cook in the same way the same quantity of tomatoes (peeled), adding them later, as they do not take so long to cook. Add salt, pepper, and one crushed clove of garlic. Let it all simmer till it has quite melted and become a soft purée; then break in, one by one and without beating them, three or four eggs. Stir quickly over the fire till the eggs are cooked, and serve at once with, if you like, slices of Bayonne ham previously fried.

§ *Eggs; sweet peppers; tomatoes; garlic; pork fat or olive oil. Bayonne ham can be added to dish.*

ŒUFS DURS   Hard-boiled Eggs

Boil the eggs ten minutes on a quick fire; put them in cold water before using; they should not be peeled till they are completely cold.

The eggs may then be cut in half lengthwise and served with a variety of sauces, such as *Béchamel*, Purée of Sorrel, Tomato Sauce, Anchovy Butter, etc.

§ *Eggs;* Béchamel *sauce (roux, milk, nutmeg) or other sauce.*

ŒUFS MIMOSA   Stuffed Eggs with Foie Gras (Cold)

These are the delicious 'Eggs Mimosa'.

Take some hard-boiled eggs, cut them in half and remove the yolks, which you chop very finely.

Take some *foie gras*, enough to fill the eggs you have, pass it through a fine sieve, and stuff the eggs with it. This should be done with a light hand and the *foie gras* should not be pressed down. Dispose your eggs in a hollow serving dish and prepare the sauce.

The sauce is a mixture of *Béchamel* and mayonnaise, one-third of the former and two-thirds of the latter; the *Béchamel* should not be too stiff or the mayonnaise too vinegary, all this being combined so as not to drown the fine flavour of the *foie gras*. It should be poured over the stuffed eggs, which should be completely covered and sprinkled all over with the chopped yolks.

§ *Eggs;* foie gras; Béchamel *sauce (roux, milk; nutmeg); mayonnaise (eggs, vinegar, oil).*

ŒUFS À LA DIABLE   Devilled Eggs

In one saucepan make a rather thin Béchamel sauce properly seasoned with salt, pepper and nutmeg; in another one cook in butter two shallots finely chopped; when they are browned add a drop of wine vinegar, a tablespoonful of French mustard, a pinch of paprika and a pinch of curry powder; stir all this well, add it to the *Béchamel* sauce, with which you incorporate the yolk of one egg and a small glass of fresh cream. Cook slowly *au bain-marie,* whipping all the time and adding one by one little pieces of butter. See that it is highly seasoned, and if necessary rectify the seasoning. Keep the sauce as hot as possible, the saucepan still standing in hot water.

Meanwhile fry your eggs either in butter, or in bacon fat according to taste, turning them once. They should be well fried outside and soft inside. Dispose them on toast previously fried. Just before serving pour the *Sauce Diable* all round and all over the eggs.

§ *Eggs;* Béchamel *sauce (roux, milk, nutmeg); paprika; shallots; French mustard; curry powder; wine vinegar; cream; butter. Bacon fat can be used for frying.*

ŒUFS FARCIS *Stuffed Eggs*

Take some hard-boiled eggs, remove the shells and cut the eggs lengthwise in half; take two fillets of anchovy for each egg and chop them very fine with the yolks. Melt a good piece of butter in a small saucepan, put in the mixture, add salt, pepper, a few chopped chives, and cook till the butter has entirely disappeared, then fill the eggs with this mixture, and serve hot with Tomato sauce.

§ *Eggs; anchovies; butter; chives; Tomato sauce (tomatoes, carrot, onion, brown roux, stock, wine vinegar, butter).*

ŒUFS EN ASPIC *Eggs in Aspic*

For each person use one egg, and first poach the eggs so that while the yolks must be soft the whites must be quite firm and set.

Place these in a fairly shallow serving dish just deep enough to allow the eggs to be covered with the jelly. Season the eggs with salt and a little lemon juice. Then pour over the jelly, which has been flavoured with six tomatoes and passed through a fine strainer. The jelly must, of course, be made of calf's foot and bones, and not gelatine. Place the dish in a cool place to allow the jelly to set, and serve cold.

§ *Eggs; lemon juice; calf's foot and bones; tomatoes.*

Fish

I understand that in Jamaica it used to be customary for the people who lived in the mountains to have their fish brought straight from the sea by relays of Negroes running through the night, so that the fish arrived delightfully fresh for breakfast (unlike the Negroes). These days are probably over.

*

POISSON GRILLÉ   *Grilled Fish*

Nothing is better than grilled fish. It seems somehow to bring out the sea flavour and to increase the quality of the flesh. Trout, sole, small turbot, salmon, cod, red mullet, mackerel, herring are delicious grilled. The principles are the same as for meat; a hot grill, greased; fish painted with butter; quick grilling at first, then slower.

Slices of fish are just painted, but a whole fish should be slightly cut; a sole lengthways, following the bone and as far in as the bone; other types of fish, unless quite small, should have a few incisions across on each side. Then the heat will penetrate into the thick part of the fish, so that the thin sides and the thicker middle will be cooked at the same time.

When the flesh is white and opaque and comes off the bone easily the fish is ready. Only then sprinkle with salt and serve at once with melted butter, *Maître d'hôtel* butter, *Béarnaise* or *Tartare* sauce or according to recipe.

§ *Fish; butter;* Maître d'hôtel *butter (butter; parsley, lemon juice). Can also be served with* Béarnaise *sauce (see p. 17) or* Tartare *sauce (see p. 19).*

FILETS DE SOLE BONNE FEMME   *Fillets of Sole Bonne Femme*

Put in a buttered fireproof dish a few sliced mushrooms, parsley and one shallot, finely chopped. Put the fillets of sole over this, add salt,

FISH

pepper, two tablespoonfuls of dry white wine and three of *fumet* of fish and poach the fish slowly.

When cooked remove the fillets and reduce the sauce by three-quarters; put back the fillets and add a few small pieces of butter, shaking the dish well so that the sauce is smooth. Just before serving glaze quickly for one minute or so in a hot oven or under a grill.

§ *Sole; mushrooms; parsley; shallot; dry white wine; fumet of fish; butter.*

FILETS DE SOLE À LA CRÈME   *Fillets of Sole, Cream Sauce.*

Cook the fillets of sole in a *court-bouillon* at the boiling-point (prepared as described and to which you add the bones and head of the fish). Boil very slowly for about four minutes and keep the fillets hot in half the stock. Reduce the other half till there are only about two tablespoonfuls left. Strain, put back the *fumet* into the saucepan, bring to the boil; add a cupful of fresh cream, salt, and a pinch of paprika; bring to the boil again, let it boil and reduce till it has thickened; finish by putting in a small piece of butter off the fire, shake the pan lightly till the butter has melted and mixed with the cream sauce, and pour over the fillets of sole, well drained, in the serving dish.

These can be served plain or adorned with all sorts of things: oysters, mussels, or mushrooms previously cooked, fresh grapes, peeled, pips removed, and cut in half, or halves of hard-boiled eggs covered with a layer of caviare. It makes a fine dish for a dinner-party.

§ *Sole;* court-bouillon; *bones and head of sole; cream; paprika; butter. Can be served with oysters, mussels, mushrooms, grapes, hard-boiled eggs or caviare.*

*

Obviously the three things which frighten people are butter, cream and wine. (I do not mention brandy or liqueurs, as these are used so sparingly and so rarely in everyday cooking that they are not worth considering.) Butter, of course, is used in large quantities, but still not so recklessly as people imagine. Also I would point out that I often advise for a dish pork fat, bacon fat or oil, according to the character of the dish.

As for cream, although expensive in itself, this is not a considerable item; a half-pint of cream goes a long way, and would be quite sufficient for, say, 'Escalopes de veau Tzarine', 'Fillets de sole', or 'Supremes de volaille' for five or six people. When used as a liaison with yolk of egg it is nearly always mentioned in tablespoonfuls.

Wine! Wine is the worst drawback, they say. It is nothing of the kind. The secret is not to put in the menu a dish which requires a little wine, unless there is some wine left over from the table. Yet, even if you have to buy it purposely, a half-bottle of cheap wine will do quite well, and, well corked, in a cool place, will keep several days. Expensive wine is not necessary for cooking – as some writers on gastronomic matters swankishly would make us believe – and for a very good reason: the flavour of the wine is not discernible; in fact, if a wine sauce, once reduced, still tastes of wine it is not a good sauce, the wine being only in these cases an ingredient contributing its richness to a harmonious ensemble in which all things should collaborate.

I would also add once more that in French cooking nothing is wasted, and a large number of delicious dishes are made of pieces left over, thereby saving the purchase of more raw materials.

*

FILETS DE SOLE DOROTHÉE *Fillets of Sole Dorothea*

The sole having been filleted, put in a small saucepan the head and bones, one onion in slices, one carrot, thyme, bay leaf, clove, salt and pepper, a glass of water and a glass of dry white wine, bring to the boil, and reduce it on a slow fire for about twenty minutes. Pass it through muslin and keep it warm. Sprinkle the fillets with salt and paprika and cook them in butter, then *flambez* them with a little good brandy; mix together this butter and brandy and the sauce previously prepared, add small mushrooms, a glass of fresh cream, a little lemon juice, and pour it very hot over the fillets. It is advisable for this dish, as for all dishes which are *flambés,* to use really good brandy, and not the kind generally sold as cooking brandy, which is useless for the purpose, having no strength and no flavour.

§ *Sole; trimmings of sole; onion; carrot; thyme; bay leaf; clove; dry white wine; paprika; butter; brandy; mushrooms; cream; lemon juice.*

SOLE NORMANDE *Sole Normandy*

Take a fine sole, skin it and put in a fireproof dish with several pieces of butter, salt, pepper, a little grated nutmeg and a glassful of good white wine. Bake it in a moderate oven for about half an hour, basting occasionally, then remove it and keep it warm while the sauce is being made. For this you want a few prawns (shelled), a dozen or so of mussels already cooked (which means simply boiling them for a few minutes in salt water with a *bouquet,* when they open and you can easily remove them from the shells), and the stock in which the mussels have been cooked.

Put in a small saucepan all the gravy from the sole, two spoonfuls of the mussel stock, the mussels and the prawns, cook it for a few minutes,

FISH

bind it with butter in which you have cooked a little flour, cook a little more, add a small quantity of cream, pour the sauce over your sole and serve very hot.

§ *Sole; butter; nutmeg; white wine; prawns; mussels; mussel stock; flour; cream;* bouquet.

SOLE EN MATELOTTE *Sole Matelotte*

This dish, although it has not the reputation of the *Sole Normande,* is a very favourite dish both in Brittany and Normandy. Skin the sole, put it in a fireproof dish, cover the sole with a mixture in equal parts of water and dry cider, salt, pepper, and a *bouquet.* Cook about twenty-five minutes, then put the gravy in a small saucepan, remove the *bouquet,* thicken as described above, pour it over the fish and sprinkle over it very fine brown breadcrumbs and serve at once.

§ *Sole; cider;* bouquet; *brown breadcrumbs; butter; flour.*

SOLE AU VIN BLANC *Sole in White Sauce*

Put the sole in a buttered fireproof dish with a good glass of white wine and two shallots chopped. Cook five or six minutes, turning it over. Remove the sauce, put it in a saucepan and add a spoonful of brown *roux,* salt, pepper, and a few small mushrooms. Reduce it a little, pour it over the sole, sprinkle with breadcrumbs, add a few pieces of fresh butter and cook in the oven for a few minutes.

§ *Sole; white wine; shallots; brown* roux; *mushrooms; butter; breadcrumbs.*

SOLES AU FOUR *Baked Soles*

Take a medium-sized sole (or two, according to the number of people), remove the black skin and the head. Put the head or heads in a small saucepan with three mushrooms cut in slices, one onion, a *bouquet,* salt and pepper, dry white wine and water. Bring to the boil, let it simmer till it has reduced by half and pour through muslin into a cup. Put aside the mushrooms, which will be used later in the dish. Put the soles in a buttered fireproof dish and pour over them the fish stock previously made, to which you add a little more white wine with a little tomato purée mixed with it. Cook slowly, basting often. When the soles are about half cooked, put in the mushrooms, sprinkle with breadcrumbs and go on cooking slowly, basting meanwhile till ready. The sauce should be a short one and the soles just slightly browned.

§ *Sole; trimmings of sole; mushrooms; onion;* bouquet; *dry white wine; tomato purée; breadcrumbs.*

SAUMON BRETONNE   *Salmon Bretonne*

Take a piece of salmon, remove the skin and bones and cut it in cubes about one inch square; sprinkle them with salt and pepper and toss them in butter together with a few slices of mushrooms for two or three minutes. Move the pan to the oven to finish the cooking, about a quarter of an hour. When cooked put the pieces of fish and mushrooms, well drained, in the serving dish. Pour butter over at the foaming stage, to which you add a little lemon juice to make a short sauce.

§ *Salmon; butter; mushrooms; lemon juice.*

SAUMON AU FOUR, SAUCE DE RAIFORT   *Baked Salmon, Horseradish Sauce*

Take a thick slice of salmon, about one pound and a half in weight, paint it with olive oil and season it with salt and pepper. Wrap it well in butter-paper, well oiled, folding the ends well, so that it cannot get undone. Bake in a moderate oven for one hour and a half. Serve with horseradish sauce.

§ *Salmon; olive oil;* Raifort *sauce (horseradish vinegar, shallots, cream).*

SAUMON EN PAPILLOTES   *Salmon Papillotes*

Take some fillets of salmon (number according to your requirements) about five or six inches long and the same number of pieces of butter paper well oiled.

Prepare in advance a mixture of mushrooms, shallots and bacon (in equal quantities) cooked two or three minutes, to which are added chopped parsley, mixed spice, salt and pepper.

Sprinkle each sheet with this flavouring mixture. Put the fillet of salmon, seasoned on both sides with salt and pepper, in the middle of the paper; sprinkle the fish itself with more of the mixture, fold carefully and bake in an oiled dish for about twenty-five minutes in a moderate oven.

§ *Salmon; mushrooms; shallots; bacon; parsley; mixed spice.*

ESCALOPES DE SAUMON VOLGA   *Escallops of Salmon Volga*

Take a piece of salmon (in the middle cut) and remove the fillets. Cut these across so as to make slices about three-quarters of an inch thick.

Trim and shape them well, and put them flat in a buttered dish, season with salt and pepper.

Put in about level with the *escalopes* of salmon some *fumet* of fish, to

FISH

which you add a little dry white wine. Bring to the boil and poach them on a slow fire till cooked (about twelve minutes). Keep them hot.

Put part of the stock in a sauté pan and reduce it by three-quarters. You have then only about a spoonful. To this add a glass of fresh cream.

Bring to the boil and let it thicken. When it is thick enough stir in a puddingspoonful of caviare and add, off the fire, a few small pieces of butter to melt in the heat of the sauce. Pour over the *escalopes* of salmon in the serving dish.

Allow one *escalope* for each person (if the salmon is fairly large; otherwise two), and one-third of a pint of cream for four people.

§ *Salmon; fumet of fish; dry white wine; cream; caviare; butter.*

TERRINE DE SAUMON   *Terrine of Salmon*
This dish is served cold and in the *terrine*. It is advisable to make it for about eight people or to serve it twice; it will keep quite well for two days in a cool place.

Take two and a half pounds of salmon, cut the best parts of it in fillets about one inch thick and four inches long, and put these in a dish for two hours with salt, pepper, a bay leaf and two glasses of sherry, turning them occasionally.

Have the flesh of some fish pounded and passed through a wire sieve (say two whitings and a slice of cod for our quantity of salmon); mash also the rest of the salmon; mix together, add salt, pepper, a piece of stale bread dipped in milk, two yolks of eggs, a few very small pieces of butter and, if you like, one truffle finely chopped.

Moisten with some of the sherry in which the salmon has soaked, butter the terrine and fill it – first a layer of minced fish, then a layer of salmon, and so on till it is full, finished by a layer of minced fish.

Cook with the lid on about an hour and a quarter in a moderate oven.

Serve with this a plain green salad and no mayonnaise, as it would drown the delicate taste of the pâté.

§ *Salmon; bay leaf; sherry; whiting or cod; stale bread; milk; egg yolks; butter. A truffle can be added.*

TRUITES À L'AUVERGNATE   *Trout à l'Auvergnate*
Clean the trout, cut them across here and there, and dry them in a cloth, sprinkled lightly with flour. Melt a good piece of butter in the pan, and when at the foaming stage put in the trout. Cook them well on both sides.

Just before serving throw in a little shallot, onion and parsley, finely chopped. Having cooked it one minute, add this to a sauce made as follows: yolk of egg in which you stir olive oil (as for a mayonnaise), vinegar, lemon juice, salt and pepper.

Put the fish in a serving dish and cover with the sauce.

§ *Trout; flour; butter; shallot; onion; parsley; yolk of egg; olive oil; vinegar; lemon juice.*

TRUITES GRENOBLOISE   *Trout Grenobloise*

The trout is cooked in foaming butter. Then, having removed that butter which has turned black, make a short *Meunière* sauce to which you add little quarters of lemon and capers.

Red Mullet can be treated in the same way.

§ *Trout;* Meunière *sauce (butter, lemon juice); lemons; capers; butter.*

TRUITES FARCIES À LA BOURGUIGNONNE   *Stuffed Trout Bourguignonne*

Take one small trout for each person; the stuffing for each trout is a quarter of a pound of salmon (once the skin and bones are removed it will be about right).

Open the trout at the back, slicing it all along, and empty it, removing the bone carefully. Stuff it with the following mixture: salmon flesh pounded in a mortar, with half a white of egg to each quarter of a pound of salmon, then squashed through a fine sieve, well seasoned and mixed with a little fresh cream.

Each trout is then wrapped in oiled paper and poached slowly (about a quarter of an hour) in red wine, with small onions, mushrooms cut in pieces, and a *bouquet*; put in also, in a muslin bag, coarsely broken pepper, a little garlic and a few cloves. For the poaching, bring to the boil and let it simmer very, very gently.

Remove the trout, unwrap them carefully, and put them in the serving dish. Remove from the sauce the *bouquet* and the bag, and let the sauce reduce by half. At the last minute put in, off the fire, in the still boiling sauce, a piece of butter in which you have worked a little flour. Stir well and pour over the fish, surrounded with onions and mushrooms, in the serving dish. Serve cold or hot, as you prefer.

§ *Trout; salmon; whites of egg; cream; red wine; small onions; mushrooms; bouquet; peppercorns; garlic; cloves; butter; flour.*

TRUITES AU VIN BLANC, I   *Trout in White Wine, I*

Cook the trout in a *court-bouillon,* to which you add a good glass of white wine. Time of cooking according to size. Drain the fish well. Serve covered with a *Beurre Blanc* sauce.

§ *Trout;* court-bouillon; *white wine;* Beurre Blanc *sauce (butter, vinegar, shallots).*

TRUITES AU VIN BLANC, II   *Trout in White Wine, II*

Have some small trout, put them in a fireproof dish, with, all round, tomatoes cut in quarters, one banana cut in thin slices, tarragon and shallots finely chopped. Pour over all this a glass of dry white wine, season well, and cook very slowly. Turn them carefully when they are about half done. When they are ready, remove the skins and keep the fish hot; let the sauce reduce a little more, then pass it through a fine sieve. Dispose the trout in the fireproof dish; add some *Sauce Hollandaise* to the sauce, little by little, over a very slow fire, whipping all the time. When it has the right consistency pour over the trout and serve at once.

§ *Trout; tomatoes; banana; tarragon; shallots; dry white wine;* Hollandaise *sauce (yolks of egg, vinegar, peppercorns, butter).*

TRUITE SAUMONÉE À LA CRÈME   *Salmon Trout with Cream*

Take a salmon trout about two pounds in weight and clean it well. Remove the skin carefully, and dip the fish in fresh cream, then in very little flour.

Put it in a long fireproof dish well buttered, cook it in a moderate oven for a few minutes, then turn it on to the other side.

Add then two glasses of sherry (or of dry white wine), let it reduce a while in a slower oven, basting well; a few minutes later add a good glass of fresh cream and finish the cooking, basting often.

Serve in the same dish.

The whole of the cooking takes a little less than half an hour, and you require about half a pint of cream for a two-pound fish.

This excellent dish is garnished with little pieces of cucumber, cut olive shaped and all the same size, cooked in salted water with a little butter in it, till soft, disposed either all round or in heaps at each end of the dish.

They should be particularly well drained so as not to spoil the cream sauce.

(A cook not used to this type of dish will find it easier to start cooking the trout with just butter for a few minutes; it will make the peeling easier. Then proceed with the recipe.)

§ *Salmon trout; cream; flour; sherry (or dry white wine). Garnish with cucumber cooked in butter.*

TRUITE SAUMONÉE EN BELLE-VUE　　　*Salmon Trout, Belle-Vue*

Take a salmon trout of the size required (the best are about two and a half to three pounds in weight, large enough for six to eight people). Put it in a *court-bouillon* at boiling-point and poach it for about twenty minutes.

Drain it well, remove the skin and put it in a long metal dish. Usually two sauces are served, a mayonnaise and a *Sauce Verte*.

The fish is surrounded by various trimmings.

These consist of hard-boiled eggs cut in half; the yolk is removed, mashed with butter, well seasoned and the cavity filled with this mixture. Others are filled with caviare. Tomatoes cut in half are scooped out and filled with either Russian salad or sardine butter; *fonds d'artichauts* or slices of poached cucumber can be treated in the same manner, but it is not advisable to use anchovies as one of the ingredients for the filling; the flavour is too strong and would kill the delicate taste of the fish.

§ *Salmon trout;* court-bouillon; *mayonnaise (egg yolks, vinegar, oil);* Sauce Verte *(mayonnaise, spinach, watercress, parsley, tarragon).*

*

As for Chinese cuisine, it is said to begin where French cooking ends, and has charm. So has the language in which recipes from that country are usually written. Out of a book dating from 350 B.C. comes, for instance, an anecdote, which is in itself a recipe, of Emperor Tay-Kong who was sadly neglecting his duties. A supremely delicious dish brought him back to his senses. It was prepared by a certain Tcheon-Yu in the following manner: He sat under a willow-tree on the shore of the lake of Ta and with a rod caught eleven carp. He kept only one, the finest, which he cleaned, emptied, stuffed with mint leaves, and put in a houang-mou *jar, which had contained rice wine for sixty years. He had poured into the jar the juice of many blood oranges and brought it to the boil, then added three clusters of the strongly perfumed white wistaria, removing them at once and replacing them with a bouquet of black peppers and herbs.*

Having taken out the carp, he then threw away the stuffing of mint leaves and replaced it by a mixture of peacocks' tongues and plovers' livers, and finished the cooking in another jar containing aromatized butter from the country of Tsou. He left the carp in the foaming butter just the time of repeating eight times: 'Kien ouy ouna te tche Ken' (whatever it may mean), cooled it in the lake, put it on a bed of ice in a casket, and sent it to the Emperor, who felt in the seventh heaven. And he was a good Emperor for ever after.

*

[68]

FISH

TURBOT AU FOUR *Baked Turbot*

Take a good sized turbot, clean it, and boil it in salted water until cooked. Remove the flesh from the bones and mince it finely, adding salt and pepper, the juice of a lemon, and some crushed nasturtium seeds, which may be obtained in bottles. Mix all this together with a little cream and place the mixture in a buttered fireproof dish, or, if you prefer it, in one little dish for each person. Sprinkle with breadcrumbs and bake in a quick oven until brown.

§ *Turbot; lemon juice; nasturtium seeds; cream; breadcrumbs.*

TURBOT AU GRATIN *Turbot au Gratin*

Take pieces of cold turbot, put them in the middle of a fireproof dish, cover with a little *Béchamel* sauce, breadcrumbs, and a few small pieces of butter. Surround the fish with purée of potatoes and bake in the oven. Serve as soon as ready.

§ *Turbot;* Béchamel *sauce* (roux, *milk, nutmeg); breadcrumbs; potato purée; butter.*

MAQUEREAU MAÎTRE D'HÔTEL *Mackerel Maître d'Hôtel*

Wash and clean the mackerel, dry them, then oil them and grill on a moderate fire. Put them for two minutes in a buttered dish over the fire and cover with a good *Maître d'Hôtel* sauce.

§ *Mackerel;* Maître d'Hôtel *sauce (butter, parsley, lemon juice).*

MAQUEREAU BRETONNE *Mackerel Bretonne*

Take some mackerel – one for each person if small, one for two people if large. Clean them well, slit them and open flat; remove the bone carefully, dry them well, rub them with a little flour and season with salt and pepper. Put a good-sized piece of butter in a pan; when at the foaming stage put in your flattened mackerel with skin uppermost; cook for two or three minutes, turn them and cook them more slowly, for about a quarter of an hour with the lid on.

Serve with a little lemon juice squeezed on at the last minute. Should the butter have become black, do not use it, but melt a little more to pour over the fish. *Whiting, herrings and soles (left whole) can be treated in the same manner.*

§ *Mackerel; flour; butter; lemon juice.*

MAQUEREAU AU FOUR *Baked Mackerel*

This is a pleasant cold-fish dish for hot weather. Slit some mackerel down the middle and remove the heads and tails. Remove the backbone, scrape the fish, wash them, and dry them well. Put them flat, or rolled, in a fireproof dish with salt, pepper (coarsely broken), grated nutmeg, one bay leaf and a small green pepper. Fill the dish level with the fish with three parts white vinegar and one-fourth water and bake in a slow oven for at least four hours.

It is important that the liquid should not boil, as the fillets must remain firm and unbroken. Serve cold with the liquid poured over through a strainer.

§ *Mackerel; nutmeg; bay leaf; green pepper; peppercorns; white vinegar.*

ROUGETS GRILLÉS   Grilled Red Mullet

Clean the fish, dry them, make a few cuts, season with pepper and salt, paint with oil and grill on a moderate fire. Serve with a *Maître d'Hôtel* or a *Beurre Blanc* sauce.

Grey mullet, brill, gurnet or herring can be grilled in the same way. Herring is best with a mustard sauce.

§ *Red mullets; oil;* Maître d'Hôtel *sauce (butter, parsley, lemon juice) or* Beurre Blanc *sauce (butter, vinegar, shallots).*

ROUGETS MARSEILLAISE   Red Mullets Marseillaise

Have some small red mullets, one for each person. Rub them all over with flour so that they are just lightly coated and fry them in hot olive oil, turning them once or twice.

Fry also in oil slices of French roll, one to each mullet. When brown and crisp remove them, rub them with a little garlic and sprinkle with saffron.

In the same oil cook for two minutes the flesh of some tomatoes, cut in pieces, allowing two to each person. Season well with salt and pepper.

Dispose in the serving dish the mullets, well drained, with the pieces of fried French bread round them, spread all over with the cooked tomatoes.

Or you can cut the French bread on the slant to make long pieces; on each you put a mullet and a layer of tomatoes over it.

§ *Red mullets; flour; olive oil; French bread; garlic; saffron; tomatoes.*

ROUGETS RIVIERA   Red Mullets Riviera

Take some red mullets (one for each person, the small ones being the best) and cook them in butter. The pan should be really hot before the butter is put in, and the fish should be well dried in a cloth sprinkled with flour. This is indispensable to prevent catching, but the fish should not be coated with flour. Cook them, turning them once.

Meanwhile pound well the flesh of a few fillets of anchovy in oil and those of one sardine. (If salt anchovies are used they should be soaked in water for six hours to remove the excess of salt.) Mix well with a good piece of butter, chopped parsley and a little lemon juice.

When the mullets are cooked, remove them, throw away the butter in which they have been cooked if any is left or if it has turned to oil; melt the prepared butter in the pan, and when hot pour all over the mullets in the serving dish. For quantities, allow four fillets of anchovy and one sardine mixed with a piece of butter the size of an egg for four red mullets. Season with pepper only.

§ *Red mullets; butter; flour; anchovies in oil; sardine in oil; parsley; lemon juice.*

ROUGETS À LA CRÈME   *Red Mullet with Cream*

Fry the red mullets in good olive oil and butter mixed in equal parts. When cooked, drain well and keep them hot in the serving dish.

For the *crème,* which is flavoured with *fines herbes,* chop finely together chervil, parsley, tarragon, one shallot and one very small piece of lemon rind. Mix well with a teaspoonful of French mustard; add then a teaspoonful of cream slightly whipped and the yolks of two eggs. Cook on a slow fire and add, one by one, six or seven small pieces of butter; season well, stir all the time and serve when it has thickened and become quite hot, but it must not boil. Add a few drops of lemon juice just before serving.

§ *Red mullets; olive oil; butter;* fines herbes; *shallot; lemon rind; French mustard; yolks of egg; lemon juice.*

ROUGETS AU FENOUIL   *Red Mullet with Fennel*

Take some red mullets, dry them well; put in a fireproof dish a mixture of butter and oil, a few pieces of fennel and two tomatoes cut in quarters, dispose your mullets over these and bake in the oven. Season them with salt and pepper and when cooked remove them to another dish and keep them hot. Add a glass of white wine and a glass of Madeira to the stock in the first dish, and go on cooking till well reduced. Pass through a fine sieve.

Prepare a *Maître d'Hôtel* butter (there should be a good amount of lemon juice in it), with this you bind your sauce; see that it is well seasoned and pour it over the red mullets in the serving dish.

§ *Red mullets; butter; olive oil; fennel; tomatoes; white wine; Madeira;* Maître d'Hôtel *butter (butter, lemon juice, parsley).*

CARPE FARCIE *Stuffed Carp*

Clean the fish well. Chop together a slice of stale bread, one hard-boiled egg, two small onions, a few leaves of sorrel, a good piece of butter, salt and pepper. Mix this stuffing well and put it in the fish. Wrap it in oiled paper and cook in a moderate oven. The time of cooking depends on the size of the carp.

It can also be cooked in butter and white wine, basting occasionally.

§ *Carp; stale bread; egg; small onions; sorrel; butter.*

BACALAO À LA VIZCAINA *Salt Cod à la Vizcaina*

Take a piece of salt cod, cut it in pieces about three inches long and soak them in cold water for twelve hours; if by that time it is still hard, boil it for a few minutes so that you can remove the bones easily, but without the fish falling to pieces.

Chop finely some onions (say two or three for about one pound and a half of salt cod) and cook them in olive oil till they are well coloured; grill three or four tomatoes and pass them through a colander. Mix the purée thus obtained with the onions and cook a little while together; then put in the pieces of cod and cook on a slow fire for about fifteen to twenty minutes.

Open a tin of red sweet peppers (pimentos) which are better for this dish than fresh ones, and drain them well. Dispose your pieces of cod together, with the purée of onions and tomatoes in the serving dish, put two or three sweet peppers on the top (cold, such as they are) and garnish with fried bread.

§ *Salt cod; onions; tomatoes; tinned pimentos; fried bread.*

FILETS DE CABILLAUD MARINÉS *Marinated Fillets of Cod*

Take a small cod, fillet it carefully, making sure that there are no bones left, and lard the fillets here and there as you would do for *boeuf à la mode*, then marinate them for a day in the following mixture: a tumblerful of dry white wine and Madeira mixed, a liqueur glassful of brandy, salt, pepper and two or three small *bouquets*, and chopped shallots.

Take a fireproof dish, butter it well, dispose your fillets of fish, garnish them with slices of fresh mushrooms; pour over the mixture in which they have been soaked (less the *bouquets*) and cook about twenty minutes in the oven, basting often. Season well, add two tablespoonfuls of fresh cream, a few small pieces of butter, shake well so that the sauce is evenly bound and serve. *Any fish of a moderate size with a rather dry*

FISH

flesh can be treated in the same way, including such fresh-water fish as carp and pike.

§ *Cod; bacon (for larding); dry white wine; Madeira; brandy; bouquets; shallots; mushrooms; cream; butter.*

HARENGS GRILLÉS *Grilled Herrings*

The best way is to grill them whole. The fish being cleaned and emptied should be simply wiped with a soft cloth, not washed; make just two or three cuts across on each side and grill seven to eight minutes. Sprinkle with salt and serve with Mustard sauce.

§ *Herrings; Mustard sauce (egg yolks, lemon juice, butter, mustard).*

HARENGS MAÎTRE D'HÔTEL *Herrings Maître d'Hôtel*

Having grilled the herrings, slit them down the back and put in a small piece of butter pounded with chopped parsley and lemon juice. Just one minute on the fire in a buttered dish, a little more lemon juice and serve very hot.

§ *Herrings; butter; parsley; lemon juice.*

HARENGS EN DIABLE *Devilled Herrings*

Fry the fish in butter at the foaming stage, when cooked paint them with mustard, sprinkle with chopped parsley and put them in a fireproof dish with a little butter and a drop of vinegar. Cook for one minute and serve with melted butter poured over the fish. The quantity of vinegar and mustard is a question of taste.

§ *Herrings; mustard; parsley; butter; vinegar.*

HARENGS MARINÉS *Marinated Herrings*

Put in a saucepan a pint of water, a pint of dry white wine and two tablespoonfuls of vinegar, one onion and one carrot cut in slices, one clove of garlic, a *bouquet,* salt and coarsely broken pepper. Bring to the boil and let it simmer for twenty minutes.

Put in half a dozen herrings (preferably with soft roes), bring to the boil again and keep just at the boiling point for about six minutes. Move the saucepan away from the fire and leave the fish in the stock till cold. Serve cold. You can use the stock again for some more herrings.

§ *Herrings; dry white wine; vinegar; onion; carrot; garlic; bouquet; peppercorns.*

ÉPERLANS AU FOUR *Baked Smelts*

Take about twenty smelts and put them in a fireproof dish, well buttered, and sprinkled with mushrooms and shallots (two of each), very finely chopped.

Season with salt and pepper, add a glass of dry white wine (or of cider) and a few small pieces of butter. Bring to the boil, and finish in a fairly hot oven. Baste occasionally.

When the smelts are cooked, put the dish on the fire a little while if it is necessary to reduce the stock more. It should reduce at least by half.

Sprinkle with breadcrumbs, add a few pieces of butter here and there, and brown in the oven or under a grill. Add a few drops of lemon juice before serving.

§ *Smelts; butter; mushrooms; shallots; dry white wine (or cider); breadcrumbs; lemon juice.*

ANGUILLES BOURGUIGNONNES *Eels Bourguignonne*

Prepare a *roux* with a piece of butter the size of a small egg, and the same quantity of flour; let it get slightly brown.

Take a pint of red wine and bring it to the boil. Season it with salt, pepper, a *bouquet* and one fillet of anchovy, finely chopped. Add a dozen button onions, previously cooked in butter.

Let the wine reduce by a quarter and put in the pieces of eel (about three inches long); cook slowly for about twenty minutes.

Make a sauce by adding the wine stock, little by little, to the *roux* you have prepared. Stir well, seeing that it is smooth and about the consistency of cream.

Dispose the pieces of eel (well drained and kept hot) in the serving dish, finish the sauce by adding to it a few pieces of butter off the fire, pour it all over the fish and garnish with fried *croûtons*. Some people add a few prunes, stoned and cut in half.

§ *Eels; brown* roux; *red wine;* bouquet; *fillet of anchovy; button onions; butter;* croûtons. *Prunes can be added.*

MATELOTE D'ANGUILLES *Stewed Eels in Claret*

Cook in butter half a dozen small onions cut in two; add a tablespoonful of flour. Boil, in another saucepan, two parts of water to one part of red wine. Pour the boiling mixture on the onions, add salt and pepper, half a dozen prunes, cut in two and stoned. Let this simmer about one hour and a half. Add your fish, cut in slices, about twenty minutes before serving. Surround the dish with *croûtons*.

§ *Eels; small onions; claret; prunes; flour; butter;* croûtons.

FISH

PETITS SOUFFLÉS DE POISSON   *Small Fish Soufflés*

A useful dish for using up remnants of fish. Take about three-quarters of a pound of cold turbot or of any boiled fish left over, mash it well and pass it through a sieve; season with salt, pepper and paprika, add the yolks of two eggs, a glass of cream, then the whites beaten to a stiff froth, mix well, put in little soufflé dishes, sprinkle with grated cheese and bake for about twelve minutes.

§ *Leftovers of turbot or other white fish; paprika; eggs; cream; cheese.*

HOMARDS ET LANGOUSTES   *Lobsters and Crayfish*

Shellfish, such as lobster or crayfish, are, if well cooked, fresh and tender, perfect. Sometimes they are tough for several reasons. The shellfish should be quite alive and kicking, so to speak, for if dying it loses its quality.

You want a saucepan with water, salt, pepper, a *bouquet* and a few drops of vinegar.

Bring it to the boil, and let it boil a few minutes, then plunge in the lobster, which will die immediately. The water having again reached boiling-point, move it away from the fire, so that it should just be 'on the boil'.

Allow twenty minutes for a small lobster, half an hour for a medium-sized one, and three-quarters of an hour for one weighing about two pounds.

Above all, leave them to cool in the stock till entirely cold; it is very important. Drain well before serving. It is always better to choose a smallish lobster. Very large ones are often disappointing.

§ *Shellfish;* bouquet; *vinegar; water.*

HOMARD À LA CRÈME   *Lobster in Cream with Brandy and Sherry or Madeira*

Have some slices of cooked lobster (properly cooked in a *court-bouillon*), pour brandy over them and set it alight. Cook them in butter for a few minutes, add salt, pepper and paprika. Beat together the yolks of two eggs, a little cream and a drop of sherry or Madeira. Blend the mixture well with the lobster and cook on a slow fire till the sauce thickens. Do not let it boil or it will curdle.

§ *Lobster;* court-bouillon; *brandy; butter; paprika; yolks of egg; cream; sherry or Madeira.*

*

We find authorities still arguing about the proper name of a well-known lobster dish. Should it be à l'Américaine *or* à l'Armoricaine? *Even the common Mayonnaise is a subject for learned discussions.*

The name of that sauce is a mystery; Grimod de la Reynière suggested that the name was wrong and that it should be Sauce Bayonnaise (*yet there was no evidence that it was a local sauce from Bayonne*) *or* Mahonnaise *in honour of the capture of the Fort of Mahon by the Maréchal de Richelieu (yet again no evidence that the sauce was created there). Carême attacked Grimod de la Reynière, criticized his suggestions and put forward another theory, that the word should be* Magnonnaise *from an old verb meaning 'stirring'. Discussions raged for fifty years or more; old dictionaries and cookery books up to 1860 adopt the name* Magnonnaise, *but the modern Larousse gives* Mayonnaise. *In all cases, I must say, whatever the spelling may be, the recipe remains the same.*

*

HOMARD À L'AMÉRICAINE   *Lobster à l'Américaine*

This famous dish is easier to make than most people think, but you must have a large live lobster or two small ones. Kill them by piercing through the head with a sharp pointed knife (the death is instantaneous), break the claws, cut the tail in several pieces, and the head in two, being careful to scrape out of the head whatever coral, or inside is there, as this will be useful for the final binding.

Put in a saucepan one tablespoonful of olive oil and one of butter; when hot put in the pieces of lobster; cook for about a quarter of an hour with the lid on, turning the pieces once or twice. Then remove the oil and butter, put in a small glass of brandy and set it alight; add then chopped onion and two tablespoonfuls of purée of tomatoes, a glass of dry white wine, pepper, salt and Cayenne pepper. Cook slowly for about forty minutes.

Dispose the pieces of lobster in a *timbale* or any deep dish and keep it hot.

Mash with a little butter the inside you have kept aside and add this to the strained sauce; just one second over the fire without boiling and pour once more through a strainer, all over the lobster in the dish. Sprinkle with chopped parsley.

§ *Live lobster; olive oil; butter; brandy; tomato purée; dry white wine; Cayenne; parsley.*

CRÊPES D'HOMARD   *Lobster Pancakes with Mushroom and Tomato Sauce*

Have ready some thin French pancakes made without sugar, and a cooked lobster. Cut the cooked lobster in small pieces, toss these for a minute or two in butter and paprika.

Meanwhile prepare a *Béchamel* sauce, to which you add a pinch of paprika and a spoonful of tomato purée. Mix this with the pieces of lobster, and stuff each pancake with the mixture. Dispose the rolled pancakes in a fireproof dish, and pour over a sauce made as follows:

Cook in butter fresh mushrooms cut in slices, thin pieces of fresh tomatoes, to which you add a sliced truffle, seasoning the red part of the lobster with a little brandy; mix well, chop finely, and bind with a little fresh cream. Cook for a few seconds, pour over the stuffed pancakes, and serve.

§ *Pancakes (without sugar); lobster; butter; paprika; tomato purée; button mushrooms; truffle; tomatoes; brandy; cream;* Béchamel *sauce (roux, milk, nutmeg).*

CIVET D'HOMARD   *Lobster Stew*

Take a live lobster and kill it by driving a sharp-pointed knife into its head, cut it in pieces and cook these in two tablespoonfuls of hot olive oil. Shake the pan well and turn the pieces over. When the shell has become red all over put in one small onion and one clove of garlic finely chopped.

Let these take colour, then sprinkle a little flour all over, so that the red pieces of lobster are almost white; cook two or three minutes, being careful that the flour does not burn.

Add a *bouquet* with one clove, and a small piece of celery, salt, and a great deal of pepper, a liqueur-glassful of rum, three-quarters of a pound of tomatoes (pips and skins removed) cut in pieces and boiling water almost level with the pieces of lobster.

Cook without a lid, at boiling-point for a minute, then more slowly for thirty-five to forty minutes, shaking well meanwhile and turning the pieces of lobster occasionally. Remove the *bouquet* before serving. The sauce should be well spiced, much reduced and fairly thick.

§ *Live lobster; olive oil; onion; garlic; flour; a* bouquet *with one clove and a small piece of celery; rum; tomatoes; pepper.*

HOMARD THERMIDOR   *Lobster Thermidor*

Take a live lobster, kill it and cut it in two, lengthways. Season the flesh with salt and pepper and grill the two halves slowly, first exposing the flesh to the fire, then the shell side, for about eighteen minutes.

Remove the flesh and cut it in fairly thin slices; toss them in butter for a few seconds only, remove them. Put in the pan a small glass of dry white wine, a teaspoonful of English mustard and a glass of cream. Bring to the boil and reduce to the consistency of thick cream. Dispose the pieces of lobster in the shells and pour the sauce all over. Glaze quickly under a grill.

§ *Live lobster; butter; dry white wine; English mustard; cream.*

LANGOUSTE BRETONNE   *Crayfish Bretonne*

Make your *court-bouillon* and cook the crayfish (tied). Let it get cold in it. When cold, take off the tail, remove the flesh whole and cut it in slices.

Take out of the head all the 'insides' (the coral, if any, the yellow-green matter and so on); pound well in a bowl.

Meanwhile make a mayonnaise; have it well spiced, add to it the pounded insides and a few capers; mix well.

Dispose the slices of crayfish in the serving dish, pour the sauce over all and arrange round it hearts of lettuce cut in half and hard-boiled eggs cut in quarters.

Sprinkle a little lemon juice over the lettuce.

§ *Crayfish;* court-bouillon; *mayonnaise (egg yolks, vinegar, oil); capers; lettuce hearts; eggs; lemon juice.*

COQUILLES ST JACQUES   *Scallops*

This recipe comes from the famous Restaurant du Chapon Fin at Bordeaux. It is a delicious dish, and by far the best way of serving a shellfish already delicious, and which, judging from the prices it fetches at fishmongers, as compared with those of crab and lobster, seems unfairly despised in England.

Wash the scallops well, boil them in salted water and chop the red part and the white part together with a tomato, a little onion, parsley, a few mushrooms, salt and pepper. Cook this for a few minutes in butter, bind it with a little *Béchamel* sauce, fill the shells with the mixture and brown in the oven.

§ *Scallops; onion; parsley; tomato; mushrooms; butter;* Béchamel *sauce) roux, milk, nutmeg).*

HUÎTRES AU GRATIN   *Oysters au gratin*

Put in a small saucepan two shallots finely chopped and fry them slightly in butter; then add parsley, two or three mushrooms chopped together very fine, breadcrumbs, salt and pepper, a little dry white wine, a small piece of fresh butter, and boil this for a few minutes. It should be rather thick. Open some large oysters, leave them in the hollow shell, and cover each of them with the above stuffing, sprinkle with breadcrumbs, add in each a little melted butter, and brown them in a moderate oven.

§ *Oysters; shallots; parsley; mushrooms; butter; breadcrumbs; dry white wine.*

MOULES   *Mussels*

Mussels should be first of all well scraped and washed in several waters. If, when washing them, you find one which seems abnormally heavy, try to open it with a knife; it may be that the shell is just full of mud.

If you find mussels opening before they are on the fire, it means that they are dead or dying.

MOULES MARINIÈRE   *Mussels Marinière*

Having cleaned the mussels put them in a saucepan with one onion and one piece of garlic chopped together, a *bouquet* of parsley and thyme, salt (very little, as sea-water will come out of the mussels), pepper, a small piece of butter and a small glass of dry white wine.

Cook on a quick fire, shaking. In five or six minutes they are ready.

Remove the *bouquet* and serve them in a deep dish, with all their stock passed through a fine strainer. This is necessary, as there is always a little deposit of grit however well you have cleaned the mussels.

In France they are served in soup plates with both a fork and a spoon.

This is the initial preparation known as '*Marinière*' out of which are made other mussel dishes.

§ *Mussels; onion; garlic; parsley; thyme; butter; dry white wine.*

MOULES BÉCHAMEL   *Mussels Béchamel*

After cooking the mussels as in the last recipe, break off the empty half-shell of each mussel and add to the strained stock two tablespoonfuls of *Béchamel* sauce.

Stir well, put back the mussels and cook one or two minutes together, adding a little chopped parsley at the last second.

§ *Mussels; onion; garlic; parsley; thyme; butter; dry white wine;* Béchamel *sauce* (roux, *milk, nutmeg*).

MOULES POULETTE   *Mussels Poulette*

Prepare the mussels as described above. Add instead of *Béchamel* a *Poulette* sauce, that is, *Béchamel* with a yolk of egg diluted in a little vinegar and a little hot cream.

When reheating the finished article just before serving, see that the sauce does not come to the boiling point.

§ *Mussels; onion; garlic; parsley; thyme; butter; dry white wine; Poulette sauce (milk, roux, nutmeg, yolk of egg, vinegar, cream).*

MOULES SAUTÉES *Mussels Sautéed*

Once the mussels are cooked and empty half-shells removed, toss the mussels in a pan with a little butter, chopped shallots, garlic and parsley and a sprinkling of breadcrumbs.

Shake well during the few minutes it takes to cook. None of the stock is used; this is a dry dish.

§ *Mussels; onion; garlic; parsley; thyme; butter; dry white wine; shallots; breadcrumbs.*

Meat

I remember, during the war, some time in 1916, we had an old fat French cook to look after our mess. We had rescued her almost forcibly from Béthune, where she had been living in a cellar, and taken her a little farther back, to Lillers, where our headquarters were. She was a clever woman, a marvellous cook, and very bad tempered. Occasionally she would produce for us a fine dish of veal Portugaise. Veal was then rare and dear, but we did not mind paying four francs a pound for such good meat. We did not mind even when we found out that the dish in question was not veal at all, but ordinary army beef, which she soaked in soda, washed and marinated for days, and heaven knows what! For her a clear profit, for us a pleasant change. Sheer robbery some narrow-minded people would say. No, a fair deal: we always felt that we had our money's worth, and this is not the cook I would quarrel with.

* * *

Listen to Laurent Tailhade about these pleasures of the table which are at the same time 'Nature's first need and Civilization's most beautiful ornament':

'Le praticien en veste blanche, qui marmitonne les ragoûts . . . C'est un grand poète, expert à créer des émotions, grace au language péremptoire des papilles gustatives.'

*

TOURNEDOS SAUTÉS *Small Fillets of Beef, Sautéed*

Take two or three fillets of steak, season them with salt and pepper and put them in a frying-pan with a good piece of butter. Fry them on a quick fire and turn them so that each side is nicely browned. Place the pan on one side so that the beef does not cook any more, but is just kept hot; then prepare the following sauce: put a piece of butter (the size of an egg) in a saucepan with a tablespoonful of flour, salt and pepper. Cook on a very quick fire until brown and stir in a little stock. You may then add some chopped mushrooms (previously browned in butter) or some chopped olives according to taste. Then put the fillets in the serving dish, pour the sauce over them, and serve very hot.

§ *Fillet steak; butter; flour; mushrooms (or olives).*

TOURNEDOS SAUCE MADÈRE *Small Fillets of Beef, Madeira Sauce*

The Madeira sauce, so often insignificant or even bad when made wrongly, is really a very good one. It is perfect with *tournedos* or little fillets of beef.

This part of the beef, which is the tenderest, is rather tasteless in itself, and that is why *tournedos* or fillet steaks are better with a sauce than plainly grilled.

It takes about two hours to make the Madeira sauce, but the preparation before the addition of Madeira is a basis for all sorts of brown sauces and will keep for several days.

Make a brown *roux* with a tablespoonful of butter, which you melt, and the same quantity of flour. Stir well and cook for two minutes or so till the *roux* has become pale brown.

Add, little by little, three-quarters of a pint of consommé (or meat stock). Bring to the boil and add one tablespoonful of purée of tomatoes, one fresh tomato cut in quarters, one onion and one carrot cut in pieces, a *bouquet*, salt and pepper. Whip well occasionally and let it simmer very slowly for about two hours. By then it should be reduced by at least a quarter, and fairly thick. If too thin, reduce it a little more.

Pass this sauce through a fine strainer into another saucepan, bring to the boil again and reduce a little more, this time quickly.

Add a port-glassful of Madeira wine, cook two or three minutes without boiling, and your sauce is ready.

Pour over the little fried *tournedos* in a serving dish. *This is also good with braised ham and with kidneys.*

§ *Fillet steak; brown* roux; *consommé or meat stock; tomato purée; tomato; onion; carrot;* bouquet; *Madeira.*

TOURNEDOS AU FOIE GRAS *Small Fillets of Beef with Foie Gras*

Cut some fillet of beef in small pieces, about one inch thick, brown these in a frying-pan, using a mixture of oil and butter, salt and pepper. In another saucepan warm some slices of *foie gras* of the same size and shape. Dry the *tournedos,* cover them with the *foie gras* and a good White Wine sauce well reduced. Serve with fried bread.

§ *Fillet of beef;* foie gras; *oil; butter; fried bread; White Wine sauce (brown* roux, *dry white wine).*

MEAT

FILET DE BŒUF À LA RUSSE   *Fillet of Beef à la Russe*

Allow one pound of fillet of beef for two people; it should be perfectly trimmed and cut in thin pieces about two inches long, rather like matches. Put in a pan a good piece of butter, have it at the foaming stage and cook your little pieces of beef, sautéing them well; needless to say, being so small, they are ready in no time. Season with salt and pepper. Remove them and keep them hot.

Meanwhile, you have melted in a little butter a small onion finely chopped (without browning it). Add a breakfast-cupful of cream, a tablespoonful of tomato purée, one of meat stock, a little lemon juice, a pinch of paprika, salt and pepper.

Bring to the boil and let it thicken, and reduce for a few minutes. Pour the sauce through a fine strainer over the pieces of beef in a deep serving-dish, bind with a small piece of butter, and serve with sauté potatoes.

§ *Fillet of beef; butter; small onion; cream; tomato purée; meat stock; lemon juice; paprika.*

PETITS FILETS DE BŒUF GRILLÉS   *Small Grilled Fillets of Beef*

Take some medium-sized fillets of beef, not too thick, beat them well, sprinkle with salt and pepper, paint them with butter and grill, if possible, over a glowing wood fire. Serve them with the following sauce:

Peel and chop very finely two small shallots, fry them in butter till brown; then add one ounce of grated horseradish, a tablespoonful of vinegar, some chopped parsley, salt and pepper. Cook slowly for ten minutes, after which add a claret-glassful of cream. Cook it again till thoroughly hot, but do not bring it to the boil.

§ *Fillet of beef; butter; shallots; grated horseradish; vinegar; parsley; cream.*

ENTRECÔTE BORDELAISE   *Steak Bordelaise*

The steak is grilled according to the usual principle – that is, painted with butter, well seared on both sides, then submitted to less heat till ready. The best piece is the rump steak, as the fillet, being more tender, is less juicy and tasty.

For the sauce put in a small saucepan two glasses of dry white wine, two chopped shallots and a *bouquet*. Reduce by three-quarters, and add one glass of meat stock and one teaspoonful of tomato purée; reduce slowly for a quarter of an hour.

Meanwhile, poach some marrow in boiling water. When soft, cut four or five thin slices and chop the rest coarsely. Add it to the sauce with a little lemon juice; see that it is well seasoned and really hot; having removed the *bouquet* put the sauce into a sauceboat.

Put your steak on a hot dish and dispose over it the slices of marrow. Serve at once. It is sometimes served with the sauce poured over it.

§ *Steak; dry white wine; shallots;* bouquet; *butter; meat stock; tomato purée; marrow; lemon juice.*

ENTRECÔTE MAÎTRE D'HÔTEL   Steak Maître d'Hôtel

Grill as before, and pour over the *entrecôte* a *Maître d'Hôtel* sauce.

§ *Steak; butter;* Maître d'Hôtel *sauce (butter, parsley, lemon juice).*

ENTRECÔTE BÉARNAISE   Steak Béarnaise

Same as before, but with a *Béarnaise* sauce.

§ *Steak; butter;* Béarnaise *sauce (yolks of egg, butter, parsley, vinegar, shallots, tarragon).*

ENTRECÔTE AU BEURRE D'ANCHOIS   Steak with Anchovy Butter

Same, but serve with a *Beurre d'anchois.*

§ *Steak; butter; anchovies.*

BŒUF PROVENÇALE   Braised Beef with White Wine and Olives

Cut in small pieces two rashers of bacon and boil them for a few minutes; put in a saucepan a glass of olive oil; when fairly hot, add your beef, cut in medium-sized squares, season well, add two onions finely cut, and sprinkle with flour, stirring all the time. After a few minutes, put in a *bouquet* and a pint of white wine and water, bring to the boil and cook slowly for about two hours and a half to three hours. At this stage of the process remove the pieces of beef and place them in another saucepan, together with the bacon and a few tomatoes peeled and cut in quarters, also a dozen or so of stoned olives. Pass the sauce in which the beef has been cooked through a fine colander or a muslin, pour it over the meat and cook again for quite half an hour, slowly, and shaking the saucepan occasionally.

This dish should be highly seasoned.

§ *Beef; bacon; olive oil; onions; flour;* bouquet; *white wine; tomatoes; olives.*

BŒUF FARCI   Stuffed Bee*f*

Cut about three pounds of rump steak in slices a little less than one inch thick. Beat and season them well.

MEAT

You have also prepared the following mincemeat: one pound of pork, half fat, half lean, one onion, one shallot, parsley, chervil, all chopped finely together, seasoned with mixed spice and salt and pepper.

Put on each slice of beef a layer of mincemeat, then two thin rashers of bacon. Arrange them on the top of each other, finishing by a slice of beef. Tie well and put it in a saucepan or a fireproof dish with a few pieces of butter, a few bones, carrots and onions (in slices) and a *bouquet*.

Add a glass of water, one of dry white wine, salt, pepper, a pinch of nutmeg and two spoonfuls of tomato purée.

Cook slowly, in the oven, or on the fire, for at least four hours, with the lid on, turning the meat once or twice during the process.

Should the gravy become too short, add a little more water and wine.

When the beef is well cooked place it in a serving-dish, remove the string carefully, and pour the gravy over all, through a strainer. Serve cold.

Make this dish the day before; it will be all the better flavoured. Keep it overnight in the refrigerator.

§ *Rump steak; pork; onion; shallot; parsley; chervil; mixed spice; butter; bones; carrots; onions;* bouquet; *dry white wine; nutmeg; tomato purée.*

BŒUF EN DAUBE   *Braised Beef*

Take three or four pounds of rump steak, cut it in thin slices, beat and season them well. Prepare some *hachis* in the following way: one pound of pork, half fat, half lean, two onions, parsley, shallots and chervil, all finely chopped together and highly seasoned. On one slice of beef put a layer of mincemeat, then a few slices of bacon, then another slice of beef, and so on till you have used the whole lot, ending by a slice of beef. Having tied the piece all round with fine string, put it in a fireproof dish on a bed of butter, bones, onion, and carrots (in slices), add the classical *bouquet,* a glass of water, salt and pepper, a little nutmeg, also a tablespoonful of tomato purée and a glass of dry white wine. Cook slowly about five hours with the lid on. When it is thoroughly cooked place the piece of beef in a deep dish, remove the string and pour over it, through a sieve, all the gravy, which, when cold, will be a succulent jelly. It is advisable to make this dish a day before so that the meat is well flavoured.

§ *Rump steak; pork; onions; shallots; chervil; butter; bones; onion; carrots;* bouquet; *nutmeg; tomato purée; dry white wine.*

BŒUF BRAISÉ AUX PETITS POIS   *Braised Beef with Green Peas*

Take a nice piece of steak, season it with salt and pepper, and put it in a casserole with a piece of butter. Put the casserole on a very quick fire and cook the beef for about ten minutes, turning it frequently. Meanwhile have some new peas shelled (use the smallest you can get) and add them to the beef with more salt and pepper. Put the lid on the casserole and let it simmer very gently for about two and a half to three hours, keeping it covered all the time.

§ *Steak; butter; peas.*

FILET DE BŒUF RÔTI   *Roast Fillet of Beef*

Take a nice fillet of beef or undercut, remove the skin and fat, tie it in a nice shape and insert here and there little bits of bacon fat, add salt and pepper and bake it, basting it often. Remove the string before serving and the fat from the gravy.

This can be served with a watercress salad and potatoes, or with a White Wine sauce, to which you add a few chopped truffles.

§ *Beef fillet; bacon fat. Truffles and White Wine sauce (brown roux, white wine) optional.*

BŒUF BOUILLI SAUTÉ   *Sauté of Beef*

Cut the beef in small cubes, also cut a dozen small onions in slices. Brown the onions first in butter or dripping, then add the meat, also salt and pepper and chopped parsley. Fry till nicely brown, stirring well. You can, if you like, add potatoes cut in cubes, in which case it is better to begin cooking the potatoes for a few minutes before adding the rest.

§ *Beef; onions; butter or dripping; parsley. Potatoes optional.*

BŒUF À LA MODE   *Beef à la Mode*

Take a piece of beef, lard it with strips of bacon, sprinkled with salt and pepper, season it on all sides, tie it well and soak it in claret for a couple of hours, turning it occasionally. About a pint would do for a piece of beef weighing about four to five pounds. Drain it and fry it in butter on all sides to close the meat, which should retain its juice during the lengthy process of braising. Put in a saucepan, pour over it the wine in which it has soaked, a liqueur glass of brandy, a cup of stock; add a little grated nutmeg, two lumps of sugar, and a *bouquet* with one clove. Bring to the boil. Then add a few onions cut in quarters, or, better still, little button onions, one calf's foot, cut in small cubes, and let the whole thing simmer really slowly for about seven to eight hours, turning it twice. At about half-time put in a few carrots, cut in slices, and previously slightly fried in butter. When cooking is finished, remove the string carefully, put the beef in a serving dish, arrange the carrots and pieces of calf's foot round the meat, and pour over, through a strainer, the gravy from which the fat must be removed. It should be delicious and soft. Serve very hot.

If you want to serve it cold the following days, this is the best way to prepare it. Remove the beef, cut it in slices, and put these in a hollow serving dish; arrange the 'trimmings', and pour the gravy evenly so as to cover the slices of meat; when cold it will be succulent jelly.

§ *Beef; bacon; claret; butter; brandy; stock;* bouquet *with a clove; onions; calf's foot; carrots; sugar; nutmeg.*

RAGOÛT DE BŒUF *Ragoût of Beef*

Take two thick rashers of bacon or of pickled pork, cut them in small cubes, and fry them lightly with a few small onions in a mixture of butter and olive oil (just enough to fry them). Add about two pounds of lean beef cut in pieces two or three inches long and the same thickness.

Toss these in the saucepan till the meat is sealed. Sprinkle in a tablespoonful of flour, stir well and cook for two minutes. Then add one clove of garlic, salt and pepper, a bouquet with rosemary, and put in enough liquid just to cover the meat. Bring to the boil, and let it simmer for about two hours.

The liquid can be red wine or white wine mixed with stock, or meat stock alone. Even plain water could be used, but the dish would lose in succulence. You can add a handful of stoned olives, or pieces of mushrooms previously cooked, about ten minutes before serving.

§ *Beef; bacon or pickled pork; onions; butter; olive oil; flour; garlic;* bouquet *with rosemary; meat stock. Red or white wine optional. Olives and mushrooms can be added.*

VEAU AUX FINES HERBES *Veal Cooked with Herbs in a Paper Bag*

Take a good-sized piece of veal, as for roasting, or, if you can, in the fillet or *longe,* and lard it all over with small pieces of fat bacon (or of pickled pork) rolled in salt, pepper, and *fines herbes.*

Chop very finely together two or three mushrooms, parsley, one bay leaf, a little thyme, and two shallots; add pepper, grated nutmeg, and a little olive oil. With all these mixed together rub the piece of veal all over and let it rest three hours. Then wrap the veal carefully in two thicknesses of buttered paper and roast it slowly in the oven, either hanging from a hook or resting on a grill in a baking tin. It should cook really slowly, and therefore a little longer than the ordinary roast veal.

When it is cooked (and it is better to have veal rather over-done than not done enough) remove the buttered paper carefully and scrape the *fines herbes* which may have stuck to the paper. Put these in a small saucepan with whatever gravy there is, a puddingspoonful of wine vinegar, salt, pepper, and a pinch of flour worked into a small piece of butter. Cook a few minutes and stir well, and use as gravy for the veal.

§ *Veal; fat bacon or pickled pork; fines herbes; mushrooms; parsley; bay leaf; thyme; shallots; nutmeg; olive oil; wine vinegar; flour.*

VEAU FARCI BRAISÉ   *Braised Stuffed Veal*

Take a good piece of veal, preferably in the ribs, but not cut into chops, bone it, trim it and put it flat on a board. Season it with salt and pepper and put on it a layer of pork sausage meat, mixed with a little chopped parsley, a tablespoonful of breadcrumbs, and moistened with a small quantity of Tomato sauce.

If there is a kidney in the piece of veal put it, skinned and trimmed, in the middle. Fold the veal, season it outside, and tie it well with a string, like a galantine. Brown it all over for a few minutes in butter.

Put it to cook in a moderate oven in a buttered dish, and resting in a bed of onions, carrots, cut in slices, a few cubes of bacon and a *bouquet*. Add a wineglassful of dry white wine, a drop of vinegar, and baste half a dozen times during the cooking, for which you should allow about twenty minutes to the pound.

Before serving remove the string and pour the gravy over the veal through a strainer, squashing the vegetables well against the sides.

§ *Veal; pork sausage meat; parsley; breadcrumbs; Tomato sauce (tomatoes, brown* roux, *stock, carrots, onions, wine vinegar, butter); onions; carrots; bacon;* bouquet; *dry white wine; vinegar; butter.*

VEAU NIÇOISE   *Veal Niçoise*

Take about two pounds of veal in the fillet, trim it well and tie it so that it keeps its shape. Brown it on all sides in a little butter, then add a few pieces of carrots and onions, also a bouquet with one clove, and a small piece of garlic. Cook the veal slowly, turning it occasionally, and with the lid on for about one hour and a half.

Meanwhile cook in olive oil two or three aubergines, peeled and cut in thin slices, and when they are nearly done – that is, soft and slightly browned – add about half a pound of peeled tomatoes, cut in quarters and with the pips removed; finish with a little chopped tarragon and parsley.

Remove the veal from the pan, cut it in thin slices and dispose them in a serving-dish. Add to the pan a small glass of sherry or Madeira and a small cup of stock. Reduce this for a few minutes.

Dispose the melted vegetables all round the slices of veal and pour the reduced gravy over all through a strainer. This dish, which should be well spiced, is at its best served cold.

§ *Veal fillet; butter, carrots; onions;* bouquet *with a clove; garlic; aubergines; tomatoes; tarragon; parsley; sherry or Madeira; stock.*

VEAU BRETONNE   *Veal Bretonne*

Take a piece of veal well trimmed, preferably in the fillet, and put it, well seasoned, in a fireproof dish with a piece of butter the size of an egg. Start cooking on the fire and, having browned it lightly on all sides, finish the cooking in a moderate oven. Five minutes before the end, put in two tablespoonfuls of meat stock (veal or chicken) and baste well. Sprinkle it all over with grated cheese, put a few small pieces of butter here and there and brown quickly in a hot oven.

Serve with a purée of onions.

§ *Veal; butter; veal or chicken stock; cheese; purée of onions.*

BLANQUETTE DE VEAU   *Veal Stew*

Cut the veal in pieces about two inches square and trim it well. (It is not necessary in this case to use the best part; on the contrary.) Have some boiling water in a saucepan with half a dozen small onions, one carrot cut in pieces, salt and pepper and a bouquet. Put in the veal, bring to the boil again, and simmer for about one hour.

In another saucepan, with a spoonful of flour and same quantity of butter, make a white *roux* and add to it little by little some of the veal stock, whipping well. Let it thicken and add more stock and so on till you have enough sauce for the veal. Then add the pieces of veal, the onions (the carrots are not usually served), and cook a little while together.

In a cup dilute one yolk of egg with a puddingspoonful of vinegar and add this binding to the veal in the saucepan, also a few mushrooms cut in slices and previously cooked for three minutes in butter. Be careful then that it does not reach boiling-point.

§ *Veal; small onions; carrot;* bouquet; *roux; egg yolk; vinegar; mushrooms.*

LONGE DE VEAU BASQUAISE — *Loin of Veal Basquaise*

Take a fine piece of veal, preferably in the fillet or ribs, boned and well trimmed. Put it in a *cocotte* on a bed of carrots and onions cut in slices, pieces of bacon, a *bouquet,* a glass of dry white wine, a little water, a small piece of butter, salt and pepper; also a calf's foot and the bones you have removed. Cook on a moderate fire, basting often. It can also be cooked in a fireproof dish in a moderate oven, if preferred.

When cooked, remove the veal and put it aside. Pass the gravy through a strainer and see that no fat is left. Meanwhile take four or five fresh sweet green peppers, remove the skin and cut them in slices; take two aubergines, treat them in the same way and cook all these in olive oil very slowly, keeping the ones separate from the others. Cook also slowly in oil a few tomatoes cut in pieces, skin and seeds removed.

Cut the veal in slices, dispose these in a flat serving dish, with aubergines, tomatoes and peppers all round and pour over the gravy, which, when cold, will be jellified.

§ *Veal; carrots; onions; bacon; bouquet; dry white wine; butter; calf's foot and bones; green peppers; aubergines; olive oil; tomatoes.*

CÔTELETTES DE VEAU GRATINÉES — *Veal Chops with Cheese*

Take some veal chops, one for each person, and trim them well. Chop finely one small onion and melt it in a piece of butter the size of a walnut; when it is light brown put in a wineglassful of meat stock and one of white wine.

Put this, when warm, in a soup plate and dip in it one by one the veal chops seasoned with salt and pepper, after which you dip them in grated Parmesan.

Put the chops in a buttered fireproof dish, sprinkle a little more grated cheese, then white breadcrumbs over all; put a small piece of butter over each and pour in the mixture of wine and stock. Cook slowly, in a very moderate oven, for about one hour and three-quarters, basting five or six times during the process.

§ *Veal chops; onion; butter; meat stock; white wine; Parmesan cheese; white breadcrumbs.*

CÔTELETTES DE VEAU À LA CRÈME — *Veal Chops in Cream*

Cook your chops in butter. Remove them and add to the butter a spoonful of cream and the juice of a lemon. Brown well and pour over the chops.

§ *Veal chops; cream; lemon; butter.*

MEAT

CÔTELETTES DE VEAU EN PAPILLOTTES *Veal Chops en Papillottes*
Prepare the following marinade: one tablespoonful of olive oil, salt and pepper, and finely chopped together parsley, two shallots, two mushrooms, and a spring onion. Marinate the veal chops (well trimmed) one day in this, turning them occasionally.

Take a piece of paper large enough to wrap up each chop, butter it well and, having it flat on the table, sprinkle it with parsley, chervil and tarragon finely chopped; put the chop previously seasoned on this, more herbs on it, and fold the paper well, turning in the edges carefully so that it does not open during the cooking.

The chops are then cooked either under a grill for three-quarters of an hour, or a little more in the oven. They are sent to the table in the paper.

§ *Veal chops; olive oil; parsley; shallots; mushrooms; spring onion; tarragon; chervil.*

ESCALOPES DE VEAU SAUTÉES *Escallops of Veal Sautéed*
Cut slices of lean veal, about one inch thick, beat them well and season with salt and pepper. Brown in butter on a quick fire, cover the saucepan and let it simmer a little. Add a glass of *jus,* and cook till there is only enough gravy left to cover the *escalopes.*

They can be served like this, or with a *Sauce Soubise.*

§ *Lean veal;* jus; *butter;* Soubise *sauce (onions, milk, nutmeg,* roux*)* optional.

ESCALOPES DE VEAU À LA CRÈME *Escallops of Veal in Cream*
Prepare as the veal *escallops* in the last recipe, then remove them and pour over them a liqueur-glassful of brandy, set them alight, then put them back in the saucepan, add a tablespoonful of brown *roux* and a tablespoonful of cream. Cover the saucepan, cook for about one hour in a moderate oven, basting occasionally.

§ *Lean veal;* jus; *butter; brandy; brown* roux; *cream.*

ESCALOPES DE VEAU PERSILLÉES *Escallops of Veal with Parsley*
Have some *escalopes* of veal, well flattened (they should not be more than a third of an inch thick) and season with salt and pepper. Prepare a mixture of white breadcrumbs, chopped parsley and garlic (this can be omitted by those who do not like garlic); dip the *escalopes* in yolk of egg, coat them with the mixture, and fry in very hot fat.

§ *Lean veal; white breadcrumbs; parsley; garlic; egg yolk.*

[91]

ESCALOPES DE VEAU VILLAGEOISE   *Escallops of Veal Villageoise*

1. Have some *escalopes* of veal (or some veal cutlets) well trimmed, season them with salt and pepper both sides and put them aside till wanted.

2. Melt a small piece of butter in a pan and when it is at the foaming stage put in the trimmings of the veal, one rasher of bacon, one onion and one carrot cut in small pieces and a bouquet. When all these have begun to cook and colour, sprinkle in a puddingspoonful of flour and cook for two minutes, stirring. Add a small glass of sherry, a tablespoonful of tomato purée (or two or three tomatoes cut in pieces), one of milk, season well, bring to the boil and let it simmer for a quarter of an hour.

3. Cook in the ordinary way some spinach, drain it and chop it well. Put this purée in a saucepan with a little piece of butter, a tablespoonful of cream, salt, pepper and nutmeg. Cook slowly, stirring, for five minutes.

4. Fry the *escalopes* in butter, dispose them on the purée of spinach in the serving dish and pour over all, through a strainer, the sauce you have prepared.

§ *Escallops of veal or veal cutlets; butter; bacon; onion; carrot; flour; sherry; tomato purée or tomatoes; milk; spinach; cream; nutmeg.*

ESCALOPES DE VEAU AUX CONCOMBRES   *Escallops of Veal with Cucumber and Cream Sauce*

This is a very good entrée in which the richness of the cream sauce contrasts most happily with the freshness of the cooked cucumber and the spiciness of the paprika. It is very simple to make successfully, the only important thing to remember is that the cream should be well reduced. The common error amongst cooks when they make a cream sauce is that they do not cook the cream properly, being apparently afraid of boiling it fiercely for a few minutes; the result is that their cream sauces are too thin (or too thick, because they add flour to obtain the proper consistency).

Having cut your *escalopes* very thin and beaten them well, you cook them in butter. When they are well cooked and nicely browned on both sides, remove them and keep them hot. You will find in the pan a residue of butter and the coagulated juices of the meat, sticking to the sides and the bottom of the pan. Scrape these well with a fork, add a tumblerful of fresh cream, a pinch of paprika, salt and pepper; stir well and bring to the boil. It should be kept boiling fiercely for a few minutes,

MEAT

stirring well till it thickens to the consistency of thick cream; this thickening is only obtained by reducing. When it has reduced sufficiently, add a few pieces of fresh butter, stirring well and keeping the pan on the corner of the fire (so as to prevent the butter turning to oil and thinning the sauce instead of thickening it more). When ready, pour it over the *escallops* and the pieces of cucumber in the serving-dish.

For the cooking of the cucumber there are two schools of opinion: either you simply boil it (skinned, of course, and cut in pieces about one inch thick) in salt water; or you cook it in very little water, and butter, the idea being that as cucumber contains a great deal of water, it will, in melting, yield a sufficient quantity for its, so to speak, stewing in its own juice. Both methods are satisfactory, but the cucumber cooked in water seems to taste fresher and cooler and is more of a contrast to the rich cream sauce.

§ *Escallops of veal; butter; cream; paprika; cucumber.*

ESCALOPES DE VEAU VIENNOISE *Escallops of Veal Viennoise*
Have your *escalopes* of veal extremely thin, well beaten and flattened; season them with salt and pepper, and dry them in flour; dip them in beaten egg, to which you add very little oil, then in white breadcrumbs, and fry in very hot fat. Being very thin and the fat very hot, three minutes on each side and they are ready, brown and crisp. Drain well, dispose a slice of lemon over each *escalope*, and pour over all a little butter melted at the foaming stage. You can adorn them, if you like, with a stoned olive, around which you place a fillet of anchovy and chopped white of egg.

§ *Escallops of veal; flour; egg; olive oil; white breadcrumbs; lemon. Can be decorated with eggs, olives, fillets of anchovy.*

ESCALOPES DE VEAU CHASSEUR *Escallops of Veal Chasseur*
Take some thin *escalopes* of veal, one for each person, and cook them in butter at the foaming stage for a few minutes. When cooked, remove them and keep them hot. Put in the same butter slices of mushroom, cook them slowly for three or four minutes, then add a few tomatoes (peeled and pips removed) cut in pieces. Cook for two minutes, add a small cup of stock, salt and pepper, and reduce to a short sauce. Put back the *escalopes*, a little chopped tarragon and parsley, cook for a few seconds more, and serve. The proportions should be two tomatoes and two mushrooms to each *escalope*.

§ *Escallops of veal; butter; mushrooms; tomatoes; stock; tarragon; parsley.*

ESCALOPES DE VEAU AUX OLIVES *Escallops of Veal with Olives*

The *escalopes* of veal should be in this case a little thicker than usual. They are slightly browned in butter in a *cocotte* or a copper pan. After that let them cook very slowly with the lid on for about half an hour.

Meanwhile, get some black olives, chop them finely, and add them to the *escalopes* about twenty minutes before serving. Season well, remove the *escalopes*, put them in the serving-dish, and dispose over all the chopped olives. Keep them hot. Add a small glass of white wine to the gravy in the *cocotte*, reduce it, and add a few drops of verjuice or lemon juice. Pour this short sauce over the *escalopes* and serve.

§ *Escallops of veal; butter; black olives; white wine; lemon juice or verjuice.*

VEAU OLIVES PROVENÇALE *Veal Olives Provençale*

Take some *escalopes* of veal, perfectly trimmed, which you beat well to flatten them, as they should be as thin as possible. Put the *escalopes* flat on the board, season them with salt and pepper and prepare the following stuffing:

Pickled pork, half lean, half fat, chopped finely and flavoured with chopped parsley, chervil and a little garlic; add just a pinch of powdered rosemary. Spread this stuffing on each *escalope* and fold it in two, seeing that the ends are well stuck together.

Melt a piece of butter in a pan, put in the *escalopes* when it has reached the foaming stage, brown them lightly on both sides and go on cooking more slowly for five minutes.

Remove the veal olives, throw away the excess of butter and put in a port-wineglassful of Madeira or sherry. Reduce by half, add a glass of meat stock in which you have diluted very little tomato purée, put back the olives and cook on a slow fire, with a lid on, for five or six minutes more.

§ *Escallops of veal; pickled pork; parsley; chervil; garlic; powdered rosemary; butter; Madeira or sherry; meat stock; tomato purée.*

AGNEAU RÔTI BÉARNAISE *Roast Lamb Béarnaise*

Roast the lamb standing on a grill in the oven, putting in the baking tin a small piece of butter, which is used for basting till the melted fat is sufficient for that purpose.

When the lamb is properly done (about eight minutes to the pound is ample for lamb), skim off the fat from the gravy. Add very little water to it and reduce it well. When it has cooled a little, blend it with a *Béarnaise* sauce.

For the sauce: put in a small saucepan two tablespoonfuls of wine vinegar, two chopped shallots and a few sprigs of tarragon. Reduce to almost nothing and let it get cool. Stir in one yolk of egg, a drop of cold water and, little by little, small pieces of butter, whipping well.

Do this with the small saucepan standing in boiling water, otherwise it might curdle. A pudding basin can be used instead of a small saucepan.

Add butter in small pieces till you have enough sauce. Pass through a fine strainer into a bowl.

Stand it in the boiling water. Add, at the end, chopped tarragon and parsley, and some of the gravy from the lamb. The consistency should be that of a mayonnaise.

The taste of tarragon is indispensable to this cause. Tarragon is available most of the year. Failing fresh tarragon, the sauce should be made with tarragon vinegar.

§ *Lamb; butter;* Béarnaise *sauce (wine vinegar, shallots, tarragon, egg yolk, butter); tarragon; parsley. If tarragon is not available use tarragon vinegar.*

AGNEAU RÔTI GRATINÉ *Roast Lamb Gratine*

Take a leg or a shoulder of small lamb and roast it in the ordinary way, basting well. It should not be too well cooked but remain pink. A few minutes before the end sprinkle all over with the following mixture, which you baste and brown quickly without letting it become more than a light golden colour.

For the mixture rub through a sieve two slices of stale white bread and mix with the crumbs one small clove of garlic finely chopped and a puddingspoonful of chopped parsley.

§ *Leg or shoulder of lamb; white breadcrumbs; garlic; parsley.*

AGNEAU RÔTI PROVENÇALE *Roast Lamb Pro vençale*

Take a leg of lamb, insert one small clove of garlic near the bone, and lard it with small pieces of fillets of anchovy about one inch long, a dozen in all. Bake it in the ordinary way, basting often. When cooked, remove it, keep it hot, and skim the fat off the gravy.

Prepare the following sauce: melt a small piece of butter in a pan, cook in it one small onion and two shallots finely chopped, and do this slowly, so that they are more melted than fried; sprinkle a little flour, stir, cook for one minute more; then add two fillets of anchovy, also finely chopped, with two or three gherkins, a puddingspoonful of tomato purée, the gravy from the lamb, and a little stock, if too short.

Mix well, cook for two minutes more, and serve. This sauce should be highly seasoned.

§ *Leg of lamb; garlic; fillets of anchovy; butter; onion; shallots; flour; gherkins; tomato purée; stock.*

AGNEAU RÔTI PRINCESSE   *Roast Lamb Princess*

Take a leg of lamb and roast it in the ordinary way, but standing on a bed of slices of carrots and onions. Meanwhile prepare:

1. A *Béchamel* sauce, keeping it a little thicker than usual, as later it will be thinned by the gravy out of the roast lamb.
2. Asparagus tips (about two good-sized bundles) which should be boiled, then well drained and tossed in butter for a few seconds over the fire.

You must time these so that both the sauce and the asparagus are ready by the time the joint is properly cooked.

Remove the joint and pass the gravy through a strainer, squeezing the vegetables against it. Skim off the fat and add the gravy (or part of it if too much) to the *Béchamel* sauce. Put in also the asparagus tips and keep hot on a slow fire.

Put the joint in the serving dish, carve it and remodel it – and pour over all the sauce and asparagus tips. Lamb cutlets can also be served in that way.

§ *Leg of lamb; carrots; onions; thick* Béchamel *sauce (roux, milk, nutmeg); asparagus tips; butter.*

AGNEAU RÔTI PIÉMONTAISE   *Roast Lamb Piémontaise*

Roast the joint as usual, and meanwhile prepare this mixture:

Take half a pound of mushrooms, clean under the tap, without peeling them if they are very fresh, cut in thin slices and chop them. Melt in a pan a piece of butter the size of a small egg, and when at the foaming stage put in the mushrooms, salt and pepper and a squeeze of lemon juice.

Cook for a few minutes on a moderate fire; the minced mushrooms should be melted, but not fried. Add a tablespoonful of cream, and cook two minutes more, stirring well.

When the joint is almost ready put the mixture, which should be dry and stiff, all over it, sprinkle with grated cheese and brown quickly in the oven.

The best piece for this dish is the saddle. Serve an extra dish of purée of mushrooms with it.

§ *Saddle or other joint of lamb; mushrooms; butter; lemon juice; cream; cheese. Serve with purée of mushrooms.*

AGNEAU RÔTI À L'ORANGE　　　　　　*Roast Lamb with Orange Juice*

The lamb is roasted, the gravy strained to remove fat, and a little orange juice added to it.

This was a favourite recipe in the eighteenth century. The lamb was sprinkled with breadcrumbs a few minutes before the end.

§ *Lamb; orange juice; breadcrumbs.*

SELLE D'AGNEAU MARINÉE　　　　　　*Marinated Saddle of Lamb*

Take a saddle of lamb, lard it, and marinate it for twenty-four hours in a well-spiced marinade (white wine *bouquet*, onions, carrots, peppercorns). Then drain it well and roast it in the ordinary way.

Put the marinade in a small saucepan, let it reduce well, squeeze through a muslin or pass through a fine strainer, add a few pieces of butter, a little stock, a small piece of butter into which flour has been worked, and a tablespoonful of redcurrant jelly and French mustard in equal parts. Cook slowly a few minutes, and pour this sauce, which should be very smooth and well seasoned, over the saddle carved in thin slices and remodelled.

§ *Saddle of lamb; larding bacon; white wine;* bouquet; *onions; carrots; peppercorns; butter; stock; flour; redcurrant jelly; French mustard.*

GIGOT D'AGNEAU AUX POINTES D'ASPERGES　　　*Roast lamb with Asparagus*

Prepare a nice leg of lamb, place it in a casserole on a bed of carrots, onions, bacon rind and broken bones, and put the casserole on a slow fire for about twenty minutes, put it aside a little while and then add a glassful of good stock, salt and pepper, cover it with buttered paper and cook it in the oven, basting often.

Prepare a *Béchamel* sauce with very little milk, add to it the gravy from the braised lamb (having skimmed off the fat), some asparagus tips cooked in the ordinary way, and sautéed in butter, and cover the lamb with this sauce. Have some more asparagus tips round the dish or at each end.

§ *Leg of lamb; carrots; onions; bacon rind and bones; stock;* Béchamel *sauce* (roux, milk, nutmeg); *asparagus tips; butter.*

SELLE D'AGNEAU FARCIE　　　　　　*Stuffed Saddle of Lamb*

Take a saddle of lamb and put it in a deep iron or earthenware *cocotte* with a piece of butter the size of an egg. Cook it a few minutes only, just enough to sear and close the meat, then put in the *cocotte* a few carrots in slices, half a dozen medium-sized onions, and a *bouquet*. Season well and cook slowly.

Meanwhile cook about a third of a pound of mushrooms; when ready mash them through a fine sieve; do the same to the onions which have cooked with the lamb, and mix the two purées together, so that it is fairly stiff, well seasoned, and very smooth.

Remove the saddle from the *cocotte* before it is quite cooked; the flesh should be quite pink; carve it in the ordinary way, and remodel it on the bone, putting between each slice a little of the purée of onions and mushrooms. Tie with a string (which you will remove carefully before serving), sprinkle with a mixture of breadcrumbs and grated cheese. Sprinkle with salt and pepper, and brown lightly in the oven. Pour over all, before serving, the gravy that is left in the *cocotte*, carefully strained.

§ *Saddle of lamb; butter; carrots; onions;* bouquet; *mushrooms; breadcrumbs; cheese.*

GALIMAFRÉE *Gallimaufry (a Gothic Recipe)*

Take a leg of lamb and remove the skin, the fat and the bone. Cut the flesh in pieces the size of a large walnut and insert into each, with a larding needle, one or two thin pieces of streaky bacon rolled in chopped parsley.

Put a small quantity of olive oil in a saucepan; when hot, put in the pieces of meat, salt, pepper and a *bouquet* of thyme and parsley. Fry them lightly, tossing them well, then put in a glass of brandy which you set alight; shake till the flames die out. Add slices of mushroom, and a little '*coulis,* anything you like', says the author. Cook very slowly till tender and squeeze in a little lemon juice.

Dispose around the meat in the dish chestnuts which have previously been cooked, and pour the sauce over all.

The *coulis* in question is not described. It must have been something to make a short sauce and give a spicy taste; cream, the burnt brandy, the liquid out of the meat and the mushrooms being the other elements in the finished sauce.

Therefore there should be just enough oil to seize the meat at the beginning, otherwise the sauce would not be nice.

§ *Leg of lamb; streaky bacon; parsley; olive oil; thyme; brandy; mushrooms; lemon juice; chestnuts.*

AGNEAU JARDINIÈRE *Lamb with Vegetables*

Take a *cocotte* or a *fait-tout* either of cast iron or earthenware, melt a little lard and cook in it for a few minutes some young carrots and some young turnips, cut in half, also a few button onions. When all these have taken colour put in your joint or saddle of lamb. Put the lid on and brown it, turning the meat on all sides so that it is properly sealed. Season with salt and pepper, and two glasses of dry white wine; put on the lid again and let it simmer for about two hours.

When the meat is properly cooked remove it, also the vegetables; skim the fat off the gravy, see that it is well seasoned, let it reduce a little, and just before serving bind it with a little fresh cream, add a little chopped parsley and tarragon. The joint should be arranged, carved and remodelled, with the vegetables around it and the sauce served in a sauceboat. New potatoes, first boiled in their skins, then peeled, and sautéed in butter are a very good accompaniment to this dish.

§ *Saddle or other joint of lamb; lard; carrots; turnips; button onions; dry white wine; cream; parsley; tarragon. Serve with new potatoes sautéed in butter.*

CÔTELETTES D'AGNEAU NORMANDE   *Lamb Cutlets Normande*

Take some lamb cutlets well trimmed and shaped, season them with salt and pepper, paint them with melted butter and coat them with white breadcrumbs. Cook them in butter in a pan and keep them hot. Meanwhile cook in butter in a saucepan some onions cut in slices, melt them slowly, and see that they are not brown; season well. When they are quite soft add a little consommé or stock and cook very slowly till the onions are a thick purée. See that it is well seasoned, arrange your cutlets on this bed of onions in a serving dish.

§ *Lamb cutlets; butter; white breadcrumbs; onions; consommé or stock.*

GIGOT DE MOUTON RÔTI   *Roast Mutton*

Trim a leg of mutton, sprinkle with salt and insert two heads of garlic near the bone. Baste often while in the oven. Should be slightly underdone. Remove the fat from the gravy before serving.

§ *Leg of mutton; garlic.*

ÉMINCÉS DE MOUTON SAUCE PIQUANTE   *Mutton Sauce Piquante*

Cut slices of cold roast mutton, warm them in butter and serve covered with a *sauce piquante*.

§ *Cold mutton; butter;* Sauce Piquante (*consommé, shallots, vinegar, capers, gherkins or garlic*).

NAVARIN PRINTANIER   *Mutton with Vegetables*

You want about one pound and a half of breast or shoulder of mutton, well trimmed and cut in pieces, and sprinkled with salt, pepper and a pinch of sugar.

Melt a piece of butter the size of a small egg, and brown the pieces of meat in it on all sides. Add two tablespoonfuls of flour, stir well, and cook about five or six minutes until the flour has become light brown. Add then a *bouquet*, and warm water level with the meat.

Bring to the boil, stirring well, so that the flour is dissolved completely, and let the ragoût simmer slowly for at least two hours.

After about one hour of slow cooking add a dozen potatoes, all about the same medium size, and half a dozen small onions. Before serving, remove the *bouquet*. The sauce should be thick and well reduced. This is the plainest method.

This dish can be made more elaborate in the following manner: at the time the pieces of meat and the flour have become browned, add two tablespoonfuls of tomato purée or four fresh tomatoes (skins and pips removed) cut in pieces; and at the same time as the potatoes and onions, a few carrots and turnips cut in slices, and a handful of peas. (If the peas are tinned add them only twenty minutes before serving.)

The *navarin* can be made also with lamb, in which case it takes less time to cook as far as the meat itself is concerned. It is essential to trim the meat well, removing skin and excess of fat, which would make the sauce unpleasantly greasy.

§ *Breast or shoulder of mutton; sugar; butter; flour;* bouquet; *potatoes; small onions.*

PORC RÔTI PÉRIGOURDINE   *Roast Pork Périgourdine*

This is a dish practically unknown in France except in Périgord, where it is, and very rightly, much appreciated.

It is made with either the leg or the fillet of pork, and in either case the skin (which in the English way becomes the crackling) is removed, the piece is boned and cooked slowly.

In those parts of France few houses have an oven (they roast on a spit, and the old bread oven is rarely used nowadays), so the prepared piece of pork is sent to the local baker, who bakes it after he has made the bread – that is, in an oven at a low temperature. To this slow cooking is due the fine quality of the dish. In Périgord it is always eaten cold.

Take a piece of pork about six pounds in weight, bone it and flatten it on the board. It should be well seasoned on both sides with lots of pepper and salt. Add two or three small pieces of garlic (this can be omitted, but it would be a mistake not to try it at least once, as the flavour it gives the meat is incomparable and the smell almost unnoticeable).

Roll the meat and tie it well with string all round, sprinkle again with salt and pepper and put it in a fireproof dish with half a tumblerful of water. Cook in a very moderate oven for about two hours, basting occasionally. Remove the string and serve in the same dish, cutting thin slices.

When served cold spread on each slice a little of the fat and gravy produced during the cooking.

§ *Leg or fillet of pork; garlic.*

CÔTELETTES DE PORC NONTRONNAISE   *Pork Chops Nontronnaise*

Take the required number of pork chops as thin as possible and trimmed. Fry them on both sides in fat. Then add seasoning and a handful of breadcrumbs (to which they always add in Périgord a little chopped garlic). Fry for a minute together, stirring well. By that time the chops are nearly done and the breadcrumbs browned. You then add a cup of hot water (or veal stock if you have any), cook for a few minutes more to reduce and thicken, and just before serving add a little vinegar or lemon juice and chopped gherkins.

The breadcrumbs should be made with stale white bread rubbed through a sieve and left to dry.

§ *Pork chops; breadcrumbs; garlic; veal stock; vinegar or lemon juice; gherkins.*

CASSOULET   *Cassoulet*

Soak for twelve hours a pound of dry white haricot beans, preferably large ones. Cook them on a slow fire with salt, pepper and one onion for about two hours.

Meanwhile, take three-quarters of a pound of pork (and, if possible, the leg or wing of a goose), cut these in pieces, brown them in butter, with salt, pepper, a little garlic chopped with parsley; then add two tablespoonfuls of tomato purée. Cook slowly for one hour. Put in the beans, a few thin pieces of bacon, one pork sausage fried and cut in slices and let all this simmer for another hour.

Put the *cassoulet* in a fireproof dish (fairly deep), sprinkle with breadcrumbs, add a few small pieces of butter and brown in the oven. Take it out, break the browned top with a spoon and stir; add a few more breadcrumbs and repeat the operation. Serve boiling hot in same dish.

This is a dish from the Toulouse district; it is made with pork, goose, duck, pickled fowl, or mutton; each place has its own tradition.

§ *Pork; if possible, leg or wing of goose; large white haricot beans; butter; garlic; parsley; onion; tomato purée; bacon; one pork sausage; breadcrumbs. Can also be made with goose, duck, pickled fowl or mutton.*

JAMBON PERSILLÉ BOURGUIGNONNE   Ham with Parsley and Burgundy

Take an ordinary ham and wash it well in fresh water. Put in a large saucepan a calf's foot, a few veal bones, a few carrots and onions cut in slices, a *bouquet* with tarragon and chervil, half a dozen shallots, salt and coarsely broken pepper, enough water and dry white Burgundy in equal parts to cover the ham. Bring it to the boil and let it simmer till cooked. Then remove, drain, and, having removed the bones, skin and gristly parts, squash together the lean and the fat with a fork (this should be only coarsely done) press it into a large salad bowl, and let it rest while you deal with the stock.

The stock should be cooked and reduced on a slow fire, then passed through a fine strainer, after which chopped parsley, a little (very little) chopped garlic, a drop of wine vinegar and a port-glassful of white Burgundy should be added to it, and the whole poured over the ham in the salad bowl. It should then be allowed to set in a cool place. It is not, as a rule, turned out of the receptacle, but served cut, in slices, as one would a pâté out of a *terrine*.

§ *Ham (uncooked); calf's foot; veal bones; carrots; onions; bouquet with tarragon and chervil; shallots; peppercorns; dry white Burgundy; parsley; garlic; wine vinegar.*

MOUSSE DE JAMBON   Ham Mousse

Take about one pound of ham, cut it in small cubes and be careful that there is no fat at all. Pound these pieces well in a mortar. Cook one small onion finely chopped slowly in a little butter, so that it melts and does not brown. Add to it a port-glassful of dry white wine, reduce this almost to nothing, then add: a puddingspoonful of paprika, a pinch of pepper, and a cup of *Béchamel* sauce. Mix well and cook slowly for fifteen minutes.

Pass all the ingredients through a sieve, put them back into the saucepan and bring to the boil; add six leaves of gelatine (melted in cold water) and mix well.

Meanwhile you have prepared half a pint of cream, well whipped.

Pour the hot mixture slowly over it and stir well. See that the seasoning is right (it should be well spiced) and pour into a soufflé dish, in which you serve it when cold.

§ *Ham; onion; butter; dry white wine; paprika;* Béchamel *sauce* (roux, *milk, nutmeg); gelatine; cream.*

FOIE DE VEAU BRAISÉ *Braised Calf's Liver*

Chop together a little parsley, onion and shallot, mix well with pepper and salt and roll in this mixture about twenty small strips of larding fat. Insert these with a larding needle into a piece of calf's liver, which you season all over with salt and pepper.

Put in a casserole a few pieces of bacon, carrot and onion, and cook this for two minutes; rest the liver on this and add a *bouquet,* a cupful of stock, a coffeespoonful of vinegar, and cook with the lid on for one hour in a moderate oven, turning the liver two or three times during the process. Serve with the sauce poured over the liver through a strainer.

It is also very good cold, and if you want the gravy to become quite jellified add a few pieces of calf's foot to the other ingredients or a little gelatine.

§ *Calf's liver; parsley; onions; shallots; larding fat; bacon; carrot; bouquet; stock; vinegar. To serve cold add calf's foot or gelatine.*

FOIE DE VEAU SAUTÉ *Calf's Liver Sautéed*

Cut the liver in thin slices and fry them in butter for one minute only on each side, seeing that they are nicely browned and stiff. Prepare a seasoning with one thin rasher of streaky bacon, one shallot and a little parsley, all finely chopped. Spread this seasoning evenly in a fireproof dish, lay the slices of liver over it, add salt and pepper, the butter in which the liver was fried, cover the dish with buttered paper and cook in a gentle oven for about fifteen minutes. A squeeze of lemon before serving.

§ *Calf's liver; butter; streaky bacon; shallot; parsley; lemon juice.*

FOIE DE VEAU FLAMANDE *Calf's Liver Flamande*

Cut slices of veal liver and toss them lightly in butter, turning them on both sides; then add, chopped together, one shallot, parsley, cibols, salt and pepper; cook a minute or two, and sprinkle with a tablespoonful of flour. Stir well over the fire, add a cupful of white wine and water mixed in equal parts and cook for about half an hour. When the slices of liver are cooked, remove them and keep them hot; let the sauce reduce by half, then put in the yolks of two eggs diluted with a little wine vinegar, a few pieces of fresh butter, the slices of liver, shake well, cook on a slow fire (see that it does not reach boiling point) a few minutes more and serve at once.

§ *Calf's liver; butter; shallot; parsley; cibols; flour; white wine; yolks of egg; wine vinegar.*

ROGNON DE VEAU LIÉGEOISE   *Veal Kidney Liégeoise*

Take a veal kidney, trim it but leave just a little of the fat which surrounds it. Melt some butter in a saucepan; when it has reached the foaming stage put in the kidney, whole, salt and pepper and brown it lightly all over. Then add a small quantity of water, or better still, of dry white wine, cover the pan and cook on a slow fire.

Meanwhile pound a few juniper berries and three or four minutes before serving, sprinkle them all over the kidney, add a little lemon juice and, just at the end, a few small pieces of butter to bind the sauce. Shake the pan well in order to do this and serve. The kidney should be rather pinkish in the middle and the whole of the cooking should not take more than about ten minutes.

§ *Veal kidney; butter; dry white wine; juniper berries; lemon juice.*

ROGNONS DE VEAU SAUTÉS   *Veal Kidneys Sautéed*

Take a veal kidney and pare it well, removing fat, skin and nerve. Cook it lightly a few minutes only in a little butter at the foaming stage; cook also in butter a few cubes of bacon, sprinkle them with a little flour, shake well for two or three seconds over the fire and add a glass of meat stock (veal or chicken preferably), a puddingspoonful of tomato purée, a teaspoonful of French mustard, a glass of sherry or Madeira, a few sliced mushrooms, salt and pepper.

Bring to the boil, reduce a little and pour over the kidneys, cut in slices in the other pan. After that just simmer for a few minutes till the kidneys are coloured and cooked. Kidneys should not cook too long or too fast, otherwise they become hard. Therefore, they should be only half-cooked before they are added to the sauce.

§ *Veal kidney; butter; bacon; flour; meat stock; tomato purée; French mustard; sherry or madeira; mushrooms.*

ROGNONS DE VEAU FLAMBÉS   *Veal Kidneys Flambés*

Take a veal kidney, trim it well as before. Melt a piece of butter the size of a small egg; when foaming put in the kidney and brown it lightly all over. Season with salt and pepper and cook for about three or four minutes.

Cut it in slices; it should be only partly done and quite red inside; pour these back into the pan, add a tablespoonful of brandy and set it alight. Shake the pan while it burns, and when the flames die out stir in a teaspoonful of French mustard, a small glass of cream, and cook for three or four minutes more.

Just before serving, squeeze over all a little lemon juice, having first sprinkled the cut lemon with Cayenne pepper. Finish with one or two small pieces of butter which melt while you shake the pan off the fire and act as a binding.

(This dish, which must be well spiced, can easily be done on a spirit lamp in the dining-room.)

§ *Veal kidney; butter; brandy; French mustard; cream; lemon; Cayenne.*

ROGNONS D'AGNEAU EN BROCHETTES *Lamb Kidneys on Skewers*

Clean the kidneys, remove the skin, the fat and the nerve in the middle; slice them in two sideways, but without parting the two pieces. Put a skewer through them. Salt and paint with melted butter. Grill for a few minutes. When ready, serve with a *Maître d'Hôtel* sauce, or put on each the following mixture: a piece of butter the size of a walnut, a little parsley and quarter of a head of garlic, well worked together.

§ *Lamb kidneys; butter; parsley; lemon juice or garlic.*

ROGNONS D'AGNEAU SAUTÉS AU VIN BLANC *Lamb Kidneys with White Wine*

Clean the kidneys and prepare them; cut in thin slices. Brown them in butter on a quick fire; add a pinch of flour, salt and pepper, a little consommé, a half glass of white wine or pale sherry. Cook only a few minutes and serve.

§ *Lamb kidneys; flour; butter; consommé; white wine or pale sherry.*

RIS DE VEAU BRAISÉ *Braised Sweetbread*

The sweetbread must be carefully pared, nerved and divested of its skin, well washed, then put in boiling water for three or four minutes and refreshed in cold water.

Put in a small saucepan, well buttered, a layer composed of one onion and one carrot cut in slices, a *bouquet* with celery; then salt and pepper and a cup of stock (preferably veal or chicken stock). Put in the sweetbread so that the liquid comes up to about one-third of the meat.

Cover the pan and bring it to the boil on the top of the stove, cook for two minutes, and finish the cooking by putting the covered pan in a moderate oven, where the sweetbread should braise for about twenty-five minutes.

When the sweetbread is cooked remove it and keep it hot, and you can serve it in several ways:

1. *Au jus*. Remove from the pan bouquet and vegetables, also excess of butter, and pour in a small glass of Madeira in which you dissolve whatever juices have coagulated in the pan. Reduce this by half, put in a tablespoonful of purée of tomato, one tomato cut in pieces and a little stock. Mix well, reduce again so that it thickens a little, and pour through a strainer over the sweetbread in the serving dish.

Peas go particularly well with this.

2. *À la crème*. Empty the pan as before, add a small glass of dry white wine and reduce by three-quarters, add then a cupful of cream and a pinch of Cayenne pepper. Bring to the boil and reduce till it thickens. Pour through a strainer over the sweetbread.

For garnishing use slices of mushrooms previously cooked in butter or, when in season, asparagus tips.

§ *Veal sweetbread; onion; carrot;* bouquet *with celery; stock.* (1) Au jus: *Madeira; tomato purée; tomato; stock.* (2) À la crème: *dry white wine; cream; Cayenne.*

CERVELLES AU FOUR *Baked Brains*

This dish can be made with brains of either calf or sheep. Having washed them well in several waters and left them to soak for two hours, so that they are perfectly white, put them in a saucepan, just covered with cold water, with salt, pepper, a *bouquet* and a teaspoonful of vinegar. Bring to the boil and cook slowly for ten minutes.

Drain them well, cut them in two if sheep's, in several pieces if calf's, and put them in a buttered fireproof dish. Take a few gherkins, a small slice of lean cooked ham and chop these together finely. Mix with a few white breadcrumbs and put them on the brains; pour melted butter with lemon juice over all and cook for five or six minutes in a moderate oven till slightly browned. Serve in the same dish.

§ *Calf or sheep brains;* bouquet; *vinegar; gherkins; lean cooked ham; white breadcrumbs; butter; lemon juice.*

CERVELLES AU BEURRE NOIR *Brains*

Put the brains for about one hour in cold water, cook them for about twenty minutes in water, salt and broken pepper, one onion, parsley, and a few drops of vinegar. Drain them well, cut in two, serve them

MEAT

with a *Beurre Noir* sauce, to which you add a little lemon juice or a few drops of vinegar.

§ *Brains; peppercorns; onion; parsley; vinegar; lemon juice or vinegar;* Beurre Noir *sauce (butter, capers).*

TÊTE DE VEAU VINAIGRETTE *Calf's Head*

Put the calf's head in cold water for three hours; then tie it in a cloth and cook in a *court-bouillon*. The *bouillon* should cover the head, even at the end of the cooking, that is, four hours later. (The brains should be cooked separately, in another *court-bouillon,* for only about half an hour, according to size.) Drain well, remove the bones, cut in large pieces and serve with a *Vinaigrette* sauce (the brains being used for the making of the sauce).

§ *Calf's head;* court-bouillon; Vinaigrette *sauce (egg yolks, gherkins, shallots, sheep or calf's brains, oil, vinegar mustard).*

LANGUE DE VEAU SAUCE PIQUANTE *Braised Calf's Tongue*

Put the tongue in hot water, dry it and remove the skin. Put in a saucepan a layer of carrots, onions, bits of bacon and bones. Add a glassful of consommé, parsley, salt and pepper; put in the tongue, cover the saucepan and cook on a slow fire for about three hours. When cooked, cut the tongue in slices and cover with a *Sauce Piquante*.

§ *Calf's tongue; carrots; onions; bits of bacon; bones; consommé; parsley;* Sauce Piquante *(consommé, shallots, capers, vinegar, garlic or gherkins).*

LANGUE À L'ITALIENNE *Tongue à l'Italienne*

Take a beef tongue, soak it in cold water for five hours, changing the water several times. Put it in a saucepan filled with cold water, bring to the boil, cook for a quarter of an hour; remove the tongue, put it under the cold water tap and peel it.

Put in a saucepan a layer of carrots, onion, tomatoes and rasher of bacon cut in pieces, also a *bouquet* and a small piece of butter. Cook all these a while, just enough to melt them, then add a glass of white wine or pale dry sherry and a pint of meat stock or consommé. Put in the tongue which should be about three-parts covered with liquid. Bring to the boil, cover with a buttered paper and finish cooking slowly for three hours and a half in a moderate oven.

When cooked, remove the tongue, skim off the fat from the liquid and reduce it to make a gravy, which you pour over the tongue. Serve with this spaghetti plainly boiled and buttered.

§ *Beef tongue; carrots; onions; tomatoes; bacon; bouquet; butter; white wine or pale dry sherry; meat stock or consommé. Serve with spaghetti.*

LANGUE SAVOYARDE *Tongue Savoyarde*

Take a fresh beef tongue, trim it well, rub it with coarse salt, coarsely broken pepper and mixed spice to which you add paprika. Keep it in a cool place, well covered with salt and spices for four or five days.

Put it in cold water with a great deal of pepper and a *bouquet*, bring to the boil slowly and cook it slowly, allowing one hour to the pound. When cooked remove the skin, keep the tongue hot and serve it with a sauceboat of melted butter and purée of turnips.

§ *Beef tongue; coarse salt; peppercorns; mixed spice; paprika; bouquet; butter. Serve with purée of turnips.*

KEBABS *Kebabs*

An Oriental dish. Cut in small squares a shoulder or a leg of lamb, put these on a silver or a wooden skewer with one thin piece of streaky bacon between each square of lamb, and half a bay leaf between each two. Grill these, well seasoned, over charcoal or under the gas. Serve with it a dish of dry rice, seasoned with salt and pepper, to which you add just a few green peas, previously cooked. The rice should be cooked in stock, not in water, but served very dry.

§ *Shoulder or leg of lamb; streaky bacon; bay leaves. For rice: rice; stock; green peas.*

BROCHETTES DE VEAU *Veal on Skewers*

Take a piece of veal in the fillet and a piece of calf's liver, also several very thin rashers of streaky bacon. Cut out of both liver and veal cubes about two inches thick. Roll them in pepper and salt and put them on a skewer alternately with a little piece of bacon between each.

Grill quickly, turning on each side. The nicest way is to have small skewers and serve one *brochette* to each person; the skewers can be of silver, plated metal, plain iron, or wood.

§ *Calf's liver; streaky bacon; veal fillet.*

CROQUETTES *Croquettes*

Not only boiled beef, but any roast meat left over can be used for this. Mince well and add about the same amount of cold mashed potatoes. Brown a few sliced onions, which you add to it. Roll in flour and fry as fritters. Serve with a *sauce piquante*.

MEAT

§ *Cold roast meat or boiled beef; potatoes; onions; flour;* Sauce Piquante *(consommé, capers, vinegar, shallots, garlic or gherkins).*

HACHIS PARMENTIER *Hachis Parmentier*

Melt a good piece of butter, add parsley, three small onions, or a large one, and shallots all chopped together. When cooked, put in your cold meat (anything left over from different dishes will do), salt and pepper, stir well and cook for a little while. Butter a fireproof dish, put in your mixture, cover with potato purée and brown in the oven.

§ *Cold meat; butter; parsley; onions; shallots; potatoes.*

Poultry and Game

EXOTIC FOOD

A good repertory of dishes ought to contain a certain choice of those that may be termed 'exotic'. But these dishes should be good according to general standards, and not only 'queer' and 'amusing'. Freakish menus should be avoided just as well as too much insularity.

It is always interesting to know what other nations are in the habit of eating, or to try to reproduce at home delicious dishes we have had abroad. In any case we must make allowance for racial idiosyncrasies: the Nordic eat compotes of fruit with chicken, the Chinese dogs and old eggs, the French snails and frogs, the Spaniards like rancid oil, and the English bread sauce. Fish and meat are often used together in Spanish cooking. The story goes that once a warrior returning from the wars had had nothing to eat for days. So being hungry, on his way home he killed a bird or two, some game, picked up a few vegetables, stopped for a bit of successful fishing, tore some garlic off the earth and, dismounting at his door, threw all these to his wife, asking her to cook them all together, and at once, as he was starving. She made some reasonable objections, both as a wife and as a cook: 'it would be a horrible mixture'. But he would not listen or wait, so she cooked all the ingredients, added rice, and the paella was born.

*

POULET RÔTI *Roast Chicken*

Nothing is more delicious than a young chicken, for instance, roasted on a spit with its tender flesh and its crisp skin. But if few of us have a spit, many cherish illusions.

There is a method of roasting which gives marvellous results; it was used in the old days and is still used in the south-west of France. Having started your bird carefully, that is standing, wrapped in thin bacon fat, on a grill in the baking dish, and basted it well, when you come to the end of the cooking, remove the fat, and colour it for a few minutes more.

Then, just before serving, drop all over the bird pork fat melted and burning. This is done slowly through a piece of paper rolled in the shape of a funnel. Set it alight as it comes out and you have drops of fat falling alight on the skin, to which they give that slightly charred taste and appearance, that crispness which is so appreciated in birds roasted in front of a wood fire.

Serve with it a plain watercress salad seasoned with salt, pepper, and very little vinegar or lemon juice; in fact, quite a dry dressing and no oil. The gravy, made with a little water added to the tin and reduced, should be what it is, short.

There is absolutely no reason why you should have out of a bird a sauceboatful of gravy, and the addition of meat stock will simply make it taste like soup and spoil the dish altogether.

§ *Chicken; bacon fat; pork fat; watercress; vinegar or lemon juice.*

POULET SAUTÉ AUX CAPRES *Chicken Sauté with Capers*

Make a white *roux* (about one ounce of butter and same quantity of flour). Stir it while cooking, but be careful the flour does not brown. Put in a tender chicken cut in five pieces, wings, legs and breast, cook them for two minutes, seeing they are well coated with *roux*.

Then add little by little veal or chicken stock, just enough to cover the pieces of chicken. As the sauce will thicken during the cooking, the sauce at the beginning should be quite liquid. Add more stock if you see that it becomes too thick. Add salt, pepper and a tablespoonful of vinegar. Cook slowly, with the lid on, in a moderate oven, say for about half an hour for a young chicken.

Meanwhile, prepare a binding with two yolks of eggs diluted with a tablespoonful of cream, a little lemon juice and capers. Add this to the chicken when ready. Mix well with the sauce. See that it is really hot, but do not let it reach the boiling point. Add chopped tarragon.

§ *Chicken; veal or chicken stock; vinegar;* roux; *capers; yolks of egg; cream; lemon juice; tarragon.*

POULET SAUTÉ À LA CRÈME *Chicken Sauté with Cream*

Take a chicken, about two pounds in weight, carve it in five pieces, wings, legs and breast, and brown these in a casserole, turning the pieces and shaking well; five minutes will do.

Add a *bouquet* with one clove, and two rashers of bacon cut in small pieces. Add also a glass of sherry or of dry white wine, salt, pepper and cook slowly for about twenty minutes with the lid on. Meanwhile, toss in butter for five minutes half a dozen mushrooms cut in slices, and cook in butter and water a dozen button onions. By the time the chicken is ready the onions are done.

Remove the *bouquet*, add the onions and mushrooms, cook for one minute more. See that the whole thing is really hot and stir in, just before serving, the yolks of two eggs diluted in very little cream.

§ *Young chicken;* bouquet *with a clove; bacon; sherry or dry white wine; butter; mushrooms; button onions; yolks of egg; cream.*

POULET SAUTÉ BOURGUIGNONNE   *Chicken Sauté with Burgundy*
In this dish, which is on the same principle as the one before, red wine is used instead of white wine and cream.

Take a young chicken, about two pounds in weight, and cut it in seven pieces – wings, legs, drumsticks and breast – fry these for two or three minutes only in butter at the foaming stage, together with a few button onions and cubes of streaky bacon. Turn the pieces, put in salt, pepper, a *bouquet* and a glass of red wine, preferably Burgundy.

Cook, with the lid on, slowly, for about twenty minutes; add then half a dozen mushrooms cut in slices and cooked two minutes in butter, remove the *bouquet* and let the dish simmer five minutes more. It is a dish with a short sauce.

§ *Young chicken; butter; button onions; streaky bacon;* bouquet; *red wine (preferably Burgundy); mushrooms.*

POULET PORTUGAISE   *Chicken Portuguese*
Take a young chicken, not more than two pounds in weight; cut it in seven pieces – the wings, the legs, the drumsticks and the breast – and season these with salt and pepper. Melt in a saucepan a tablespoonful of olive oil and butter mixed, and cook in this the pieces of chicken till they are browned on all sides.

Add one small onion and two shallots finely chopped and a port-glassful of Madeira. Stir well, cook for one minute, then add a small glass of stock and a tablespoonful of tomato purée. Season well, cover the pan and cook for about twenty minutes on a slow fire.

Meanwhile, peel some tomatoes, cut them in pieces, and cook them in butter for two or three minutes. Remove the pieces of chicken to the serving-dish, put the pieces of tomatoes over them, add a little chopped parsley, and pass through a strainer the sauce from the saucepan.

§ *Young chicken; olive oil; butter; onion; shallots; Madeira; stock; tomato purée; tomatoes; parsley.*

POULET BÉARNAISE *Chicken Béarnaise*

This is an old-fashioned dish from Béarn. Take a young chicken, about one and a half pounds in weight; cut it in seven pieces: the wings, the legs, the drumsticks and the breast.

Melt in a pan a piece of pork fat the size of a small egg. When melted and hot, fry the pieces of chicken on all sides, just a few minutes only, in order to colour them.

Chop finely one onion and grate one carrot; fry this also for a few minutes in a little pork fat.

Take a fireproof casserole (preferably earthenware), put in the pieces of chicken, the minced carrot and onion; add one slice of lean ham cut in small cubes, salt, pepper, a tablespoonful of water (or of dry white wine) and cook in a moderate oven, with the lid on, for about a quarter of an hour.

Add then two or three tomatoes (peeled, pips removed and cut in small pieces), cook five minutes more and serve in the casserole.

Needless to say, in Béarn they also add a little chopped garlic with the tomato.

§ *Young chicken; pork fat; onion; carrot; lean ham; tomatoes. White wine and garlic optional.*

POULET BISCAYENNE *Chicken Biscayenne*

You want for this dish a young tender chicken not more than two pounds in weight. Cut it in five pieces – wings, legs and breast.

Melt in a pan a tablespoonful of pork fat or bacon, put in the pieces of chicken, turn them once, cook one minute and sprinkle them with a little flour.

Stir well and add one small onion and one clove of garlic chopped.

Let this cook two or three minutes, then add four or five tomatoes (pips and skins removed) cut in pieces, and a sprig of sage.

Season well, put the lid on and cook fairly slowly for twenty-five minutes, shaking occasionally.

§ *Young chicken; pork fat or bacon; flour; onion; garlic; tomatoes; sage.*

POULET SAUTÉ MARENGO *Chicken Sauté Marengo*

The sauté of Poulet Marengo *is, so to speak, a period dish. The story goes that in June 1800, the Austrian army was routed by the French. Bonaparte asked his victorious generals to dinner. Unfortunately, the transports had been left behind in the advance, and there was nothing in the only cart which had followed except the chef, Dunan, and a few kitchen utensils.*

It was difficult to arrange a meal. Fortunately, a few chickens were found in a destroyed farmhouse, also some tomatoes. There was brandy in a flask, white wine in a bottle, a little oil in one of the pans, and wild garlic in the fields. In half an hour a dish was improvised, the chicken cut in pieces and fried in oil for a few minutes, then sprinkled with brandy, and the sauce made with the wine, the chopped garlic and the tomatoes cut in pieces added to the chicken. The name? That of victory. Such is the origin of the Poulet Marengo *which is still prepared now in the same manner, except that we now adorn it with mushrooms,* croûtons *and fried eggs.*

Carve the chicken (again not more than two pounds in weight) in seven pieces – legs, drumsticks, wings and breast; put in a saucepan two tablespoonfuls of oil and a small piece of butter, and when hot add the pieces of chicken. Brown them lightly on all sides, then reduce the fire and cook about twenty minutes. Remove the pieces and put in the same oil a dozen mushrooms, cut in quarters, three tablespoonfuls of rather thin tomato sauce, a drop of brandy, and cook this five minutes.

Put back the pieces of chicken, see that it is well seasoned and cook a little more all together. Before serving add a squeeze of lemon and chopped parsley.

Some people add at the same time as the brandy a small glass of dry white wine and a little chopped garlic or shallot. Should the sauce become too short during the cooking dilute it with a small amount of stock. Serve with *croûtons* and fried eggs, crisply fried also in oil.

§ *Young chicken; olive oil; butter; mushrooms; tomato sauce (brown roux, tomato purée, bouillon, nutmeg, butter); brandy; lemon juice; parsley;* croûtons; *eggs. Dry white wine and garlic or shallot optional.*

POULET LYONNAISE *Chicken Lyonnaise*

Take a plump young chicken, joint it and place the joints in a casserole in which you have melted plenty of butter. Cook on a quick fire, turning the joints often. Then add a quarter of a pound of mushrooms and a tomato cut in little pieces. Cook for a few minutes more and add a glass of dry white wine, a little beef juice, and a few drops of old brandy, season with salt and pepper, and cook for twenty minutes. Remove the pieces of chicken and keep them hot; add to the sauce some chopped parsley, and, if you like it, a tiny piece of finely chopped garlic, and let it reduce a little. Pour the sauce over the chicken and serve very hot.

§ *Young chicken; butter; mushrooms; tomato; dry white wine; beef juice; old brandy; parsley. Garlic optional.*

POULET AU GRATIN *Chicken au Gratin*

Cut in small pieces the meat left of a roast chicken, put them in a fireproof dish and cover with a *Béchamel* sauce and grated cheese, surrounded by purée of potatoes. Brown in the oven.

§ *Leftovers of chicken;* Béchamel *sauce (*roux, milk, nutmeg*); cheese; potatoes.*

COQ-EN-PÂTE, SAUCE PÉRIGUEUX *Coq-en-Pâte, Sauce Périgueux*

Prepare a chicken for roasting, well seasoned inside and outside. Start it in butter in a flat saucepan, then roast it in the ordinary way, basting often with butter.

Have a piece of *foie gras*, which you cut in small cubes, and two or three truffles, which you trim and chop. When the chicken is almost done (allow about twenty-five minutes for a bird weighing two pounds) stuff it with this mixture.

Meanwhile, you have prepared the batter for the crust as follows:

Have on the board half a pound of sifted flour in a heap. Make a hole in the middle and add two whole eggs, one by one, three ounces of butter, a pinch of salt and half a glass of tepid water, working the batter in the ordinary way.

When smooth and firm, flatten it on the board to a layer about half an inch thick and large enough for the chicken to be wrapped in it. When wrapped, paint with yolk of egg, put it in the serving dish and bake ten to twelve minutes in a moderate oven.

For the *Sauce Périgueux* chop the trimmings of the truffles finely and cook them in a small saucepan with a glass of Madeira. Reduce by half, season well and add twice the quantity of much-reduced stock and a puddingspoonful of tomato purée. Cook slowly eight to ten minutes and taste; it should be highly seasoned and the flavour of tomato must not be noticed; if too pronounced, add a little more Madeira and cook a few minutes longer.

Finish by a binding of butter, off the fire.

§ *Chicken; butter;* foie gras; *truffles; shortcrust pastry; yolk of egg; Madeira; stock; tomato purée.*

SUPRÊMES DE VOLAILLE À LA CRÈME *Chicken Suprême with Cream Sauce*

A *suprême* is the wing or the breast of a bird, skin removed, with the bone scraped of all flesh as is done with a lamb cutlet and cut short. Cook the *suprêmes* in butter (a piece the size of a small egg for four wings or breasts) at the foaming stage till the outside begins to show white, then turn them and cook the other side. They should be pleasantly browned. Add to the butter in the pan a third of a pint of cream, a pinch of paprika, salt, pepper, bring to the boil, and reduce till the cream has reduced and thickened. Finish by stirring in a small piece of butter off the fire and pour over the *suprêmes* of chicken in the serving dish, add slices of mushrooms previously cooked in butter, or asparagus tips in season.

§ *Chicken wings or breasts; butter; cream; paprika; mushrooms or asparagus tips.*

SUPRÊMES DE VOLAILLE STRASBOURGEOISE — *Suprêmes of Chicken Strasbourgeoise*

Take as many wings or breasts of chicken as you want, allowing one for each person. Trim neatly into *suprêmes* – that is, remove the skin and scrape away all flesh from the bone, as you do for lamb's cutlet, so that the bone is clean and bare, and nothing is left but the best and whitest meat.

Melt some butter in a pan already hot, and when it has reached the foaming stage put in your *suprêmes* and cook them, turning them once or twice. They should be just a little browned on the outside and seasoned with salt only. Remove them and keep them hot.

Add to the butter in the pan fresh cream in sufficient quantity (a teacupful to two *suprêmes*), a pinch of paprika, salt, and pepper; bring to the boil on a quick fire, so that the cream boils and reduces; to this you add a piece of *foie gras,* the size of a small egg, mashed through a fine sieve, and cook a minute or two more, till the sauce has the consistency of thick cream. Finish with a few small pieces of fresh butter put in one by one, and well mixed with the sauce by shaking the pan.

Meanwhile, have some spaghetti cooked in the ordinary way and well drained; add a few small cubes of *foie gras* and pieces of truffle, mix well, and toss all this lightly for a minute in butter. Place your *suprêmes* on this mixture in the serving dish, with the cream sauce poured over.

§ *Chicken wings or breasts; butter; cream; paprika;* foie gras; *spaghetti; truffles.*

SUPRÊMES DE VOLAILLE SMITANE — *Suprêmes of Chicken Smitane*

This sauce, which is of Russian origin, is usually served with game or tiny spring chickens; it is also good with *suprêmes* of chicken. Cook them in butter as described in the last recipe.

For the sauce, use the same pan and the same butter, only if there is too much butter left, throw it away. The pan must be almost dry.

Cook in it two shallots and half an onion chopped very finely till they melt and begin to brown; put in a port-glassful of dry white wine, bring to the boil and reduce almost to nothing.

Then put in the pan a third of a pint of cream, a pinch of paprika, bring to the boil and let it reduce and thicken. See that it is well seasoned and pour over the *suprêmes* in the serving dish through a fine strainer.

This sauce should really be made with sour cream, but a good result can be obtained by adding a little lemon juice to fresh cream. The taste of the Sauce Smitane must be slightly acid.

§ *Chicken wings or breasts; butter; shallots; onion; dry white wine; paprika; sour cream, or fresh cream and lemon juice.*

JAMBES DE POULET GRILLÉS   *Grilled Legs of Chicken*

Make a few incisions in the thickest part of the flesh and rub the legs all over with prepared English mustard (not too liquid), then roll in white breadcrumbs. Put a few small pieces of butter on each leg and grill them slowly, turning once or twice. Serve with a Mustard Sauce.

§ *Chicken legs; English mustard; white breadcrumbs; butter; Mustard Sauce (egg yolks, lemon juice, butter, mustard).*

POUSSINS POLONAISE   *Spring Chicken Polonaise*

You can use either the really small chicken which is just large enough for one person, or what shops call the 'two-portion bird' – these take two or three minutes more to cook than the others.

Start cooking them in foaming butter in a pan on the top of the stove, season them and finish them in a fairly hot oven in the same pan; about a quarter of an hour is enough. Keep them hot. Melt a good piece of butter in a pan; when it is at the foaming stage put in a handful of white breadcrumbs and one hard-boiled egg chopped very finely.

Fry for two minutes; when the breadcrumbs begin to brown add chopped parsley and sprinkle the mixture over the *poussins* in the serving dish. Add a few drops of lemon juice and finish by pouring all over them butter melted at the foaming stage. The *poussins* should be well covered with the mixture.

§ *Spring chicken; butter; white breadcrumbs; egg; parsley; lemon juice.*

POULARDE ALBUFERA   *Chicken Albufera*

You want a plump tender fowl, which you cook about forty minutes on a bed of vegetables (slices of carrot, of onion, bits of bacon and a *bouquet*) in a sauté-pan. It should be stuffed with cooked rice, prepared as for a pilaff, and mixed with little cubes of *foie gras* and slices of truffle. Start the bird on the fire for a few minutes and finish it in the oven. About half-way through the cooking add a glass of dry white wine.

Meanwhile, prepare a *Velouté* of chicken. To a small quantity of white *roux* add chicken stock, bring to the boil, and let it thicken for twenty minutes. Pass through a strainer and add the gravy to it (fat skimmed off) out of the fowl. Mix well, and add to this two ounces of *foie gras* squashed through a sieve. A few minutes before serving finish the sauce with a little lemon juice, a pinch of Cayenne pepper and cream, and pour all over the fowl in the serving dish. There should be some extra rice all around it and an extra sauce-boat of sauce.

For the rice: into about an ounce of butter at the foaming stage put one onion finely chopped, and let it melt without browning. Add one large cup of rice, and fry till it loses its transparency. Then add two cups of liquid (same size of cups, as rice absorbs twice its volume of liquid) with salt and pepper, stir well, bring to the boil, and when boiling put it in a moderate oven, covered with a buttered paper and with the lid on. Cook seventeen minutes. By that time the rice has absorbed the liquid and is done as it should be. Stir in a small piece of butter, and it is ready for use.

The pan to use is a low sauté-pan, and the liquid to add to the rice should be in this case half consommé, or white stock, and half water.

§ *Chicken; carrots; onion; bacon pieces;* bouquet; *cooked rice;* foie gras; *truffles; dry white wine;* roux; *chicken stock; lemon juice; Cayenne; cream; consommé or white meat stock.*

BROCHETTES DE FOIES DE VOLAILLE   *Grilled Chicken Livers*
Cut the chicken livers in squares; take the same number of thin slices of bacon and put one between each piece of liver on a skewer. Cook on a slow fire, turning many times. Serve with *Maître d'Hôtel* sauce.

Turkey and duck livers may be done in the same way.

§ *Chicken livers; bacon;* Maître d'Hôtel *sauce (butter, parsley, lemon juice).*

*

Above all, as I have said before, do not be afraid of simplicity. Pretentiousness is always wrong. And spare your friends the ideal dinner according to that marvellous person, 'the connoisseur of bad food'. Everything is, of course, perfect: the soup, which is thin and anaemic, full of nondescript flotsam and jetsam of doubtful origin and of faded flavour; the fish which is upholstered with a white sauce trimmed with parsley and lined with flour; the bird or joint, desiccated (if a chicken belonging to the sporting variety with muscular legs) and swimming in a brown sauce which might have been a gravy soup the day before, and surrounded by watery potatoes and French beans fresh from the Turkish bath; the sweet, something jellified and mysterious, the secret of which is only known to a few members of the household; the savoury, cheese straws made of bricks; then oceans of unripe figs, of stony pears, of opaque grapes, of hard marrons glacés, of gritty chocolate; and the coffee . . . one can only say of the coffee that it leaves one speechless.

Well, as I have said before, a perfect dinner, a perfect bad dinner. Though there is some kind of superior, and perverse satisfaction in tasting that kind of perfection, it is somewhat distressing, prosaically to have to stop at the coffee-stall on the way home for an honest sandwich and a cup of 'white' coffee.

*

OIE FARCIE LANDAISE *Stuffed Goose Landaise*

Take a young goose, prepare it for roasting and stuff it in the following manner: About a quarter of a pound of breadcrumbs, a quarter of a pound of sausage meat, the liver chopped, and a handful of olives stoned and cut in half, a spoonful of anchovy butter and a little chopped parsley.

All this should be well seasoned with salt, pepper, a little nutmeg, mixed together and bound with one egg. Before stuffing the goose, sprinkle the inside with a little lemon juice; stuff it, close the opening and wrap the bird with very thin slices of pork fat.

Roast, basting often, and half an hour before the end remove the slices of fat, so that the goose becomes nicely coloured.

Serve with potatoes baked in the goose fat. The gravy must remain as it is, and not spoilt by the addition of anything else. Remove excess of fat if necessary. This fat is delicious and can be used in cooking.

The time of cooking for an average bird is two and a half hours, beginning with a hot oven and reducing to moderate.

The anchovy butter is simply done by chopping and pounding fillets of anchovy in oil and working in well the same quantity (or a little more if the anchovies are very salt) of butter.

§ *Goose; breadcrumbs; sausage meat; olives; parsley; Anchovy Butter (anchovy fillets, butter); nutmeg; egg; lemon juice; pork fat slices.*

DINDE FARCIE *Roast Stuffed Turkey*

Take a turkey about nine to ten pounds in weight. (There is no

Recipes of Boulestin

point in having a larger bird unless you are particularly fond of cold turkey. As it is, the one chosen will do once hot, once cold, once for *rissoles,* and the bones, etc., will be the making of a perfectly good soup.)

For a turkey of that size you want for the stuffing one pound and a half of sausage meat and the same quantity of chestnuts.

1. Sausage Meat. This can be bought ready-made. If made at home (which is very easy) you want two-thirds of lean pork and one-third of fat. It should be minced through the third knife of an ordinary mincing machine. Either way the meat once minced or bought should be seasoned with salt, pepper, a pinch of mixed spice and a tablespoonful of brandy. You can also add to it one truffle finely chopped. (Truffles can be bought in bottles containing even one only; some shops also have 'truffle peelings', which are cheaper and quite satisfactory for this purpose.)

2. Chestnuts. These should be partly cooked first; no good result will be obtained if they are put in raw, as they have not got time to cook properly. Once the skin is removed, they can be partly grilled, fried or boiled.

3. Add the chestnuts without breaking them to the minced meat and fill with this the inside of the turkey. Sew the opening, and wrap the bird with thin slices of unsmoked fat bacon; tie with a string. Stand it on a grill in a baking dish containing a little meat stock and cook in a very moderate oven about fourteen minutes to the pound. About twenty minutes before the end remove the slices of bacon so that the bird becomes well coloured; during this time baste often with melted fat or butter.

4. Remove the turkey and put it in the serving dish. Add to the baking dish two or three tablespoonfuls of veal stock or of hot water, cook for two minutes, strain and serve in a sauceboat. Garnish the turkey with three-quarters of a pound of Chipolata sausages previously fried.

> § *Turkey; sausage meat; chestnuts; mixed spice; brandy; unsmoked fat bacon; meat stock; veal stock; Chipolata sausages. Truffle or 'truffle peelings' can be added.*

*

We all have our recipes for stuffing turkeys, with truffles and sausage meat after the French tradition, with chestnuts in the English fashion, even with oysters in the American manner.

But somehow truffles seem more than anything else connected with the festivities of Christmas. They are exquisite, and should be eaten by themselves, cooked either in port wine or champagne in a hermetically sealed little terrine or wrapped up in several greased papers under the ashes of a wood fire.

One further reason why fresh truffles taste so exquisite is that we have waited for them and that, apart from their intrinsic qualities, they have the charm of evanescence. Only for a few weeks can we enjoy them, like strawberries in summer. So that they give us the thrill of an ideal long pursued, fugitively attained; not only their own (the issue is larger), they fill their predestined place, they appeal to our sense of perfection, and they leave us just in time, before we have become tired of them.

Truffles, of course, stand for Périgord, and, no doubt, it is only in a remote country like Périgord that we can feel the months moving, things growing, and the charm of the revolving seasons.

There, during October, they receive, after days of faithful waiting, that other gift of nature, the cèpes: *and the oak forests are full of their autumnal scent. There, they have seen the prickly shells of the chestnuts slowly opening and the ripe fruit falling; they have cooked these either blanchies (the peasants will throughout the winter eat them and drink white wine when they go to each other's cottages for the* veillée*) or roasted on charcoal, and the wood fires perfume the house.*

But truffles are our finest Christmas present from Nature, truffles, the one thing which man has never managed to improve, force or grow, which modern science has not been able to interfere with, that mysterious and delectable fungus which, unaided by an animal, man would not even have been able to find.

What are truffles; where do they come from; how do they grow? So many mysteries. They were known in the Roman Empire, in Greece, and Alexandre Dumas says that 'les Barbares en passant sur elles les foulerent aux pieds et les firent disparaître'. Anyhow, truffles apparently disappeared from Europe and reappeared, just as mysteriously, in the early part of the eighteenth century.

It is a cruel story of man's selfishness. We are in Périgord, here is an oak forest. There ought to be truffles, but our sense of smell is obtuse; the pig comes to our help: he smells, he hunts, he digs, and when, with delighted gruntings, he has more or less unearthed the truffle, by way of thanks we bang him on the nose with a stick.

I always wonder if the bits of potatoes which we give him as a consolation prize taste to him like the truffle he has just found. Does he know he is deceived?

*

DINDE TRUFFÉE *Turkey with Truffles*

Have a well-fattened young turkey ready for roasting. Take eight or ten truffles, peel them and cut them in quarters; boil the skins for two minutes in a glassful of sherry, chop them finely and mix them with about one pound and a half of pork sausage meat and two chopped chicken livers; season well and stuff the bird with the mixture, to which you add the pieces of truffles. Cut two of the truffles in thin slices which you insert between the skin and the flesh of the bird. Roast in the ordinary way, basting often. Remove the fat before serving the gravy.

The turkey should be well seasoned inside before inserting the stuffing, and the stuffing should be put in at least the day before you roast the bird so that the flesh is well flavoured. Serve, if you like, chip potatoes and a plain salad of watercress.

§ *Turkey; truffles; sherry; pork sausage meat; chicken livers.*

CROQUETTES DE DINDE *Turkey Croquettes*

One gets tired of everything, even of the best cold turkey; this is a very good way of using up the remnants. Scrape off the white flesh, trim it and cut it in small pieces, also cut in the same way some good ham (about quantities, if you have half a pound of turkey you should use a quarter of a pound of ham). Peel three ounces of mushrooms, chop them finely and cook them in butter: add a cupful of consommé and let it reduce by about half. Put in a little more butter, salt, pepper, chopped parsley and spices; cook slowly for ten minutes, pass through a sieve and bind with a yolk of egg. Then pour the sauce over the pieces of turkey and ham, mixing well. The mixture, which you let grow cold, should be of such a consistency that you can then, when quite cold, make croquettes with it, but it must be fairly soft all the same.

Beat an egg well, drop the mixture by small quantities at a time, roll in egg, then in breadcrumbs, again in egg and finish by another coating of breadcrumbs. Fry in very hot fat, drain well and serve with a sauce, according to taste.

§ *Cold turkey; cooked ham; mushrooms; consommé; butter; parsley; spices; eggs; breadcrumbs.*

CANARD BRAISÉ AUX NAVETS *Braised Duck with Turnips*

Take a duck prepared as for roasting and begin cooking it in a pan in butter at the foaming stage, just enough to colour it well on all sides.

Make a brown *roux* in a saucepan with a puddingspoonful each of butter and flour. Add little by little a tumblerful of meat stock, a tablespoonful of tomato purée, a *bouquet*, and reduce for a few minutes, whipping meanwhile. Put back the duck, seasoned, put the lid on and cook slowly for about half an hour.

Take a few small onions and three or four turnips, which you cut in pieces about two inches long, all more or less the same size, and fry them lightly in a pan with butter and a little sugar. When they are golden brown add them to the duck, shake well and cook slowly for twenty-five minutes more. Remove the *bouquet* before serving.

(If the turnips are old and tough, peel them thickly, instead of scraping; that will remove the fibrous part.)

§ *Duck; butter;* brown *roux; meat stock; tomato purée; bouquet; onions; turnips; sugar.*

CANARD AUX OLIVES *Roast Duck with Olives*

Roast the duck for about half an hour. Put in a saucepan a tablespoonful of brown *roux*, one of consommé, one of white wine; wash, peel, and stone a good many olives; add them to the sauce and cook a few minutes. This sauce being ready, finish cooking the duck in it.

§ *Duck;* brown *roux; consommé; white wine; olives.*

RAGOÛT DE CANARD *Ragoût of Duck*

Make a little brown *roux*, add a little chopped onion, and put in, whipping well, a tumblerful of half meat stock, half dry white wine, salt, pepper, a *bouquet*; add the remnants of a roast duck, and cook slowly for twenty minutes.

Add then eight or ten pork Chipolata sausages previously grilled or fried, and a few stoned olives. Cook for a few minutes more. Garnish with croûtons. Remove the *bouquet* before serving.

§ *Cold duck;* brown roux; *onion; meat stock; dry white wine; bouquet; pork Chipolata sausages; olives;* croûtons.

CANARD SAUVAGE AUX BIGARADES *Wild Duck with Bitter Oranges*

Take some wild ducks, allowing one for two or at the most three people, as only the breast is really good and tender; it should be carved in thin slices.

Put a piece of butter in a shallow saucepan and roast the ducks in it, baste often, allowing about twenty minutes in a fairly quick oven.

Remove the ducks and keep them hot. Put very little flour in the saucepan and make a little *roux*, add a glass of port wine and one of veal stock; stir well and finish cooking the ducks in that for ten minutes.

Meanwhile, put in a small saucepan a little castor sugar and melt it. When it turns yellow put in a liqueur-glassful of curaçao. Add the sauce from the ducks, the skin of one orange (pith carefully removed) cut thin and small, like matches, and a little lemon juice.

Bring to the boil and cook a minute or two.

Skin the birds and pour this sauce all over; serve with it quarters of Seville orange, carefully peeled with a very sharp knife, made hot in a small saucepan.

The only possible vegetable with this dish is potatoes in some form, soufflées, sautées, Anna or Macaire.

§ *Wild ducks; butter; roux; port wine; veal stock; castor sugar; curaçao; Seville oranges; lemon juice.*

CANARD SAUVAGE AU PORTO *Wild Duck with Port*

This is a very good way of serving wild duck, which is rather dull roasted. Put the bird in a flat saucepan and roast it in a very hot oven, not more than fifteen minutes, so that it is only partly cooked. Baste often and season well. When ready, remove the bird and carve fillets out of the breast and best part of the legs. Put in a saucepan a tablespoonful of claret and one of port, very little *jus*, or stock, and a piece, no bigger than a nut, of butter in which you have worked a little flour, and reduce this sauce at least by half. Meanwhile, put the fillets in another saucepan, pour in a liqueur-glassful of brandy and set it alight. Keep them hot. Add to the reduced sauce whatever blood and gravy may be in the dish where you have carved the bird, a tablespoonful of fresh cream, a little lemon juice, reduce again, see that it is well seasoned; add, at the last minute a few pieces of butter, one by one, stirring well and pour this sauce through a fine strainer (or squeeze it through a muslin) over your fillets in the serving dish.

§ *Wild ducks; claret; port; jus or stock; butter; flour; brandy; cream; lemon juice.*

*

ROASTING GAME

There are many pleasant ways of cooking game, and there is no reason why it should always be served roasted with bread sauce. About roasting there are several things which are very important. A bird should be salted inside before roasting; it makes the whole difference to the taste of the meat; also it should be wrapped up in very thin, fat bacon, and frequently basted. When it is served in a carefully warmed dish, the gravy should be poured over it, and no stock of any kind added to this gravy, which must keep its own specific taste. The only way to make gravy, if necessary, is to pour a little salted hot water in the baking pan and scrape well the sides on which the essential and succulent juices of the meat have solidified.

Grouse is better plainly roasted and especially cold, but pheasant is better with sauce; poached, with a cream sauce and braised celery, it is exquisite, or served braised with sauerkraut. There is the elaborate and perfect Partridge Souvarof with its accompaniment of truffles and foie gras, *and the homely Perdreau en casserole, for which, incidentally, you do not require absolutely perfect birds.*

*

PERDREAU À LA RUSSE *Partridge à la Russe*

Take a partridge and put inside it a piece of butter in which you have worked salt, pepper, and lemon juice. Wrap the partridge in thin fat bacon and cook it in a flat saucepan, in a moderate oven, the bird resting on a bed of lean bacon, carrots and onions all cut in small pieces. Baste often, cook for about half an hour, unwrap it and keep it hot. Meanwhile cut finely one small onion and two shallots, and melt these slowly in butter; add a small glass of dry white wine and reduce it by three-quarters; then put in a cup of cream, a pinch of paprika, a few drops of lemon juice, bring to the boil, and let it reduce for a few minutes.

Pour through a strainer over the partridge in the serving-dish.

§ *Partridge; butter; lemon juice; fat bacon; lean bacon; carrots; onions; shallots; dry white wine; cream; paprika; lemon juice.*

PERDREAU À L'ANGLAISE *Partridge à l'Anglaise*

Take one or two young partridges, cut them in two, but do not quite separate the two halves, which you open and flatten as you do a small chicken for grilling.

Marinate them for two hours in the following mixture: Oil, salt, pepper, bay leaves, thyme, and parsley, turning them once or twice. Grill the birds, starting with a fierce fire, on both sides, and reduce the heat; turn them once or twice. Serve with a *Rémoulade* sauce.

§ *Partridges; oil; bay leaves; thyme; parsley;* Rémoulade *sauce (shallots, onion, parsley, chervil, oil, vinegar, mustard).*

PERDREAU POCHÉ *Poached Partridge*

The 'poaching' in this case is in connexion with the cooking, not the catching of the bird. This is the plainest of all recipes, yet an exquisite dish in which you get the full flavour of the game entirely unspoilt by any condiment – the perfection of simplicity.

Take a perfect bird, young and fat, salt it inside and outside, wrap it in vine-leaves and put it in another wrapper, well tied, of thin fat bacon. Cook it in boiling water for thirty-five to forty minutes; this depends on the size of the bird, but, in any case, a little more time than for roasting should be allowed. Then put it in iced water till cold.

Remove the wrappers and you will find a partridge with a fine flesh, pink, tender, juicy and full of its own lovely perfume. Eat it plain or with just a green salad very lightly dressed.

§ *Partridges; vine leaves; thin fat bacon.*

FILETS DE PERDREAUX AUX BIGARADES   *Fillets of Partridge with Bitter Oranges*

Roast your partridge in the ordinary way (not forgetting to sprinkle the inside of the bird with salt, and to roast it between two rashers of fat bacon). Do not joint the bird, but carve away slices of the meat as you would do for a duck, and keep them hot.

Make a *roux,* add to it a little veal or beef stock and cook for a few minutes. Then add to this the broken bones of the partridge, salt, coarsely broken pepper, half a glass of dry white wine, the gravy from the roasted partridge, a little of the rind (peeled off very thin) of an orange, and one bay leaf. Bring to the boil, let it reduce, pass through a sieve and skim off the fat.

Fry some *croûtons;* dispose your fillets of partridge on them, put them in a dish and cover them with your sauce, to which you have added a few minutes before the squeezed juice of an orange.

§ *Partridges; fat bacon; roux; veal or beef stock; peppercorns; dry white wine; an orange; a bay leaf; croûtons.*

*

Brillat-Savarin holds the view that, if cooked fresh, a pheasant is not as good as a good fowl. It should be kept, he says, eight days at least, and not plucked till the last minute, as the perfume is kept more perfect within the feathers. The right moment to eat it is when the flesh begins to change colour and smell slightly; then the bird has reached its maximum of succulence. For most people this may be too much of a good thing. This is not the usual French opinion, which is in favour of highness; indeed, this is obvious, otherwise the word faisande, *which means high, would not have been coined and would not be used now in connexion with game generally.*

*

FAISAN FARCI   *Stuffed Pheasant*

Prepare a stuffing with pork sausage meat, a few chicken livers, one chopped truffle, salt and pepper, a little parsley – all this well mixed and bound with the yolk of an egg and very little cream (the mixture should be fairly stiff) – stuff the bird with it and cook it, wrapped in bacon in

POULTRY AND GAME

the usual way, but in a moderate oven. When it is about three parts cooked add to the baking tin a claret-glassful of Madeira or sherry, a spoonful of tomato purée (a little hot water if necessary), salt, pepper and grated nutmeg. Finish cooking, basting often.

Before serving remove the wrapper of bacon, put the pheasant in a dish, with *croûtons*, spread with *foie gras*, all round, and pour the sauce over the whole.

§ *Pheasant; pork sausage meat; chicken livers; truffle; parsley; yolk of egg; cream; Madeira or sherry; tomato purée; nutmeg; croûtons; foie gras.*

FAISAN AUX POMMES   *Pheasant with Apples*

Prepare the pheasant as for roasting. Melt some butter in a saucepan and brown the bird on all sides. Finish the cooking in a moderate oven, basting well and allowing about thirty minutes for an average-sized bird.

Meanwhile, peel and cut in thin slices half a dozen eating apples; cook them in butter. When they are nearly done dispose half of these at the bottom of an earthenware *cocotte*; put the pheasant in this; place the rest all round the bird, season well and add two or three tablespoonfuls of cream.

Put the lid on the *cocotte* and cook in a moderate oven for about fifteen minutes. Serve in the *cocotte*.

§ *Pheasant; butter; apples; cream.*

FAISAN À LA CRÈME   *Pheasant in Cream*

Have a pheasant trussed as for roasting, season it inside with salt and pepper and brown it on all sides in butter. Put the saucepan in a moderate oven and go on cooking the bird, basting often, for thirty to thirty-five minutes, according to size.

When the pheasant is cooked, remove it, put in the pan a tablespoonful of brandy, a glass of *fumet* of game and two glasses of cream. Cook for two or three minutes and reduce, put back the bird, stir and baste well, cook for a few minutes more and serve in the same saucepan or casserole in which it has been cooked.

§ *Pheasant; butter; brandy;* fumet *of game; cream.*

CROQUETTES DE FAISAN   *Pheasant Croquettes*

This is a typical example of frying in deep fat. There should be lots of it, so that the croquettes do not touch each other and can revolve freely, and it should be very hot so that the coating of breadcrumbs is fixed straight away and forms a dry and crisp outside.

The croquettes themselves are made as follows: remnants of roast pheasant and a very small quantity of lean cooked ham, chopped finely, well seasoned and pounded through a sieve.

Add a little *Béchamel*, one yolk of egg (or two, according to quantities), and mix well. The mixture should be fairly stiff.

Shape the croquettes rather small, dip them in beaten eggs, roll them in white breadcrumbs, and fry as described.

§ *Cold pheasant; lean ham;* Béchamel *sauce* (roux, *milk, nutmeg); eggs; white breadcrumbs; fat for frying.*

CAILLES FOURRÉES — *Stuffed Quail*

Have some fat quails and stuff them with minced meat prepared as described below. Put in a deep fireproof dish or a *cocotte* two or three rashers of fat bacon, one onion and one carrot cut in slices, salt, pepper and a pinch of mixed spice, also two juniper berries crushed. Dispose the quails on this bed and cook slowly till ready (about a quarter of an hour). Pour the gravy through a muslin over the quails in the serving dish.

Stuffing: There are several ways of stuffing quails, the best are the following:

1. Mince finely remnants of roast chicken, one or two mushrooms, add very little breadcrumbs, mix well, season with pepper and salt and bind together with marrow fat.

2. Mash some *foie gras*, season it with salt and pepper, a pinch of mixed spice, add a little fresh cream, a teaspoonful of port wine, the yolk of an egg, and mix well.

When the quails are stuffed with either of these preparations the opening should be sewn (the thread to be removed before serving). Some people cook the birds for a minute or two in butter before putting them in the *cocotte*.

§ *Quails; fat bacon; onion; carrot; mixed spice; juniper berries. For stuffing, either (a) cold roast chicken, mushrooms, breadcrumbs and marrow fat; or (b)* foie gras, *mixed spice; cream; port; yolk of egg.*

CAILLES AUX RAISINS — *Quail with Grapes*

Melt a small piece of butter in a pan or a little casserole, put in your quails and just colour them on all sides; add salt and pepper and finish cooking in the same pan for about twelve minutes in a hot oven. Add (for four quails) half a tumblerful of veal stock well reduced, bring to the boil, put in a teaspoonful of grapefruit juice and lemon juice mixed, a few peeled grapes (pips removed), cook for one minute more and serve.

§ *Quails; butter; veal stock; grapefruit juice; lemon juice; grapes.*

CAILLES EN RAGOÛT   *Ragoût of Quail*

Take some quails, cut them in two and toss them for a minute or two in a pan with a little pork fat and a sprinkle of flour. Add then a cup of consommé or of veal stock, salt, pepper, a *bouquet,* a few fresh mushrooms and pieces of globe artichokes. Cook very slowly, and when it is nearly ready add the juice of an orange.

Other small birds can be treated in the same manner.

§ *Quails; pork fat; flour; consommé or veal stock; bouquet; mushrooms; globe artichokes; orange juice.*

BÉCASSE FLAMBÉE   *Woodcock Flambée*

First put in a small pan half a glass of claret and half a glass of port wine, salt, pepper, Cayenne pepper and two or three pieces of lemon peel. Cook till it is reduced by three-quarters.

The woodcock, seasoned, should be roasted in a dish in a quick oven, often basting with butter; allow six or seven minutes only.

Remove it, and to the gravy in the dish add a small glass of Madeira, one of stock and very little tomato purée. Mix well, cook two minutes and keep this gravy hot.

Cut the bird in half, put the pieces in the pan with the reduction of wine, add a glass of brandy and set it alight, shaking well.

This finishes the cooking of the bird and gives the necessary flavour.

Meanwhile, chop the 'insides' and mash them well with a piece of butter and a little *foie gras.* Spread part of this mixture on pieces of toast (one to each half-woodcock) and cook these one minute under the grill.

Place the pieces of bird on the pieces of toast and keep them hot in the serving dish.

Put in the pan the rest of the mixture, mix well with what is left of the reduction of wine, add the gravy previously prepared, bring to the boil and pour (through a fine strainer) over the woodcock in the dish.

Allow half a woodcock to each person. With this dish no green vegetables should be served, only potatoes of a dry kind, like straw or soufflées.

§ *Woodcock; claret; port; Cayenne; lemon peel; butter; Madeira; stock; tomato purée; brandy;* foie gras; *toast.*

SALMIS DE GIBIER *Ragoût of Game*
All birds can be served en salmis which is the 'Salmigundy' of the old cookery books and all salmis are prepared in exactly the same manner.

Prepare the bird or birds as for roasting, with inside a little salt and butter, but roast only for ten minutes to a quarter of an hour, according to size. Then carve the bird in the ordinary way and put the pieces in a saucepan.

Chop the carcase, liver, neck, etc., coarsely; put them in another saucepan with two or three shallots (chopped finely), salt, pepper, a tablespoonful of purée of tomato, a *bouquet* and a glass of red wine; bring to the boil and let it simmer till it has reduced by half. Pass the sauce through a strainer and add to it gravy from the roasted bird and blood which has come out in the carving. Add also a cupful of *fumet* of game.

Mix well, pour over the pieces of bird in the saucepan, add a drop of Madeira wine, a few slices of mushrooms previously cooked for five minutes in butter and cook for ten minutes on a slow fire. Serve with *croûtons* all round the dish.

You can also make it for a change with dry, white wine instead of red, and add a little lemon juice; it makes a different kind of salmis with a pleasant sharp taste.

§ *Game; fat bacon; shallots; tomato purée;* bouquet; *red wine; fumet of game; Madeira; mushrooms; butter;* croûtons. *Dry white wine and lemon juice can be used instead of red wine.*

CHEVREUIL *Venison*
Venison can be prepared in many pleasant ways, and should be served with a sauce of a sharp kind which contrasts with the sweetness of the meat itself. If the venison is tender it need not be marinated unless you have to keep it for a day or two.

It can be marinated in plain oil or the marinade can be made in the following manner:

Marinade: Cut finely one onion, one carrot, one shallot, add a *bouquet* with celery, two cloves, and cook this in very little oil for one minute; add half a pint of vinegar, bring to the boil and cook for a quarter of an hour. Pass through a strainer and pour it cold over the piece of venison, previously sprinkled with salt and pepper.

Turn the piece several times during the twelve to twenty-four hours which the meat should marinate. The aim of the marinade is to make the meat more tender and to remove the excessive gamey taste it may have; also it is used for the making of the sauce.

The meat should be carefully boned and trimmed, and will be improved if larded; it should be kept underdone, allowing only nine to ten minutes to the pound. Before putting in the oven drain it well and wipe it with a cloth, cook well greased with butter in a hot oven, basting well.

Venison is usually served with a purée of chestnuts or of celery and a sauce like *Poivrade* or *Grand Veneur*.

§ *Venison; bouquet with celery; cloves; olive oil; onion; carrot; shallot; vinegar.*

FILETS DE CHEVREUIL SAUTÉS   *Fillets of Venison Sautéed*

Cut some thin slices from a piece of venison which has not been marinated, and put them in a fireproof china dish. Put in a saucepan a glass of wine vinegar, a bay leaf, a sprig of thyme, one onion with a clove, one chopped shallot, parsley and a small piece of cinnamon. Bring to the boil and cook five minutes. Pass through a fine strainer, let it get cold and pour this marinade over the slices of venison. Let this stand one hour in a cool place.

Melt some butter in a *sauteuse,* cook the fillets (they should not be too well cooked) and put them in the serving dish. Add to the butter in the *sauteuse* a glass of brandy, the marinade, a little consommé or stock and a small piece of butter worked in with flour; reduce for a few minutes, whip well, pour over the fillets, and cook a little more.

If you want to have a garniture with it, you can serve either purée of chestnuts and redcurrant jelly or, more subtly, slices of eating apples fried in butter.

§ *Venison; wine vinegar; shallot; parsley; thyme; onion; clove; cinnamon; butter; brandy; consommé or stock; butter; flour.*

CIVET DE LIÈVRE   *Jugged Hare*

When preparing the hare keep all the blood, to which you add a little claret or vinegar so that it does not coagulate. Cut the hare in smallish pieces.

Put in a saucepan some butter, a few small onions, and a rasher of streaky bacon cut in small pieces. When well browned remove onions and bacon, and use the same butter to fry the pieces of hare; they should be fried for a few minutes only, after which you add a little flour, salt and pepper, parsley, and a tumblerful of claret and stock mixed in equal parts. Add also the onions and bacon previously fried, also the pieces of hare, then the blood. Stir it well, put the lid on, and let it simmer for at least two hours and a half. Remove parsley before serving.

The hare, to be good, should not weigh more than about six pounds, as the flesh of bigger hares is liable to be tough.

§ *Hare; claret; small onions; streaky bacon; butter; flour; parsley; stock. Vinegar optional.*

CIVET DE LIÈVRE LIMOUSINE *Fricassée of Hare Limousine*

Cut the hare in smallish pieces and marinate them for three hours in a little olive oil, a small glass of brandy, salt, pepper and slices of onion. Turn the pieces occasionally.

Fry in butter a dozen cubes of streaky bacon or of pickled pork with a few button onions. Cook for a few minutes and sprinkle in a tablespoonful of flour.

Stir well, and cook two or three minutes, then add the pieces of hare, well drained, and cook them, stirring well, until the flesh has stiffened.

Add a *bouquet*, one clove of garlic, and enough red wine to cover the pieces of hare. Cook on a slow fire, with the lid on, for three hours.

See that it is highly seasoned, remove the *bouquet*, and add a dozen or so of chestnuts previously cooked in meat stock. Cook a few minutes more, and serve.

If you have the blood of the hare, add to it a little vinegar to prevent coagulation, and stir it in, little by little, five minutes before serving; it will act as a binding and will improve the dish.

§ *Hare; olive oil; brandy; onion; streaky bacon or pickled pork; button onions; flour;* bouquet; *garlic red wine; chestnuts; vinegar.*

RÂBLE DE LIÈVRE ALSACIENNE *Saddle of Hare Alsacienne*

Take a saddle of hare and marinate it for two days in the following mixture: a glass of dry white wine, one of vinegar, carrots, onions cut in slices, salt, coarsely broken pepper and a *bouquet*.

Turn the saddle two or three times a day, so that it is well soaked. Then drain it and fry it a few minutes only in olive oil.

It should be browned all over, but quite red inside. Drain it well again, and keep it hot.

Put in a pan the marinade (strained) and reduce it by three-quarters; add to it two or three tablespoonfuls of *fumet* of game or of stock, a tablespoonful of redcurrant jelly and a teaspoonful of mustard, and cook together a few minutes.

Carve the saddle in fillets and put these in a fireproof serving dish. Pour the sauce over through a fine strainer, and put for a few minutes on a slow fire – just enough to finish cooking the meat.

POULTRY AND GAME

Add, immediately before serving, a small piece of butter in which you have worked a little flour which will thicken and bind the sauce.

Put *croûtons* round the dish, and serve with a purée of chestnuts or of celery.

§ *Saddle of hare; dry white wine; vinegar; carrots; onions; peppercorns; bouquet; olive oil; fumet of game or stock; redcurrant jelly; mustard; butter; flour;* croûtons; *purée of chestnuts or of celery.*

LAPIN SAUTÉ   *Sautéed Rabbit*

Take a young rabbit, clean it, wipe it with a cloth, and cut it in pieces. Put in a pan a piece of butter the size of an egg, and when at the foaming stage put in the pieces of rabbit, adding salt, pepper, and a pinch of mixed spice. Cook on a quick fire, tossing occasionally. In about a quarter of an hour it is ready. Throw in then two or three shallots finely chopped and a small glass of dry white wine; cook for five minutes more on a slower fire and sprinkle with chopped parsley before serving.

§ *Rabbit; butter; mixed spice; shallots; dry white wine; parsley.*

LAPIN À LA FLAMANDE   *Rabbit à la Flamande*

The rabbit is cut in pieces, fried a few minutes in butter with half a dozen button onions, a *bouquet* of thyme and parsley and slices of bacon. Add a tumbler of red wine, a little vinegar and seasoning.

Cook slowly with the lid on for about one hour or a little less. Half-way through remove the onions, the *bouquet* and the bacon, and add a few prunes, stoned and cut in half, also a handful of seedless raisins.

Serve with *croûtons,* fried in bacon fat, round the dish.

A chicken can be treated in the same manner.

§ *Rabbit; button onions; thyme; parsley; red wine; vinegar; prunes; seedless raisins;* croûtons.

PURÉE DE LAPEREAU   *Purée of Young Rabbit*

A very good dish can be made with young rabbit. Bone it, and pound the flesh in a mortar, pass this through a fine sieve, add salt, pepper, a little nutmeg, a teaspoonful of Tomato sauce, a little good stock, and boil it for a little while to the consistency of thick cream. Serve with fried *croûtons.*

§ *Rabbit; nutmeg; Tomato sauce (tomatoes, onions, carrots, wine vinegar, brown* roux, *stock, butter); nutmeg; stock;* croûtons.

PÂTÉ DE LAPIN   *Rabbit Pie*

Have two young rabbits, joint and bone them, put the pieces in cold water for one hour; then put them in a saucepan just covered with cold water, adding salt, pepper, two onions and a little sage. Bring to the boil and cook gently for about twenty minutes.

Move the pieces of rabbit to a pie dish with chopped parsley, a few pieces of bacon, slices of hard-boiled egg and a dozen stuffed prunes. Mix well, add a pint of stock well seasoned and cover with paste for pie crust. Bake till the pastry is cooked and nicely brown.

For the Stuffed Prunes: Soak the prunes in water for a day and dry them well, stone them and fill with the following mixture: half an onion and parsley finely chopped, to which you add pork or bacon also minced; season with salt and pepper, add just enough breadcrumbs to bind the mixture, fry in butter for a few minutes and stuff the prunes.

§ *Rabbits; onions; sage; parsley; bacon; egg; stock; pastry; prunes; breadcrumbs. Pork optional.*

Pickled Meats and Pâtés

PETIT SALÉ, I *Pickled Pork, I*

Petit salé is a kind of pickled pork. It is usually made in large quantities at the time, as it keeps for a long time. But it can also be prepared in small quantities.

Take several pounds of pork, preferably from the neck or the breast, or the parts of the animal which are streaky. Cut them in pieces, about three or four inches long.

Get a large earthenware jar with an opening narrower than the bottom. Put at the bottom a layer of thyme and bay leaves, then a thick coat of salt. It is necessary to use the coarse grey salt, unrefined, sea salt being preferable to rock salt. Take a piece of pork and rub it well over with salt, then another, till you have made a layer of meat, all the pieces being well pressed against one another; then another thick layer of salt, and so on, till you have filled the jar or come to the end of your stock of pork. Cover the jar with a piece of cloth, then with the lid. If the jar has no lid, a piece of board over the cloth with something heavy over it will do. Keep in a cool place at least ten days before using.

When you take a piece, take it with your fingers; do not dig in the jar with a fork, and replace the salt carefully.

§ *Pork (preferably neck or breast); thyme; bay leaves; coarse salt.*

PETIT SALÉ II *Pickled Pork, II*

The other way of making *petit salé*, by pickling in *saumure*, is equally good. Take a jar, put bay leaves and thyme as before and fill it with water, leaving of course room for the pieces of pork. Put in salt, a handful at the time, and stir with a wooden spoon to make it dissolve. Go on adding salt till you reach the saturation point, that is to say, when the water cannot dissolve any more salt (which you will know by putting an egg in it; it floats if the water is saturated). Then put the meat in and keep covered in a cool place.

If you make a large quantity, do not forget when you reach the bottom pieces to wash them in several waters before using, otherwise, no doubt, they would be too salt.

§ *Pork; bay leaves; thyme; coarse salt.*

CONFITS D'OIE *Preserved Goose*

Take a well-fattened goose. Cut it in pieces, legs, wings, neck, breast, etc. Remove carefully all the fat attached, also the fat inside the bird. Put the meat for twenty-four hours in a jar with coarse salt, thyme and bay leaves. Melt the fat in a large saucepan with a spoonful of water and one pound of pork fat. When well melted, put in the parts of the goose and cook on a very slow fire for four hours (drying the pieces well before you put them to cook). Then put them in an earthenware jar and pour the fat over. When cold, cover the jar as for *petit salé*. Your *confit* in a few days is ready for use.

When you want a piece take it out and see that none of the others are exposed to the air. It is advisable to melt again part of the fat and pour it afresh over the *confits*. They will keep for months. In Perigord the stock for the year is usually prepared about Christmas time.

Confits *are also made with ducks and turkeys, and, after all,* petit salé *is only a cheaper and coarser form of* confits.

§ *Goose; coarse salt; thyme; bay leaves; pork fat.*

RILLONS *Potted Pork*

In the origin *rillons* were the scraps of meat left at the bottom of the big pan in which the meat of a whole pig was cooked for the purpose of making fat for the needs of the household. They were then seasoned and kept in small pots. But those days are over, and *rillons* are now made on a smaller scale.

Take several pounds of streaky pork, cut it in small pieces and roll them well in salt and lots of pepper. Put all this in a large saucepan with a tumblerful of salted water and cook on a moderate fire. Stir often to help the melting of the fat and the evaporation of the water. Cook till the pork meat is a nice brown colour. When the fat stops smoking it is cooked.

Remove them from the fire and squeeze through a sieve. Taste them, add more seasoning if necessary, put them back in the saucepan and cook a few minutes more. Then put them in earthenware pots and pour slowly the melted fat over them, so that it fills the tiny spaces left in the *rillons*. Go on pouring till you have on the top a layer of pure fat about half an inch thick. Cover with paper and the lid. *Rillons* are very good cold as a kind of coarse pâté, as hors d'œuvre, and also used for different dishes.

§ *Streaky pork.*

RILLETTES *Potted Pork*

Variation on the same theme. Get several pounds of pork, some fat, some lean, chops or legs, and chop it very finely. Begin the cooking. Also boil in a *court-bouillon* without vinegar a piece of pig's liver (half a pound for about three or four pounds of *rillettes*); when well cooked pound it well, add it to the pork meat, mix well, add salt and a good deal of pepper. Bring to the boil, stirring all the time, and then cook more slowly till ready. Remove from the fire, stirring occasionally, so that the fat and the lean remain well mixed. Wait till the fat is half set to put in pots.

For both these pâtés the proportion of fat and lean is rather a question of taste. On the whole, the best is half and half, which you usually get in using the streaky parts of the pork for the *rillons*, and a pound of lean to a pound of fat for the *rillettes*.

§ *Lean and fat pork;* court-bouillon *without vinegar; pig's liver.*

GALANTINE *Galantine*

Take two pounds of veal, one pound of streaky pork, a quarter of a pound of liver and mince it fairly fine together, but keep a few nice thin pieces of veal apart. Mix the mince well on the board, add one shallot and a little parsley chopped, spices and a good deal of salt and pepper. Butter a deep pie dish, put in a layer of minced meat, a rasher of bacon, a slice of veal sprinkled with seasoning, another rasher, more minced meat and so on until the terrine is full. Cover with buttered paper and cook in a moderate oven for an hour and a quarter. Put a weight over it and let it grow cold. It will be better if made twenty-four hours before it is to be eaten. Serve in the dish.

Can also be made with hare or rabbit instead of veal.

§ *Veal; streaky pork; liver; shallot; parsley; spices; bacon.*

PÂTÉ DE VOLAILLE *Pâté of Chicken or Duck*

Bone a chicken, and put aside the white meat. Mince the rest with half a pound of lean veal, half a pound of lean pork and a quarter of a pound of pork fat. Season well and add a few chopped truffles. Take a jar, put first a layer of minced meat, then alternately a very thin rasher of bacon, white meat of chicken, bacon, minced meat, and so on till the pot is full. Cook for one hour and a quarter in a *bain marie* in a moderate oven.

The same can be done with duck, in which case it would be a pity not to add some fine truffles, the peelings of which should be added, cooked for a few minutes in a liqueur glass of port wine to the minced meat. It should cook about a quarter of an hour longer.

§ 1. *Chicken; lean veal; fat and lean pork; truffles; bacon.*

2. *Duck; lean veal; fat and lean pork; truffles; port wine; bacon.*

PÂTÉ DE FOIE GRAS *Pâté de Foie Gras*

Take half a pound of streaky pork, pass it through the mincing machine, add salt and pepper. Get three or four truffles, peel them and cut them in three or four pieces, chop the skins and add them to the minced meat. Take a *foie gras* (duck's or goose's) about one pound and a half in weight. Put in some truffles here and there.

Take a *terrine* or earthenware jar, coat the bottom of it with the minced meat; a few truffles, the *foie gras,* a few truffles, a coat of minced meat. Cover the pot, cook about one hour and a quarter in a *bain marie* in a moderate oven. Let it get tepid, then press it slightly, drain whatever gravy there is in the jar and fill with melted pork fat or, better still, goose fat. A coat of pork fat on the top, a sheet of thin paper overlapping the edge, and put the lid on. Keep in a cool place, but not damp.

§ *Streaky pork; truffles;* foie gras; *pork fat. Goose fat optional.*

PÂTÉ DE FOIE *Pâté de Foie*

Take, say, one pound of liver, remove the skin and nerves carefully and chop the meat, mixing it with three-quarters of a pound of bacon fat. Pass it through a sieve, and season well with salt, freshly ground pepper and nutmeg. Take a *terrine* and line it with very thin slices of streaky bacon; put in your minced meat, and cook (with a buttered paper over it) in a moderate oven for a little more than one hour. Let the pâté get cold in the larder with a weight over it. Serve in the *terrine* in which it has cooked.

§ *Liver; bacon fat; nutmeg; streaky bacon.*

TERRINE DE GIBIER *Game Pâté*

You can use for this pâté any game you have by you – partridge, pheasant, hare or rabbit. The procedure is always the same. Cut some nice fillets out of whatever game you are using and season them with salt and pepper; also prepare some minced meat (the proportions should be one part of minced meat to two parts of game) in the following manner: pork, streaky bacon, lean veal, a little stale bread, parsley, one onion and one shallot finely chopped, one truffle in slices, spices, salt and pepper. These should be finely minced and well mixed.

Take an earthenware *terrine,* grease it with pork fat and fill it, beginning with one bay leaf at the bottom and a layer of minced meat, then a layer of game, a thin piece of fat bacon, a layer of meat and so on till the *terrine* is full, ending with minced meat and a slice of fat bacon. Stand the *terrine* in a tin full of hot water and bake in a moderate oven for about one hour and a half.

While it cooks, put in a small saucepan full of water, bones and scraps of game, one onion, with a clove, one carrot cut in slices, *bouquet* and a calf's foot. Bring to the boil and let it simmer till well reduced. When the *terrine* is cooked, remove it from the oven. You will find that the pâté has shrunk; empty out most of the fat it has yielded and fill in with your reduced stock (through a fine colander), which will become a jelly when cold. Put a weight over the pâté and put it away to cool. It will keep for weeks if (when it has become tepid), you pour over it melted fat and cover it with a piece of greased paper. If you intend to eat it at once, this is not necessary. In any case, it is better to keep it a day.

§ *Game; pork; streaky bacon; lean veal; stale bread; parsley; onion; shallot; truffle; spices; pork fat.*

Vegetables

VEGETABLE DISHES

It is a great mistake always to serve two vegetables as an accompaniment to a meat course. At least one vegetable, potatoes, is quite enough, and the practice both extravagant and monotonous of what clubs called 'the vegetables of the day' (or what the cook calls 'a second vegetable') should be discouraged. Why have with any meat course, say, potatoes and either French beans, or spinach, or young carrots, plainly boiled, simply because it is a habit? It may be that the taste of these vegetables does not go especially well with the flavour of the meat dish; it may be also that the flavour of these vegetables is not at its best when only plainly boiled. So why not make two courses instead of one and have, in the French fashion, a course of meat and potatoes and a separate vegetable course, both at their best? It costs hardly a penny more and is far pleasanter, indeed it will excite even the most jaded appetite.

Needless to say, the vegetables must be young and tender. It seems, somehow, a ghastly tragedy to see these admirable English raw materials cooked ever so primitively in plain water, or allowed to go till over-mature by a gardener, more anxious of size than of flavour. However, if we live in London we must be content with the best we can get at the greengrocer's, but if we have a garden we must be firm and not be afraid of breaking the gardener's heart; our peas must be small, our broad beans under age, and our lettuces gathered in their youth.

They must also be specially prepared; boiling is only a preparation for the finished article, and the finished article is well worth the extra trouble. Simple as these dishes are we seem somehow far from the days when 'sharp hunger' was the only seasoning of

'Our Cambrian fathers sparing in their food.
   Their sallading was never far to seek,
   The poignant water-grass, or sav'ry leek . . .'

But then perhaps they felt about it as Nebuchadnezzar did according to that old Oxford prize poem:

'Nebuchadnezzar ate the rank green grass
With herds of oxen and the savage ass,
   And murmured as he cropped the unwanted food,
   It may be wholesome, but it is not good.'

ARTICHAUTS VINAIGRETTE *Artichokes Vinaigrette*

The cooking of globe artichokes is a simple affair. Remove the hard short leaves near the stalk and the stalk altogether, and cook standing in boiling salted water, and not quite covered with water. Cook for about three-quarters of an hour and without a lid on the saucepan. When you can easily remove a leaf they are ready. They must be thoroughly well drained. Serve hot or cold with a *Vinaigrette* sauce. The *fonds* cut in small pieces and tossed for one minute in butter are delicious in omelettes.

When very young, small and fresh, artichokes can be eaten raw, with salt, as hors d'œuvre.

§ *Globe artichokes; Vinaigrette sauce (eggs, gherkins, shallot, capers, oil, vinegar, mustard).*

ARTICHAUTS À L'ITALIENNE *Artichokes à l'Italienne*

Take some artichokes, remove the leaves and the heart and keep only the bottom, which you trim well. Throw them in cold salted water. Boil them well and keep them in a cloth. At the same time prepare the following sauce: a tumblerful of consommé, a piece of butter the size of a walnut and a pinch of flour; mix well; cook slowly, then add a tablespoonful of grated cheese and a spoonful of white wine. Do this over the fire, stirring all the time. Cook about a quarter of an hour. Arrange the artichokes in a buttered dish, pour the sauce over, sprinkle with breadcrumbs and brown in the oven.

§ *Globe artichokes; consommé; butter; flour; cheese; white wine; breadcrumbs.*

ARTICHAUTS À LA BARIGOULE *Artichokes à la Barigoule*

Take some artichokes, cut off three-quarters of the leaves and remove the smaller ones which are near the stalk. Put them in boiling water and cook them about ten minutes. Remove them and dip them in cold water. Then remove all the inside, leaving only the heart and the outer circles of leaves, and fill them with a mixture prepared as follows:

Put in a saucepan one onion, one shallot and a few mushrooms very finely chopped, a piece of butter the size of a small egg, a little olive oil and cook on a moderate fire about ten minutes; then add parsley and a rasher of bacon chopped together, salt and pepper, a 'drop' of white wine, a tablespoonful of beef stock, a teaspoonful of purée of tomatoes.

Fill the artichokes with this mixture; place over each a very thin rasher of bacon and tie them with some thread.

Put in a fireproof dish pieces of carrots and onions, one bay leaf, and whatever scraps of meat and small bones you have by you; add a tablespoonful of beef stock. Place your artichokes on this bed and bring to the boil, keeping the dish covered. Put it aside a few minutes, remove the lid, baste the artichokes, cover them with oiled paper and finish cooking in a moderate oven, basting occasionally.

When ready, remove the strings and bacon. Serve the artichokes covered with gravy obtained by squashing through a sieve all the ingredients in which they have cooked.

I should like to add that this dish – which dates from the end of the eighteenth century – is far more complicated to describe than to make; in any case, it is well worth the trouble.

§ *Globe artichokes; onion; shallot; mushrooms; butter; olive oil; parsley; bacon; white wine; beef stock; tomato purée.*

FONDS D'ARTICHAUTS FLORESTAN　　*Artichoke Bottoms Florestan*

The bottoms of the artichokes previously boiled are put on a purée of spinach (properly prepared with mashed spinach, a little butter and cream), covered with a thin layer of *Mornay* sauce, sprinkled all over with grated cheese, and browned quickly.

§ *Globe artichokes; spinach; butter; cream;* Mornay *sauce (roux, milk, nutmeg, egg, cheese); cheese.*

ARTICHAUTS VÉRONÈSE　　*Artichokes Véronèse*

Have some globe artichokes as fresh as possible and small; remove all the leaves till you get to the tender whitish part. Cut off the stalk and cut the artichokes in quarters, removing also the 'hay' if there is a great deal. (If the artichokes are young, there will be hardly any.)

Boil them (in boiling salted water) till soft, and drain them well.

When cold, dispose them gently in the serving dish and pour over all a *Sauce Verte*.

§ *Globe artichokes;* Sauce Verte *(eggs, vinegar, oil, spinach, watercress, parsley, tarragon).*

ASPARAGUS

Gastronomic writers become positively lyrical over asparagus: 'It is a charm,' writes the author of The Book of the Table, *'when we know that it is a lily, near of kin to the lily-of-the-valley, we are not surprised at its power over us. When we hear that it is ranked with the asphodels, we are ready to believe that the fields of asphodels in which the blessed roam in Elysium must be beds of asparagus . . .'*

ASPERGES GRATINÉES   *Asparagus with Cheese*

Scrape and wash some green asparagus and cook them in salted boiling water. Prepare in a small saucepan the classical mixture of butter and flour, cook it a few minutes, add milk, let it thicken and pour it over the asparagus (using only the tender green part, cut in small pieces) in a fireproof dish. Sprinkle well with grated cheese (Parmesan and Gruyère mixed in equal parts) and brown in the oven.

Asparagus tips are also very good cooked à la poulette *in the manner described for young carrots.*

§ *Asparagus; butter; flour; milk; Parmesan cheese; Gruyère cheese.*

ASPERGES MALTAISE   *Asparagus Maltaise*

Have some good-sized asparagus and serve them hot with the following sauce:

Put in a small saucepan two tablespoonfuls of wine vinegar and a little pepper, bring to the boil and reduce at least by half and let this get cool. Put in a bowl the yolks of three eggs, a quarter of a pound of butter cut in small pieces and the reduction of vinegar. Cook standing in boiling water, whipping all the time. When the sauce begins to thicken, add a drop of cold water, a few more small pieces of butter, the juice of half a blood orange and a teaspoonful of grated rind.

This sauce, like Béarnaise, Mousseline, etc., will be spoiled if it reaches more than a moderate degree of heat.

§ *Asparagus; wine vinegar; yolks of egg; butter; blood orange.*

BEIGNETS D'ASPERGES   *Asparagus Fritters*

Take some asparagus tips about three inches long, cook them in the ordinary way, drain them, and refresh them for one minute in cold water. Drain again carefully, roll them lightly in flour, dip them in beaten egg, tie them in little bundles, and fry in deep fat. Serve on a napkin with quarters of lemon.

§ *Asparagus; flour; egg; fat; lemon.*

AUBERGINES

So we reach summer; we have now the full-bodied summer vegetables, sometimes of exotic origin, which give our dishes a spicy quality perfect in hot weather.

The best of these is the aubergine or eggplant, which can be served in many ways, and is obtainable for several months. This attractive vegetable is not yet used as much as it is abroad, but no doubt it will have the success which both bananas and grapefruit have had in a few years.

I have seen recipes beginning, 'Boil the aubergine first . . .' This is asking for disaster. If the aubergines are to be plainly fried, they are cut in very thin slices and fried in very hot oil. If they are to be stuffed or used in any other way, they should be cut in half lengthways, then again fried in oil on both sides till the flesh is soft and almost transparent, then treated according to recipe.

As for people who find them indigestible, they should cut them in half, sprinkle them with salt, and leave them for about one hour and a half. The salt will bring out the water, which is the indigestible part; after which they are cooked according to recipe. (This does not apply to fried aubergines.)

AUBERGINES AU FOUR *Baked Aubergine*

Aubergines can be cooked with cream in the following manner. Peel the aubergines and cut them lengthways in thin slices; fry these in oil and when cooked drain them well, also sprinkle them with salt. Meanwhile, prepare a fairly thick *Béchamel* sauce; pour a little of it into a fireproof dish (adding a little gravy or *jus*), then put in a layer of aubergines, more *Béchamel,* more aubergines, and so on, finishing by a covering of sauce. Cook slowly in the oven. You can, if you like, add a little grated cheese or incorporate with the sauce a little purée of tomato for a change.

§ *Aubergines; oil;* Béchamel *sauce (roux, milk, nutmeg); gravy or jus. Grated cheese or tomato purée can be added.*

AUBERGINES FARCIES *Stuffed Aubergine*

They may be stuffed in different ways, but the preliminary preparation remains the same: cut them in two lengthways, cut the flesh all round near the skin and across several times without spoiling the skin. Fry them in a little oil, turning them occasionally till the flesh has become transparent and soft.

After this scoop out the flesh carefully with a spoon, chop it finely and mix it with either of these:

1. Mushrooms and tomatoes (skin and pips removed), chopped finely and partly cooked in butter.
2. Minced cooked mutton and tomato sauce.
3. Chopped mushrooms, half cooked, and grated cheese.
4. Chopped fillets of anchovy, and breadcrumbs.

In any case, you fill the aubergine skins with the preparation you prefer and brown it in the oven, or under the grill in a buttered fireproof dish.

§ *Aubergines; oil.*
Stuffing: *mushrooms; tomatoes; butter*
mushrooms; grated cheese
fillets of anchovy; breadcrumbs.

AUBERGINES À LA TURQUE *Aubergine à la Turque*

Allow one-half aubergine for each person. Cut them in two lengthways and sprinkle them with salt. One hour later wipe them well and fry them in oil on both sides. When the flesh is soft, scoop it out and chop it.

Meanwhile, cook separately a handful of rice and one or two sweet peppers. Chop these together, add them to the flesh of the aubergines and to the flesh of two tomatoes just cooked for one minute. Season with salt, pepper, paprika and a pinch of saffron. Fill the aubergine skins with this mixture, put them in a buttered fireproof dish, and brown in the oven or under the grill.

§ *Aubergines; olive oil; rice; sweet peppers; tomatoes; paprika; saffron.*

AUBERGINES À L'ITALIENNE *Aubergine à l'Italienne*

Peel the aubergines, cut them in thin slices, roll them lightly in flour and fry them in hot olive oil.

Remove them and fry for two minutes only, in the same oil, the same quantity of tomatoes (pips and skin removed), cut in slices. Take a buttered fireproof dish and put in it a layer of aubergines, one of tomato and so on till the dish is full.

Pour on the top a small quantity of tomato sauce, just to cover, sprinkle over all grated cheese, half Parmesan, half Gruyère, put here and there a few small pieces of butter and brown in the oven.

§ *Aubergines; flour; olive oil; tomatoes; Tomato sauce (tomatoes, carrot, onions, wine vinegar, brown* roux, *stock, butter); Gruyère cheese; Parmesan cheese; butter.*

AUBERGINES SOUFFLÉES   *Souffléed Aubergine*

Cut the aubergines in two and cook in oil as previously described. Having chopped the flesh finely, mix it with about the same quantity of *Béchamel* sauce, add grated cheese, yolks of eggs (one yolk to each aubergine), then the whites well whipped, fill the skins, dispose these in a buttered fireproof dish and cook like a soufflé in the oven. Cook for eight to nine minutes only.

§ *Aubergines; olive oil; flour;* Béchamel *sauce (roux, milk, nutmeg); cheese; eggs.*

AUBERGINES NAPOLITAINE   *Aubergine Napolitaine*

Cut the peeled aubergines lengthways in thin slices. Sprinkle with salt and leave in a dish for one hour and a half. Drain well, dip them lightly in flour and fry them in hot olive oil.

Take about the same quantity of cold mutton carefully trimmed, mince it finely and add a little chopped onion melted in butter, with salt, pepper and mixed spice.

Put in a buttered fireproof dish the slices of aubergines and over each a layer of minced meat. Sprinkle on the top grated cheese and white breadcrumbs. Pour melted butter over all and brown quickly in a hot oven or under a grill. Serve in the same dish, with a sharp Tomato sauce.

§ *Aubergines; flour; olive oil; cold mutton; onion; mixed spice; cheese; white breadcrumbs; butter; Tomato sauce (tomatoes, carrot, onions, wine vinegar, brown roux, stock, butter).*

AUBERGINES BOUCALAISE   *Aubergine Boucalaise*

Allow one aubergine for two people. Cut them in two, lengthways; sprinkle with salt, making cuts across with a sharp knife. Leave them for an hour or so.

Then scoop out the flesh and wipe it well to remove the water which has oozed out.

Put some olive oil in a frying-pan (about two tablespoonfuls for four aubergines). When hot, put in the flesh of the aubergines cut in smallish pieces; cook these on a slow fire so that they melt and do not brown and fry.

When they are becoming soft and transparent, add a few slices of mushrooms and cook a few minutes more. Add, three minutes before serving, a little chopped garlic and parsley.

This vegetable, which should be highly seasoned, is served either as a separate dish or with a roast meat, preferably fillet of veal.

§ *Aubergines; olive oil; mushrooms; garlic; parsley.*

CHOU VERT *Green Cabbage*

Take some small green cabbages, boil them in salted water, drain them well, mash them thoroughly, add, over the fire, butter, salt, and pepper, and what is usually called a 'drop' of vinegar.

They are also excellent simply sauté, in which case you begin by boiling them as before; then remove them before they are completely cooked, drain them well, and fry them in hot butter, and season just before serving.

§ *Cabbage; butter; vinegar.*

CHOU VERT VENDÉENNE *Green Cabbage Vendéenne*

Take several green cabbages, clean them well, removing the hard parts, and cut them coarsely. Put these in salted water at the boiling point; cook them fast, uncovered. When cooked, drain them well, mash them, reheat them, and add in the serving dish salt, pepper and a good piece of butter, which must melt in the heat of the cabbage and not on the fire. The taste of fresh melted butter is indispensable to this dish. Some people add a drop of wine vinegar.

§ *Cabbage; butter. Wine vinegar optional.*

CHOU SURPRISE *Cabbage Surprise*

Take a savoy cabbage, remove the damaged outside leaves and wash it well. Cook it in boiling salt water, and when almost cooked remove it and refresh it in cold water. Drain well and cut out the harder middle part; fill the space with a few chestnuts and Chipolata sausages previously cooked.

Tie the cabbage so that it keeps its shape and put it in a saucepan on a bed of pieces of carrot, of onion and of bacon; add salt, pepper, grated nutmeg and a little water. Cook very slowly, with lid on, on a low fire or in the oven for two hours. Put the cabbage in a deep serving dish and pour the sauce over it through a strainer, squashing the vegetables with a spoon.

§ *Savoy cabbage; chestnuts; Chipolata sausages; carrots; onions; bacon; nutmeg.*

CHOU FARCI *Stuffed Cabbage*

Take a large white cabbage, boil it about a quarter of an hour in salted water. It must be cooked enough for you to open the leaves without breaking them. Remove it, drain it well and open it. Once open, stuff it with either sausage meat or the following mixture: sausage meat, veal, bacon, garlic, parsley, shallots, minced together and highly seasoned. Give the cabbage its original shape and tie it with string. Put the prepared cabbage in a fireproof dish with butter, a spoonful of consommé, salt and pepper, and cook in a moderate oven, basting often. Remove the string before serving.

You can, if you like, make instead of one cabbage several miniature ones, by surrounding a ball of minced meat with a few leaves. It is rather better and easier to serve.

§ *Cabbage; sausage meat; veal; bacon; garlic; shallots; butter; consommé.*

CHOU FARCI À LA RUSSE *Stuffed Cabbage à la Russe*

Take a large white cabbage, remove the outside leaves and boil the best and largest leaves carefully, being careful not to break them. Chop together a few slices of rumpsteak, and fry this (with minced onion and shallots) in butter; also fry about the same quantity of pork sausage meat. Mix together on a board, chop again, season well and add about the same quantity of boiled rice. Mix again, add a little gravy and put some of the mixture on each cabbage leaf. Roll and shape it like a fat sausage and place in a fireproof dish. Cover with *bouillon* and simmer till almost all the *bouillon* has reduced. Serve with a Tomato sauce. This dish is one that requires to be highly seasoned.

§ *Cabbage; rump steak; onions; shallots; butter; pork sausage meat; rice;* bouillon; *Tomato sauce (tomatoes, onions, carrots, brown* roux, *wine vinegar, stock, butter).*

CHOU ROUGE FLAMANDE *Red Cabbage Flamande*

Cut the cabbage in quarters, removing the hard parts, wash it well and cut it fairly fine. Put in a saucepan (preferably earthenware) a piece of butter the size of an egg, melt it, add salt, pepper, a tablespoonful of vinegar, then the cabbage, and cook, stirring occasionally, with the lid on for one hour and a half on a slow fire. Add then two eating apples cut in quarters, a tablespoonful of sugar and cook slowly for another hour. Serve very hot in the saucepan.

§ *Red cabbage; butter; vinegar; apples; sugar.*

CHOU ROUGE DANOISE *Danish Red Cabbage*

This is a very good accompaniment to goose, duck, wild duck, plover and pork.

Cut very finely a red cabbage and cook it slowly in an earthenware saucepan with a glass of red wine, one of redcurrant jelly, and half a glass of wine vinegar. Put in about three or four ounces of butter (according to the size of the cabbage), or, better still, goose fat, a little sugar, and salt.

Cook slowly for two and a half to three hours.

Red cabbage is also very pleasant, raw, cut very finely, plainly seasoned with salt, pepper and vinegar – as an hors d'œuvre salad.

§ *Red cabbage; red wine; redcurrant jelly; wine vinegar; butter or goosefat; sugar.*

CHOU ROUGE À LA TYROLIENNE *Red Cabbage Tyrolienne*

Take a red cabbage, clean it and remove the core; cut it in smallish pieces and put it in an earthenware saucepan with a little pork fat and a piece of smoked bacon. Season well and cook a few minutes and add a cup of either stock or water. Cook slowly, stirring occasionally, about three hours. About half an hour before the end add a dozen chestnuts, previously cooked (first boiled, then lightly fried in pork fat or butter).

Serve as a separate vegetable dish or with roast game.

§ *Red cabbage; pork fat; smoked bacon; stock; chestnuts; butter.*

CHOUX DE BRUXELLES *Brussels Sprouts*
À L'ITALIENNE, I *à l'Italienne, I*

Wash and clean some Brussels sprouts, drain them well and cook them in boiling salted water on a quick fire for about a quarter of an hour. Meanwhile, put in a small saucepan a piece of butter the size of an egg, and a spoonful of flour and cook this for five minutes, stirring and mixing well; add about a pint of milk, bring to the boil and let it thicken; it is then time to add seasoning, a little grated nutmeg, the juice of a lemon and grated cheese. Then put your sprouts (well drained once more) in the sauce and cook a little more on a slow fire, bringing to the boil. Needless to say, it is no use being mean about the sauce, and the quantities given above, which would only do for a small quantity of sprouts, should be increased accordingly.

§ *Brussels sprouts; butter; flour; milk; nutmeg; lemon juice; cheese.*

CHOUX DE BRUXELLES *Brussels Sprouts*
À L'ITALIENNE, II *à l'Italienne, II*

Having boiled your sprouts and drained them well (they should be as small as possible), toss them in a little butter and add some chestnuts previously boiled and shelled, and also tossed in butter. Mix well, season and finish the two together. There should be about a fourth of chestnuts to three-fourths of sprouts.

§ *Brussels sprouts; chestnuts; butter.*

CHOUX DE BRUXELLES MORNAY　　　　*Brussels Sprouts Mornay*

Put your sprouts, cooked and very well drained, in a flat fireproof dish with *Béchamel* sauce covering them. Sprinkle with grated cheese and brown in a fast oven or under the grill.

§ *Brussels sprouts;* Béchamel *sauce (roux, milk, nutmeg); cheese.*

CHOUX DE BRUXELLES SAUTÉS　　　　*Sautéed Brussels Sprouts*

Having the sprouts boiled and very well drained, fry them in butter so that they are slightly browned. Season and serve.

§ *Brussels sprouts; butter.*

CHOU-FLEUR POLONAISE　　　　*Cauliflower Polonaise*

This can be done in two ways; but in either case the cauliflower is boiled in salted boiling water with a drop of vinegar. It should be kept fairly firm. When cooked, remove it, drain it well, and break it in little bunches, not using the main stalk. You can then:

1. Either place these, seasoned with salt and pepper, in a buttered fireproof dish, sprinkle them with chopped yolk of egg and white breadcrumbs, put here and there a few pieces of butter, and brown quickly in the oven or under a grill; or

2. Having spread the pieces of cauliflower, sprinkle all over hard yolk of egg and parsley chopped together; meanwhile melt an ounce of butter in a pan, when it is foaming throw in a handful of white breadcrumbs, fry for two seconds, and pour all over the cauliflower, and serve.

It is advisable to cook a cauliflower in a saucepan just large enough to hold it, so that it does not move in boiling and get damaged; cook it head downwards; if there is any scum forming it won't spoil its appearance.

§ 1. *Cauliflower; vinegar; yolk of egg; white breadcrumbs; butter.*
　2. *Cauliflower; vinegar; yolk of egg; parsley; butter; white breadcrumbs.*

CHOUX-FLEURS FRITS　　　　*Fried Cauliflower*

Boil a good-sized cauliflower in salted water, and when it is nearly cooked remove it carefully and dry it in front of the fire. Then break off the top into little pieces, and fry them in butter until nicely browned. Sprinkle with salt and pepper. Add a few lumps of butter and serve at once.

§ *Cauliflower; butter.*

VEGETABLES

CHOU-FLEUR À LA MENTHE *Cauliflower with Mint*

Having boiled the cauliflower and drained it well, put it in the serving dish and pour over all a good quantity of mint sauce.

§ *Cauliflower; mint sauce.*

PURÉE DE NAVETS *Purée of Turnips*

Peel the turnips and cook them with a small piece of butter, a pinch of sugar, salt and just enough water to cover them. Cook slowly until they almost melt; mash them well and pour through a sieve. Put back the purée thus obtained in the saucepan over a slow fire and dilute it with a small quantity of fresh cream; put in also a few slices of hard-boiled egg. This purée should not be too thick.

§ *Turnips; butter; cream; egg.*

NAVETS BRAISÉS *Braised Turnips*

Take some young and tender turnips. Peel them; it is advisable to do this rather thickly, as sometimes the outside part is stringy.

Put in a pan a piece of butter (about half an ounce for one pound of turnips) and cook the turnips slowly. When they have started colouring and softening, sprinkle a little sugar all over and put in a small cup of meat stock.

Let them simmer very slowly till soft. At that time, the stock having almost disappeared, put in a white sauce made like a *Béchamel* or an ordinary white sauce, but with a squeeze of lemon juice in it.

§ *Turnips; butter; sugar; meat stock; white sauce or* Béchamel *sauce (*roux, milk, nutmeg*); lemon juice.*

POUSSES DE NAVETS *Turnip Tops*

They should be well washed, and only the sound leaves used. Put them in boiling salted water and cook them quickly, uncovered, for about a quarter of an hour. When ready drain them well in a colander and press them in a cloth.

You can then either chop them coarsely, just buttered and seasoned; or make a proper purée with the addition of butter and cream.

§ *Turnip tops; butter or butter and cream.*

CAROTTES SAUTÉES *Sautéed Carrots*

Have some carrots boiled and drained; let them get tepid, then cut them across in thin slices, and fry them lightly in butter at the foaming stage. Sprinkle with salt and chopped parsley and serve.

(There should be no excess of butter; use only just enough to cook the carrots; better put too little at the beginning and add a little more later than to have at the end liquid butter turned unpleasantly to oil and wasted.)

§ *Carrots; butter; parsley.*

CAROTTES NOUVELLES À LA POULETTE *New Carrots à la Poulette*

Take some small new carrots, scrape them lightly, and cook them in salted boiling water; drain them well and keep them hot. Put in a saucepan a piece of butter the size of an egg and a tablespoonful of flour; cook this a few minutes and see there are no lumps. Then add a glass of water, a little milk, salt and pepper, and cook the sauce about a quarter of an hour. Just before serving stir in a yolk of egg, a little cream and chopped parsley, and pour it over the carrots. Needless to say the sauce must not reach the boiling point after the addition of the yolk of egg.

§ *New carrots; butter; flour; yolk of egg; cream; parsley.*

CAROTTES VICHY *Carrots Vichy*

Take some young carrots, scrape and wash them and cut them in very thin slices. Put a good piece of butter in a saucepan, then your carrots, sprinkle with salt, a little sugar and, if necessary, add later some more butter. Cook on a medium fire till the carrots are soft and nicely browned. The mixture of the salt, the sugar, the butter and the little water left on the carrots combine in the process of cooking to make a really delicious dish; but you must use new carrots.

§ *New carrots; butter; sugar.*

CAROTTES À LA CRÈME *Carrots with Cream*

Have some young carrots; if really small leave them whole, otherwise cut them in two or in four quarters and keep them more or less the same size. Cook them in a saucepan with just enough water to cover them, a piece of butter, a pinch of salt and a little sugar (in the proportion of one puddingspoonful of sugar and two of butter for a pint of water).

Bring to the boil and boil till the water has almost entirely disappeared. Reduce the heat and cook, shaking occasionally till the carrots are soft and glazed. Add a little hot cream, enough to make a short sauce, reduce a little and serve. If the carrots are not new and a little hard, parboil them first.

§ *Carrots; butter; sugar; cream.*

CAROTTES FRITES *Fried Carrots*

The carrots should be young and tender, scraped, washed and dried, then cut across in thin slices.

Melt in a frying-pan a spoonful of fat (for a small bundle of carrots) and let it get hot. When it smokes, put in the carrots and a pinch of salt. Cook on a moderate fire, turning the carrots occasionally. When they are soft (feel one with the point of a kitchen knife) and pleasantly browned, they are done.

Remove the excess of fat, if any, sprinkle a little pepper and a little sugar all over, and serve.

§ *Young carrots; fat; sugar.*

FRICASSÉE DE BETTERAVES *Fricassée of Beets*

Have three cooked beets (preferably baked); peel them, cut them in slices and put them in a saucepan with a good piece of butter, salt and pepper. Cook slowly, shaking occasionally, for a quarter of an hour; add a sprinkling of flour, stir well, then a glass of milk, bring to the boil, cook for another ten minutes, stirring, and add chopped parsley just before serving. The sauce should be a short one and well seasoned.

§ *Cooked beetroot; butter; flour; milk; parsley.*

PURÉE DE POIS VERTS *Purée of Peas*

Quite a good purée can be made both with new peas and the shells. Remove the string parts and cook them in boiling water and salt. When they are soft press them hard against the sides of the pan, drain them again in a strainer and mash them through a sieve together with the peas (which should be cooked in the same way and seasoned with parsley and one small onion). See that it is the right consistency, and finish by adding a few pieces of butter. Warm it up, stirring, and serve.

§ *New peas; parsley; small onion; butter.*

PETITS POIS AU LARD *Peas with Bacon*

Take some peas and cook them in very little water and a piece of butter. Put in also the heart of a lettuce cut in four pieces, four or five small button onions, salt and pepper, and two rashers of bacon cut in small pieces. The best for this is not the ordinary bacon, but the kind known as 'green' bacon, or pickled pork. If at the end of the cooking the sauce is getting a little short, add a small quantity of hot water; see that it is properly seasoned and serve at once. In Périgord they use pork fat instead of butter.

§ *Peas; lettuce; green bacon or pickled pork; pork fat or butter.*

POIS À LA FRANÇAISE *French Peas*

Put your peas into a saucepan with a piece of butter, using a quarter of a pound to each quart of shelled peas. Add the heart of a lettuce cut in quarters, a few button onions, a *bouquet,* a pinch of sugar, salt and pepper, and a small cup of water. Bring to the boil quickly and after that cook slowly, with the lid on, for about three-quarters of an hour or a little more, adding water, if necessary.

Before serving remove the *bouquet* and reduce the liquid if there is too much; finish by adding a few pieces of butter, off the fire, so that they just melt. Some people like this dish fairly sweet.

§ *Peas; butter; lettuce; button onions;* bouquet; *sugar. Sugar optional.*

POIS À L'ÉTOUFFÉE *Peas à l'Étouffée*

This is a mixture of both English and French methods and it combines both flavours. It should really be served as a separate vegetable dish, like the peas *à la Française.*

Put the peas with two button onions cut in quarters, a *bouquet* of parsley, chervil and mint, a few small pieces of butter, salt and pepper, a pinch of sugar and a small cup of water. Bring to the boil and boil fast with the lid on, and shaking often till the peas are soft (for about twenty to twenty-five minutes).

Look at the peas occasionally, and if they are getting too dry add a little hot water. There should be just a short sauce at the end, so if there is too much liquor left, reduce it before serving.

§ *Peas; button onions; parsley; chervil; mint; butter; sugar.*

POIS MÉLANGÉS *Peas and String Beans*

Have some peas and some string beans – same quantity of both – boiled, well drained and hot.

Put them in a saucepan over the fire, shake them well, season and put in a good piece of butter, which should just melt, and a little parsley and chervil chopped together.

§ *Peas; string beans; butter; chervil; parsley.*

HARICOTS VERTS *String Beans*

Get some string beans, break the ends and boil them in boiling water with salt and pepper. Drain them well, put them in a saucepan with a good piece of butter, salt and pepper, and cook them for a few minutes on a slow fire, shaking them often.

VEGETABLES

You can serve them with a *Maître d'Hôtel* sauce, or fry them slightly in butter. They should be in any case rather highly seasoned.

§ *String beans; butter. Can be served with* Maître d'Hôtel *sauce (butter, parsley, lemon juice).*

HARICOTS VERTS À LA CRÈME   *String Beans with Cream*

Do not cut the string beans after the English fashion, but break both ends, tearing off the part which is 'stringy' and throw them in boiling water with salt and pepper. When cooked (they should be quite firm still) drain them well and keep them hot.

Meanwhile you have cooked a wineglassful of red wine vinegar till reduced by one third, and also removed it from the fire. Now, in another small saucepan mix some cream and the yolks of two eggs; cook this over a slow fire till it just begins to thicken, adding the vinegar little by little and stirring all the time. Pour this mixture over the string beans, mix well, season, add chopped parsley and cook for a few minutes more. Squeeze a quarter of a lemon over it just before serving.

§ *String beans; red wine vinegar; cream; yolks of egg; parsley; lemon juice.*

HARICOTS VERTS À LA LANDAISE   *String Beans à la Landaise*

Take a sufficient quantity of string beans and cook them in boiling salted water. When they are quite soft strain them thoroughly, and let them get cold. Then melt some butter in a frying-pan, add the beans and some grated cheese, a mixture of Gruyère and Parmesan being the best. Fry the beans for a few minutes, and serve very hot. This dish should really be made with the *mange-tout* kind of bean, but as they are difficult to get the others make a good substitute, especially if you add a few haricot beans to the others in the frying-pan, having, of course, soaked and boiled them before.

§ *String beans; butter; Gruyère cheese; Parmesan cheese.*

HARICOTS VERTS BÉARNAISE   *String Beans Béarnaise*

Take the required quantity of string beans, clean and boil them in the ordinary way; drain them well and add small pieces of tomato flesh and little shreds of lean ham.

Season with salt and pepper, mix well, add a good piece of butter and cook slowly for a few minutes.

In the south-west of France they use pork or goose fat instead of butter and add a little chopped garlic. The proportions should be two or three tomatoes and one small slice of ham to each pound of string beans.

§ *String beans; tomatoes; lean ham; butter or pork or goose fat. Garlic optional.*

HARICOTS MÉLANGÉS   *Mixed Beans*

This is a mixture in equal parts of white haricot beans and of string beans. It is advisable to cook them separately, as they do not take the same time to cook; the white beans about one hour and a half (if fresh) in boiling salted water and without the lid on; the string beans in the same way for about twenty or twenty-five minutes. Cut the string beans if they are large.

Drain them well and dry them over the fire for one or two minutes in a saucepan, mix them, put in a good piece of butter divided in small pieces. Toss them for a little while over the fire, but do not let the butter become brown; it should be just a little more than melted; sprinkle in chopped parsley and serve.

§ *String beans; white haricot beans; butter; parsley.*

HARICOTS BLANCS   *White Beans*

Take a pound of haricot beans. Soak them for twelve hours. Put them in a saucepan with lots of water, salt, broken pepper, one carrot, one onion, parsley; bring to the boil, skim well and let it simmer for three hours. Drain well, leaving only a tablespoonful of the juice, add butter and serve.

§ *Haricot beans; peppercorns; carrot; onion; parsley.*

HARICOTS ROUGES,   *Red Haricot Beans,*
BOURGUIGNONNE   *Bourguignonne*

Wash and soak some red haricot beans, put in a saucepan one carrot, one onion, a piece of streaky pickled pork, and a good piece of butter. Brown well on a moderate fire, then add a good glass of claret, a teacupful of beef stock, salt, pepper, *bouquet,* the haricot beans and just enough water to cover them if necessary. Bring to the boil, and let it simmer actually for hours. Before serving cut the pork in small pieces, remove *bouquet,* carrot and onion. Some people let this cook slowly (with the lid on) in the oven for a whole day.

§ *Red haricot beans; onion; carrot; streaky pickled pork; butter; claret; beef stock; bouquet.*

VEGETABLES

FÈVES *Broad Bean*

Broad beans are rather unfairly neglected by cooks; still, well prepared, they are excellent. There are several ways of serving them. If very young and tender the skin need not be removed, but if they have grown rather big it is advisable to skin them.

On the Continent broad beans, when small, are eaten raw with salt, by way of hors d'œuvre. When bigger they are cooked in lots of salted boiling water (for about twenty minutes) well drained and served with butter or Poulette sauce; they are usually flavoured with parsley and summer savory, chopped together. (The annual herb summer savory is used specially in connexion with broad beans.)

Broad beans are also very good with a *Maître d'Hôtel* sauce.

§ *Broad beans; butter or* Poulette *sauce (roux, milk, nutmeg, yolk of egg, vinegar); parsley, summer savory.*

FÈVES AU LARD *Broad Beans with Bacon*

Put in a saucepan a small piece of butter, in which you cook two rashers of streaky bacon cut in small pieces (or better still, pickled pork), sprinkle a little flour, stir well, put in the cooked broad beans, pepper, a few leaves of savory and parsley chopped finely, a little of the stock in which they have cooked, cook a little while and serve.

§ *Broad beans; butter; streaky bacon or pickled pork; flour; savory; parsley.*

PURÉE DE FÈVES *Purée of Broad Beans*

Having boiled the broad beans with a *bouquet* of parsley and savory, in this case for just a quarter of an hour, refresh them under the cold tap and drain them well. Finish cooking them with a piece of butter, and sprinkle in a little flour. Stir well and when they are soft mash them; add whatever is necessary of the stock in which they were first cooked, to give the purée the right consistency.

See that it is well seasoned; put it back in the saucepan and dry it over the fire. When it is really hot, stir in, off the fire, a small piece of butter, and serve.

§ *Broad beans; parsley; savory; butter; flour.*

ÉPINARDS AU JUS *Spinach with Gravy*

Prepare in exactly the same way as chicory with gravy (see p. 161), but cook a little longer. You can, if you like, add a tablespoonful of cream.

§ *Spinach; consommé,* jus *or gravy; butter. Cream optional.*

ÉPINARDS AU GRATIN *Spinach with Cheese*

Take some spinach; wash and clean well and cook in salted boiling water, drain well and put it in a fireproof dish with a good piece of butter, salt and pepper.

Take about a quarter of a pound of mushrooms, peel them and cook them in a small saucepan, with water, a little vinegar and a small piece of butter. When cooked, chop them very fine. Add a teaspoonful of flour, a liqueur glassful of sherry and a tumblerful of milk. Cook for about twenty minutes, add a little cream if you like.

Pour this over the spinach, sprinkle with breadcrumbs and grated cheese, with here and there a few small pieces of butter, and brown in the oven.

§ *Spinach; butter; mushrooms; vinegar; flour; sherry; milk; breadcrumbs; cheese. Cream optional.*

OSEILLE AU JUS *Sorrel with Gravy*

Take a good quantity of sorrel (it reduces a great deal), remove the stalks and centre vein and wash it well. Put it in a saucepan with a piece of butter and let it melt slowly, stirring occasionally with a wooden spoon.

Make a *roux* and add to it some consommé and let it cook, stirring all the time. Then add to this, little by little and alternately, the purée of sorrel and a little stock, season it well and put it in a fireproof dish (it is then too liquid) to be cooked slowly, covered with a buttered paper in the oven for about one hour. Finish by adding one or two eggs well beaten; mix well, cook a few minutes, add a few pieces of butter, and serve.

§ *Sorrel; butter; roux; consommé; stock; eggs.*

PURÉE D'OSEILLE *Purée of Sorrel*

Wash and clean the sorrel, remove the hard portion of the bigger leaves, poach it in boiling water for about ten minutes. Drain it well, chop it, put it in a saucepan with a piece of butter, salt, pepper, and a tablespoonful of consommé; let it simmer for a little while.

§ *Sorrel; butter; consommé.*

POIREAUX EN HACHIS *Chopped Leeks*

Take a bundle of leeks, remove the outside leaves and all the green part which might be hard. Wash them well and cook them in hot salted water till tender (if they are large cut them in pieces). Drain them well; there must be no water left at all. Chop them very finely or squash them through a sieve. Put in a saucepan a good piece of butter; melt it; put in the leeks, a pinch of flour, season with salt, pepper and grated nutmeg; cook a little while stirring well; add a cupful of cream and cook a little longer; at the last minute bind with two yolks of egg. Serve with cutlets or escalops of veal; or as a separate vegetable dish, garnished with *croûtons* all round the dish.

§ *Leeks; butter; flour; nutmeg; cream; yolks of egg.* Croûtons *if separate dish.*

ÉPINARDS FLORENTINE *Spinach Florentine*

Clean and wash thoroughly one pound of spinach, having first carefully removed the stalks; cook it in boiling salted water; when cooked drain well. Refresh with cold water and squeeze well so that there is not a drop of water left, then pass through a fine sieve. Put in a saucepan a piece of butter about the size of an egg, put in the purée of spinach, season well (the addition of a little nutmeg is recommended), add about one tablespoonful of flour (or potato flour), mix well, stirring over the fire with a wooden spoon. Add a glass of milk, a little cream, bring to the boil, remove to the corner of the stove, then put in, one by one, four yolks of egg, stirring well all the time.

Whip the four whites to a froth and add them in turn, also two tablespoonfuls of finely grated cheese (Parmesan and Gruyère), and follow then the usual procedure as you would for any other soufflé. Sprinkle with a little grated cheese, if you like, before putting in the oven.

§ *Spinach; butter; nutmeg; flour or potato flour; milk; cream; eggs; Parmesan cheese; Gruyère cheese.*

ÉPINARDS À LA BOURGEOISE *Spinach à la Bourgeoise*

Clean the spinach well and, having washed it in several waters, drain and dry it. Put it in a thick saucepan with a good piece of butter (about a quarter of a pound for one pound of spinach), and cook, stirring well, on a fairly quick fire.

When cooked, that is soft and melted, stir in one slice of cooked lean ham cut in small cubes, and just before serving, a handful of very small *croûtons* (fried in butter or in bacon fat).

Serve at once, as a separate dish.

§ *Spinach; butter; lean cooked ham;* croûtons.

FENOUIL *Fennel*

The best for eating is the Florentine or sweet fennel, the *finocchio* of

Italy, where it is very popular. It can be served raw as hors d'œuvre salad, plainly seasoned with French dressing; cooked, it can be treated exactly like celery or endive.

§ *Fennel; French dressing. See also the recipes for celery and endive.*

ENDIVES *Endive*

Have the required quantity of Belgian endives (one pound would do for four people), remove the damaged leaves and wash well. Take a flat saucepan or a baking tin, butter it well all over. Put the endives flat in it, add salt, the juice of half a lemon and just enough boiling water to cover them. Bring to the boil and cover them with buttered paper; go on cooking for half an hour or more. When they have become soft and transparent they are cooked. Drain well and prepare according to recipe.

§ *Endives; butter; lemon juice.*

ENDIVES FLAMANDE *Endive Flamande*

To the endives add from the beginning little cubes of pickled pork. When ready, add a little butter and serve with the juice.

§ *Endives; pickled pork; butter; lemon juice.*

ENDIVES MEUNIÈRE *Endive Meunière*

Having drained the endives well, melt some butter in a pan and when at the foaming stage put it in your endives, flat at the bottom and not overlapping. After two or three minutes they are pleasantly browned. Turn them and cook for two minutes more; then dispose them in the serving dish, add salt and pepper and lemon juice. Should the butter in the pan have become too black, throw it away and melt quickly another small piece of butter, which you pour foaming over the endives in the serving dish.

§ *Endives; butter; lemon juice.*

ENDIVES MORNAY *Endive Mornay*

Well drained, covered with a Mornay sauce in a fireproof dish. Brown and serve.

§ *Endives; butter; lemon juice;* Mornay *sauce (roux, milk, nutmeg, cheese, yolk of egg).*

ENDIVES MILANAISE *Endive Milanaise*

Cook the endives as usual. When cooked, drain them well and put them in a buttered fireproof dish. Add a little salt and sprinkle them with grated cheese. Brown quickly in the oven or under the grill. Just before serving melt a piece of butter the size of an egg. When at the foaming stage pour it over the endives and serve at once.

§ *Endives; butter; cheese.*

CHICORÉE AU JUS *Chicory with Gravy*

Clean the chicory well, wash it in cold water, poach it for five minutes in boiling water. Drain it well by squeezing in a sieve, chop it, put it in a saucepan, with salt, pepper, butter, a little consommé, *jus*, or gravy, and let it simmer for a little while.

§ *Chicory; consommé,* jus *or gravy; butter.*

PURÉE DE CHICORÉE *Purée of Chicory*

As salad reduces to next to nothing in cooking, it is advisable to allow one chicory for each person; wash it well, remove the outside leaves, and cook it for about half an hour in boiling water; put it under the cold tap and drain it well, chop it very fine. Prepare a *roux* in a saucepan, add the chicory, salt and pepper, and cook it on a slow fire for about a quarter of an hour. Add, one by one, a few small pieces of butter, then a little fresh cream, and serve either with fried bread or poached eggs over it. It makes a good entrée for luncheon.

§ *Chicory;* roux; *butter; cream; fried bread or poached eggs.*

ENDIVES AU JUS *Endives with Gravy*

Wash and clean your endives, keep only the heart, poach them five minutes in hot water. Drain them well. Put them in a dish with butter, a little *jus* or consommé, salt and pepper, and cook for about twenty minutes in a covered dish or in a moderate oven, basting often.

§ *Endives;* jus *or consommé; butter.*

LAITUES AU JUS *Lettuce with Gravy*

Prepare and cook in exactly the same way, but a little less.

§ *Lettuce;* jus *or consommé; butter.*

LAITUES AU FOUR *Baked Lettuce*

Take some lettuces and remove the outside green leaves. Throw them in salted boiling water and cook for a few minutes. Remove most of the water and finish cooking in a closed dish on a slow fire. Drain well and put them in a buttered fireproof dish, cover with a *Béchamel* sauce, sprinkle with breadcrumbs and brown in the oven.

§ *Lettuce;* Béchamel *sauce (roux, milk, nutmeg; breadcrumbs).*

MOUSSE DE LAITUE *Lettuce Mousse*

Have four good-sized lettuces (either the cabbage kind or the cos), clean them well and put them in boiling salted water. Boil them one minute and let them simmer three or four minutes more.

Boil also two floury potatoes, or one fairly large one – not more than a quarter of a pound.

Pound both the potatoes and the lettuces (well drained) and mix them well over the fire; add the yolks of three eggs, cook one minute more, see that it is well seasoned, and add, lastly, four whites of egg beaten to a stiff froth.

Fill a well-buttered Charlotte mould, stand it in boiling water and cook fifteen minutes in a moderate oven. Or use an ordinary soufflé dish, cook in the ordinary way about three minutes less and serve in the dish.

§ *Lettuce; potatoes; eggs.*

CÉLERI *Celery*

Clean it well, remove the bad stringy parts, cut off the green part about seven or eight inches from the heart, slice it in two and cook it in boiling salted water till soft, that is for about a quarter of an hour. This is, in any case, the initial preparation.

§ *Celery.*

CÉLERI AU JUS *Celery with Gravy*

Having prepared the celery, allowing one head for each person, remove it, drain it well and fold it in two. Make a *roux* and add to it meat stock, stir well, bring to the boil and let it thicken; add more stock to thin it, whip well, let it thicken again and so on for half an hour or so or anyhow till you have enough to cover the celery.

Place the folded celery in a flat saucepan. Cover it with the sauce and cook very slowly till it is reduced at least by half. Add a little purée of tomato, a little meat gravy, mix well, see that it is well seasoned, reduce a little more and serve.

§ *Celery;* roux; *meat stock; tomato purée; meat gravy.*

CÉLERI GRATINÉ *Celery with Cheese*

Dispose the pieces well drained and folded in two in a fireproof dish. Cover with very little *roux* diluted with meat stock and tomato purée and pour over the pieces of celery, just enough to moisten them.

VEGETABLES

Sprinkle with white breadcrumbs, grated cheese; pour over all melted butter and brown slowly in the oven.

§ *Celery; roux; meat stock; tomato purée; white breadcrumbs; cheese; butter.*

CROQUETTES DE CÉLERI *Celery Croquettes*

This is a very pleasant and useful way of serving celery, when, though 'in', it is not nice and white enough for eating raw. Wash and clean the celery in salted water, dry it well in a cloth, cut it in small pieces and cook it in boiling water, on a quick fire, for about a quarter of an hour. Drain it well and chop it fine. Then put it again in just enough water to cover it and boil it for about three-quarters of an hour under a buttered paper. Make a *roux* with flour and butter, add, little by little, about a cupful of hot milk, salt and pepper and cook till fairly thick, add the chopped celery and cook a little more. Then bind it with a yolk of egg (or two according to the amount of sauce made and celery used). Let it get cold; it should then have the consistency of batter. Make little fritters, roll them in whipped egg, sprinkle with breadcrumbs and fry in very hot fat.

§ *Celery; roux; milk; eggs; breadcrumbs; fat.*

*

CUCUMBERS

This delicious vegetable, which in England is better than anywhere else, can be used in other ways than sliced around salmon. Cooked, it retains its quality of proverbial coolness. It is perfect cut in thick slices and boiled in salted water, then served with a cream sauce; it contrasts pleasantly with the richness of the sauce. It makes a good vegetable dish, served with, say, a poulette *sauce or stuffed and braised like a tomato.*

*

CONCOMBRES *Cucumbers*

Cucumbers are delicious when properly cooked. They should be cut in four or six pieces, peeled, cooked in hot water with salt and a little vinegar for about ten or fifteen minutes, and served with either a sauce *Poulette* or *Maître d'Hôtel* (chopped parsley cooked with butter and lemon juice). They are very good cut in thin slices and fried.

§ *Cucumbers; vinegar;* Poulette *sauce (roux, milk, nutmeg, yolk of egg, vinegar) or* Maître d'Hôtel *sauce (parsley, butter, lemon juice).*

CONCOMBRES AU JUS *Cucumbers with Gravy*

Peel and cut the cucumbers as above, place them raw in a dish, sprinkle them with salt and add a few slices of onion. An hour later remove the onions and drain the cucumbers, which you place in a saucepan over a bed of fat bacon, on a slow fire. Meanwhile, make a brown *roux,* add stock and a little tomato sauce, pour this over the cucumbers which should be cooked about half an hour on a slow fire. Serve the sauce, passed through a sieve, over the cucumbers.

§ *Cucumbers; onion; fat bacon; brown* roux; *stock; Tomato sauce (tomatoes, onions, carrots, wine vinegar, brown* roux, *stock, butter).*

CONCOMBRES À LA CRÈME *Cucumbers with Cream*

Take some cucumbers, peel them, remove the seeds, cut them in pieces about two inches long, and cook them in boiling water (with salt and a little vinegar) till soft. Drain them well and keep them hot. Make a white *roux,* add a glass (or more, according to quantity required) of milk, stir well, cook a quarter of an hour or so, add more milk if it thickens too much, season well, add a little lemon juice and two yolks of egg; also, just before pouring the sauce over the cucumbers in the serving dish, add a little cream and a few small pieces of butter.

§ *Cucumbers;* roux; *milk; lemon juice; yolks of egg; cream; butter.*

CONCOMBRES FARCIS *Stuffed Cucumbers*

Choose some rather fat cucumbers, peel them and cut them in pieces about three inches long, and scoop out some of the flesh to make a cavity large enough to hold a certain amount of stuffing.

For the stuffing: Fry in butter one onion, finely chopped, together with one rasher of streaky bacon cut in very small pieces; add a few mushrooms and tomatoes, some of the cucumber flesh and parsley, also finely chopped; cook a few minutes in butter and stir in a few white breadcrumbs, then stuff the pieces of cucumber.

Put these in a flat saucepan on a bed of bacon rind, pieces of onions, of carrots, of tomatoes and a little consommé. Cook on a moderate fire and finish browning in the oven. Serve with the gravy poured over through a strainer. Some people parboil the pieces of cucumber first.

§ *Cucumbers; onions; streaky bacon; mushrooms; tomatoes; parsley; butter; white breadcrumbs; bacon rinds; carrots; consommé.*

COURGES FARCIES *Stuffed Marrow*

Cut the marrows in half (the small green ones are better for this

VEGETABLES

dish) and boil them in salted water until they are quite tender. Meanwhile the following mixture should have been prepared. Fry one or two tomatoes in butter and mash them with some grated cheese, a cupful of pork sausage meat, salt and pepper. Stir well and stuff the marrows with the mixture, then sprinkle them with breadcrumbs, add a few little pieces of butter, and bake them in a quick oven until nicely browned.

§ *Small marrows; tomatoes; pork sausage meat; cheese; butter; breadcrumbs.*

COURGETTES AU BEURRE   *Baby Marrows with Butter*

When the little vegetable marrows are very small, that is not more than three inches long, they are delicious boiled in salted water. They should not be peeled, just cooked whole and served with fresh butter added in the serving dish, with chopped parsley and salt.

§ *Courgettes; butter; parsley.*

TOMATES FARCIES   *Stuffed Tomatoes*

Cut the tomatoes in two by the middle, remove the seed and salt them. Fill them with either of the following stuffings:

1. Chop an onion, brown it in butter, add chopped mushrooms, breadcrumbs, parsley, salt and pepper, a little consommé.
2. Chop an onion, brown it in butter, mix with sausage meat, add salt and pepper.

Fill the tomatoes, sprinkle with breadcrumbs, put a tiny piece of butter on each and cook in a moderate oven.

§ *Tomatoes; breadcrumbs; butter.*
    Stuffing: 1. *Onion; mushrooms; breadcrumbs; parsley; butter; consommé.*
             2. *Onion; butter; sausage meat.*

CHAMPIGNONS À LA CRÈME   *Mushrooms with Cream*

Cook your mushrooms whole in butter, lemon juice, salt and pepper. When they are cooked, remove them and keep them hot. Let the butter reduce, then add a glass of fresh cream, stir well, bring to the boil, let it reduce, after which you put back the mushrooms with a little chopped parsley and let the whole simmer for a few minutes.

§ *Mushrooms; butter; lemon juice; cream; parsley.*

CHAMPIGNONS AU VIN BLANC   *Mushrooms with White Wine*

Wash the mushrooms in cold water and cut them in two or three pieces; cook them slowly in butter for five minutes; add a little lemon juice, salt, and a good deal of freshly-ground pepper; when they are done (which takes five minutes more only, as they should remain fairly firm), remove them and reduce the sauce, add a small glass of dry white wine, and reduce again. Put back the mushrooms, chopped parsley, and a few small pieces of butter.

Melt this by shaking the pan off the heat and serve the moment the butter has just melted. It must not be kept waiting either on or off the fire, as the butter would turn unpleasantly to oil.

§ *Mushrooms; butter; lemon juice; peppercorns; dry white wine; parsley.*

CHAMPIGNONS AU FOUR   *Baked Mushrooms*

Clean about a dozen mushrooms in cold water; if quite fresh they need not be peeled. Cut off the stalks, cook the mushrooms slowly in pork fat or olive oil, turning them once. Two or three minutes will do, as they must remain firm. Remove them.

Chop together the stalks, a little bacon fat and parsley (also a little garlic, if permitted), and fry these in the same fat.

Put this mince over the mushrooms in a fireproof dish, add half a tumbler of water and one teaspoonful of wine vinegar, salt and pepper; cook in a slow oven about half an hour and serve in the same dish. You can, instead of vinegar, add, at the last minute only, lemon juice.

§ *Mushrooms; pork fat or olive oil; bacon fat; parsley; wine vinegar or lemon juice. Garlic optional.*

PURÉE D'OIGNON   *Purée of Onions*

Cook five or six onions cut in slices in milk and salted water for a few minutes; drain them well and finish melting them very slowly with a little butter. They must not get brown. Add salt, pepper, a pinch of nutmeg and about the same quantity of *Béchamel* sauce (rather thin) as there is of melted onions.

Mix well and cook slowly in the oven till it has become quite thick. Mash them, add then a small amount of grated cheese and a tablespoonful of cream. Mix well, see that it is really hot, and serve. The final consistency should be that of a thick purée; should you want it finer, pass through a sieve.

§ *Onions; milk; nutmeg;* Béchamel *sauce (milk, nutmeg, roux); cheese; cream.*

VEGETABLES

OIGNONS À LA CRÈME *Onions with Cream*

Boil in salted water three or four big onions. Dry them. Put in a fireproof dish one ounce of butter and melt it. Cut your onions in small quarters and put them in the butter till they get a golden colour; then add two rashers of streaky bacon cut very thin. Cook in the oven for a quarter of an hour. Remove the dish and keep it aside till it is only tepid. Then add one beaten egg, a spoonful of cream, mix well together and put back in the oven till golden brown.

§ *Onions; butter; streaky bacon; egg; cream.*

CHAMPIGNONS GRILLÉS *Grilled Mushrooms*

Choose the largest mushrooms you have, clean and wash them well and cut them across in pieces as regular as possible. Cut slices of stale bread in pieces about the same size, and put all these (two pieces of mushroom, one of bread, two of mushroom, and so on) on a skewer – one *brochette* for each person – season well and grill carefully. Serve at once, and just before serving pour over the *brochettes* melted butter in which you have squeezed a little lemon juice.

§ *Mushrooms; stale bread; butter; lemon juice.*

GRATIN DE CHAMPIGNONS *Mushrooms with Cheese*

Have some mushrooms, wash them under the cold tap; if they are really fresh there is no need to peel them. Cook them covered with a buttered paper for five or six minutes in butter with pepper and a little lemon juice. Remove them, add a glass of sherry to the butter and lemon in which they have cooked, and reduce by half. Add then a small quantity of thin *Béchamel,* same quantity of fresh cream, and bring to the boil. Let it boil and thicken. See that it is well seasoned. Put the mushrooms in a fireproof dish, cover them with the sauce, sprinkle all over with grated cheese and brown quickly. Serve in the same dish.

§ *Mushrooms; butter; lemon juice; sherry;* Béchamel *sauce (roux, milk, nutmeg); cream; cheese.*

CHAMPIGNONS FARCIS AU POISSON *Mushrooms Stuffed with Fish*

1. Take some fresh mushrooms, choosing the largest possible. Cut the ends of the stalks and carefully sever the stalks from the mushrooms. Cook for a quarter of an hour in butter, adding at the last salt and pepper. Chop together finely any remnant of white fish you have by you, the mushroom stalks, parsley and a tiny piece of garlic. Add a whole egg and mix well; fill the mushrooms with this mixture, sprinkle

with breadcrumbs, put a small piece of butter on each, and cook in the oven in a buttered dish for about a quarter of an hour. Serve on *croûtons*.

Needless to say, this dish can be varied by the addition of lobster, mussels or scallops.

2. Another way of serving this is with a sauce. Make a very much reduced stock with the bones and head of fish, white wine, *bouquet* and slices of onions, let the mixture reduce, adding a few pieces of fresh butter last.

3. Should you be using mussels, reduce the stock obtained in the cooking of the mussels, add it to flour lightly cooked in butter, and cook as you would a *Béchamel*. Put the mushrooms in the dish, with the sauce and the *croûtons* round the dish, so that they do not get sodden.

§ 1. *Mushrooms; butter; shellfish or leftovers of white fish; parsley; garlic; egg; breadcrumbs; fried bread.*

2. *Mushrooms; butter; shellfish or leftovers of white fish; parsley; garlic; egg; fish stock; white wine; bouquet; onions.*

3. *Stuffed mushrooms (as above); mussel stock; mussels; flour; butter;* croûtons.

PURÉE DE CHAMPIGNONS *Purée of Mushrooms*

Take some fresh mushrooms (about one pound), wash them and cut them in small pieces. Cook them with a small piece of butter, salt, pepper and lemon juice. When they are soft mash them well and add about the same quantity of rather thin *Béchamel* sauce, a little piece of butter, cook for one minute, see that it is well seasoned and serve.

This purée makes a particularly fine garniture (for a dinner party) for lamb cutlets, escalopes *of veal or* suprêmes *of chicken.*

§ *Mushrooms; butter; lemon juice;* Béchamel *sauce (roux, milk, nutmeg).*

CÈPES BORDELAISE *Cèpes Bordelaise*

Wash and clean your *cèpes* (an edible fungus), cut them in slices, and fry them in oil and butter, with salt and pepper, and shallots, garlic and parsley chopped together.

§ Cèpes; *oil; butter; shallots; garlic; parsley.*

CÈPES FARCIS *Stuffed Cèpes*

Choose some fine *cèpes,* wipe them well and cut off the stalks. These you chop very finely and mix with the same quantity of breadcrumbs;

add one or two rashers of streaky bacon, parsley, and a little garlic minced together. Mix and season this stuffing.

Dispose the mushrooms in a fireproof dish with some stuffing over each one and cook in the oven for about fifteen minutes, after which you add a little Tomato sauce or purée of tomatoes (rather thin). Put back in the oven and cook till the top is slightly browned. Serve in the same dish or, if you use an entrée dish, be careful not to waste the delicious gravy made by the tomato sauce and the juice from the *cèpes*. Just before serving squeeze a little lemon juice. This dish is very good even when made with the tinned *cèpes*.

§ Cèpes; *breadcrumbs; streaky bacon; parsley; garlic; Tomato sauce (tomatoes, brown roux, wine vinegar, onions, carrot, stock, butter) or tomato purée; lemon juice.*

CÈPES À LA MONSELET — *Cèpes à la Monselet*

Cèpes can be cooked in the following manner recommended by Monselet, a distinguished writer and gourmet who died about 100 years ago.

Cut them in slices and *sauté* them with a large quantity of good butter in a large frying-pan, season well, add just a little chopped garlic and a shallot, also finely chopped, and just at the end a pinch of parsley. As soon as the mushrooms are cooked and beginning to get browned remove the pan from the fire; and for, say one pound of mushrooms, bind well with four yolks of eggs mixed with a glass of fresh cream. Shake the pan well and do not put on the fire again; the heat of the butter is sufficient for the *liaison* to be perfect and the sauce to be hot.

§ Cèpes; *butter; garlic; shallot; parsley; yolks of egg; cream.*

TRUFFES AU XÉRÈS — *Truffles in Sherry*

Wash your truffles well in water, and brush them with a very hard brush to remove the earth which usually sticks to them. Peel them. Put them in a small saucepan with a pinch of salt and enough sherry to cover them well. The saucepan should be kept closed all the time they are cooking, that is, two hours on a very slow fire.

Truffles cooked in that way – or indeed in any way – should be eaten by themselves as a delicacy. Needless to say, I am speaking of fresh truffles, which are in season only for a short time in the winter. Preserved ones are good enough for flavouring pâtés and sauces, but not for this special dish or the following one.

§ *Truffles; sherry.*

TRUFFES AU LARD   *Truffles with Bacon*

Wash and peel as before, salt them slightly and wrap each one in a very thin piece of streaky bacon. Wrap each again in three oiled papers well closed. Put them for three-quarters of an hour in a dish in a moderate oven. If you are lucky enough to have wood fires in your house, put the truffles under a heap of warm ashes, put a few burning cinders over them and cook for half an hour. That is the true and infinitely better way.

§ *Truffles; streaky bacon.*

PURÉE DE MARRONS   *Purée of Chestnuts*

Having peeled, boiled and mashed the chestnuts, add salt and pepper, a little stock to thin the purée, whip well over the fire and finish by stirring in, off the fire, a small piece of butter.

§ *Chestnuts; stock; butter.*

MARRONS BLANCHIS   *Steamed Chestnuts*

Remove the thick skin only of the chestnuts and boil them ten minutes in salted water. Peel them and let them get nearly cold. Take a narrow and deep saucepan, put at the bottom water and a few potatoes and steam your chestnuts. Serve with fresh butter.

§ *Chestnuts; potatoes; butter.*

FARCE AUX MARRONS   *Chestnut Stuffing*

This stuffing is remarkably good for roast goose or duck. Take a quarter of a pound of onions, cut them in thin slices and cook them slowly in pork fat or butter till golden brown. Peel about a pound of chestnuts (both skins should be carefully removed), add them to the onions, also salt, pepper and a little more fat or butter. Cook very slowly till the chestnuts are reduced to a pulp and stir well before stuffing the bird.

§ *Chestnuts; onions; pork fat or butter; onions.*

POTIRON GRATINÉ AU LARD   *Pumpkin with Cheese and Bacon*

Take four large slices of pumpkin, peel them and carefully scrape away all the pips. Then boil the vegetable in water with plenty of salt. When cooked, remove it, draining off all the water and drying it in front of the fire. Then mash it well, adding pepper, and more salt if necessary. Meanwhile, some thin rashers of streaky bacon should have been crisply fried and broken into little pieces. When these ingredients are prepared, take a well-buttered fireproof dish and fill it with alternate

VEGETABLES

layers of pumpkin and pieces of bacon. Pour over the dish the fat obtained from frying the bacon, and sprinkle with breadcrumbs. Bake in a quick oven until nicely browned.

§ *Pumpkin; streaky bacon; breadcrumbs.*

SOUFFLÉ DE POTIRON *Pumpkin Soufflé*

Pumpkin – which is used by fairies to make coaches for Cinderellas and by the French peasants for soups – is, if properly treated, a delicious vegetable; *en soufflé* it is at its best. Take a pound of pumpkin, peel and clean it and put it in a saucepan with a tumblerful of salted water; cook it for half an hour on a moderate fire, after which drain it well and mash it through a fine sieve. Add little by little about two tablespoonfuls of flour and a glass of milk; mix well, and add to the mixture first about one ounce of butter and three tablespoonfuls of castor sugar (or more according to taste), then the yolks of two eggs mixed with two teaspoonfuls of kirsch (or brandy), and last the two whites well whipped. Put the mixture in a well-buttered fireproof dish, sprinkle with sugar and cook in a moderate oven for about twenty minutes. Serve immediately.

§ *Pumpkin; flour; milk; butter; castor sugar; eggs; kirsch or brandy.*

POTATOES

Potatoes are used constantly in the menu, from the soup to the sweet course. In the form of flour they are used for thickening, cakes, soufflés and suchlike, but as these cannot properly be called 'potato dishes', they are not included in this collection.

Boiling. Potatoes are always boiled in cold salted water. It is advisable to boil them in their skins, which prevents them from breaking and being saturated with water. In any case new potatoes should always be boiled in their skins. Some people prefer steaming to boiling. Small steamed potatoes are a perfect *garniture* for *ragoûts* and boiled fish like turbot and salmon.

Baking. Potatoes are always roasted in their skins, either in the oven or under hot ashes.

Frying. The most important things in frying potatoes are:

1. To have the potatoes well dried after you have washed and cut them up; the best way to obtain this is to wipe them with a dry cloth.
2. To have the fat really boiling, which is when you see a blue smoke

arising. The best fats are either good oil or a mixture of pork and beef fat (the best being round the kidney) in equal proportions. You first melt the two fats together and then put them in a deep frying-pan after having passed the fat through muslin.

This fat can remain in the pan and can be used for everything which requires deep frying, excepting, of course, fish. Clarify the fat from time to time by bringing it to the boil and then throwing in a drop of cold water, which causes any particles of solid matter to drop instantly to the bottom. This must be done with great care as the cold water creates a sort of explosion in the fat and a great deal of boiling steam arises.

It is undoubtedly worth while to have a frying basket in the pan. Some are made to rest on the handles of the pan, which is very useful for draining. It can be used for many things, such as fritters, croquettes, fried potatoes, soufflés, etc., and makes deep frying so much easier.

POMMES DE TERRE FRITES *Fried Potatoes*

Like all simple things, fried potatoes are often very badly done. They should be golden brown, crisp and dry, and served the moment they are ready. Never fry potatoes in a frying-pan. You want a deep vessel full of fat (which must not be used for anything else). It is very important, after you have cut your potatoes in whatever shape you like best, to dry them well in a cloth. It is equally important that the fat should be very hot. Throw in your potatoes. They must be literally and freely swimming in boiling fat. When golden brown, remove them, drain them well and sprinkle with salt.

They are easily drained if you fry them in a wire basket. It is advisable to throw them on a large piece of white paper, which will absorb what is left of the fat. The sprinkling of salt will finish the drying besides giving them taste.

§ *Potatoes; fat.*

POMMES FRITES PAYSANNE *Fried Potatoes Paysanne*

Cut some potatoes in smallish cubes, dry them well and fry them in very little pork fat (or goose fat if any available); stir them well and a few minutes before serving add very little chopped garlic; then at the last minute chopped parsley; sprinkle with salt when in the serving-dish and serve at once. There should be no fat left in the pan at the end of the cooking.

§ *Potatoes; pork or goose fat; garlic; parsley.*

VEGETABLES

POMMES DE TERRE FRITES *Fried Potatoes with*
AUX FONDS D'ARTICHAUX *Artichoke Bottoms*

Take three artichokes, break off the leaves and the heart and keep only the bottom part, trim it well and cut it into four pieces. Add them to about three-quarters of a pound of potatoes prepared for frying. Fry together and sprinkle with salt.

§ *Potatoes; globe artichokes; fat.*

POMMES PAILLE *Straw Potatoes*

Cut some yellow potatoes as thin as straw, dry them well, and throw them into a deep dish full of boiling fat. In a few minutes they will be crisp and golden, after which you drain them well and sprinkle with salt.

§ *Potatoes; fat.*

POMMES RISSOLÉES *Potatoes Rissolées*

Choose some small potatoes or cut large ones in oblong pieces. Wipe them well and put them in a pan with a good piece of butter. Cook very slowly (for about half an hour), shaking occasionally with the lid on. They will be crisp and brown outside, soft and buttery inside. There should be only one row at the bottom of the pan, therefore a large flat saucepan is the best for this purpose. Salt before serving.

§ *Potatoes; butter.*

POMMES RISSOLÉES AU MENTHE *Potatoes Rissolées with Mint*

Take some new potatoes, scrape them, or if the skin is very thin, just brush them in water. Put them in a flat saucepan with a good piece of butter. Cook slowly with the lid on, shaking occasionally. When ready (in about twenty minutes) remove the butter, if it has not been all absorbed by the potatoes, sprinkle with salt and fresh mint finely chopped and add one small piece of butter. Shake well and serve.

§ *New potatoes; butter; mint.*

POMMES SAUTÉES *Sauté Potatoes*

These are often wrongly prepared. Boil some potatoes in their skins (preferably the yellow 'soapy' kind, floury ones being no good for this purpose); peel them and let them get cold; then cut them in thin slices and toss these in butter at the foaming stage in a frying-pan till golden brown.

Two important things to remember: The pan must be hot before you put in the butter; you cannot do too many potatoes at the same time, as it would not be possible to toss *(sauter)* them freely. Salt before serving.

§ *Potatoes; butter.*

GRATIN DE POMMES DE TERRE			*Gratin Potatoes*
Put in a buttered fireproof dish slices of cold boiled potatoes; sprinkle with grated cheese and brown in the oven or under the grill.

§ *Potatoes; cheese; butter.*

PURÉE DE POMMES DE TERRE			*Purée of Potatoes*
This is very different from ordinary mashed potatoes. Boil some floury potatoes in their skins, peel them and mash them well, add a little butter, salt and pepper; put them back into the saucepan (well wiped) and stir them for one minute over a slow fire. Add little by little hot milk, and whip well; go on whipping and adding hot milk until you have a light and soft purée the consistency of very thick cream. See that it is well seasoned, stir in another little piece of butter, and serve.

The drier the potatoes are when you begin (hence the cooking in the skin and the initial drying), the more milk they will absorb and the more creamy the purée will be.

§ *Potatoes; butter; milk.*

PURÉE DE POMMES SOUFFLÉE			*Purée of Potato Soufflé*
Cook in salted water some white floury potatoes, drain them well, put them in a clean saucepan and dry them over the fire so that they are not watery. Mash them well – there must not be a single lump left – put in salt and pepper, a good piece of butter and a tablespoonful of hot milk. Beat this well and work it over the fire, add the yolks of two eggs and another tablespoonful of milk, more even if it looks too thick, then put in the whites of the two eggs well whipped. Mix thoroughly, and bake in a hot oven for about a quarter of an hour.

Another attractive way of serving this dish is the following: Instead of boiling the potatoes, bake them in their skins in the oven, then cut them in two, scrape out the inside, prepare as described above and refill the empty skins with the purée instead of putting it in a dish. Finish baking in the same way.

§ *Potatoes; butter; milk; eggs.*

POMMES SICILIENNE			*Potatoes Sicilienne*
First make a very good purée of potatoes, using, if possible, cream instead of milk. Then take a small orange, cut it into slices (using the

rind as well), remove the pith and pips, dry each slice in a cloth, fry them for a few minutes in butter, and chop them into little pieces. Fry also one or two finely chopped shallots and add them to the orange. Mix this well with the purée, add salt and pepper, and form into little balls. Place these in a buttered fireproof dish and bake in a quick oven for a few minutes so that the balls are nicely browned.

The flavour of orange in this way of doing potatoes goes especially well with goose, in the same way that an orange salad is a good accompaniment to wild duck.

§ *Potatoes; cream; butter; an orange; shallots.*

POMMES DE TERRE FARCIES   *Stuffed Potatoes*

Take some large potatoes, peel them and scoop out a good-sized hole in each. Boil what you have scooped out in the ordinary way, and when cooked, drain it and mash it well.

Prepare the stuffing with either sausage meat or a mixture of pork and veal and, chopped together, a little bacon and parsley. Mix well with the mashed potatoes you have prepared, season well and moisten with a little stock.

Stuff the potatoes, put them in a buttered fireproof dish with a teacupful of stock and a small piece of butter on top of each potato. Bake in a moderate oven, basting often till the potatoes are cooked, that is about one hour.

§ *Potatoes; sausage meat or pork and veal mixture; bacon; parsley; butter.*

POMMES DE TERRE DUCHESSE   *Potatoes Duchesse*

Cook in their skins in the oven large floury potatoes; when cooked, mash them and add yolk of egg, mixing well (one to a quarter of a pound of potatoes). Add a little butter and work the mixture well. Season with salt, pepper and a little grated nutmeg. Put this mixture on a floured board and let it cool. Cut in equal-sized squares, paint these with yolk of egg, and bake brown on a greased tin in a hot oven.

§ *Potatoes; nutmeg; yolk of egg.*

POMMES DE TERRE GRATINÉES   *Potatoes with Cheese*

Bake in the oven in their skins some large floury potatoes, having first washed and scrubbed them well. When they are well cooked cut them in two and remove the pulp, taking care not to damage the skin. Work the pulp with a little butter, grated cheese, a little fresh cream,

Recipes of Boulestin

salt and pepper. Fill the skins, sprinkle with grated cheese and brown in the oven or under a grill.

§ *Potatoes; butter; cheese; cream.*

GÂTEAU DE POMMES DE TERRE *Potato Cake*

To some mashed potatoes, well seasoned, add a little onion (thin slices, fried brown) and a few bits of cooked bacon. Mix well and press this like a cake about one inch thick in a frying-pan very hot and buttered. Shape the cake with a knife, so that it is a little smaller than the bottom of the pan.

Shake it while it cooks. It should be quite free in the pan. When a little smoke rises and the cake makes a kind of rustling noise when you shake it, it is done. Put a plate on the top of it and turn the pan upside-down so that the nicely browned bottom of the cake becomes the top.

§ *Mashed potatoes; onion; bacon.*

BEIGNETS DE POMMES DE TERRE *Potato Fritters*

Boil in their skins a few potatoes, peel them and mash them well; to be certain that they are reduced to a soft purée, pound them in a mortar; season with salt and pepper, add a piece of butter (a quarter of a pound to a pound of potatoes) and milk to moisten the mixture, which should be fairly stiff.

Bind with two whole eggs, mix thoroughly and cut in smallest pieces which you roll in flour before frying in deep fat.

§ *Potatoes; butter; milk; eggs; flour; fat.*

POMMES DE TERRE ARMORICAINE *Potatoes Armoricaine*

Take some large floury potatoes, scrub them well and bake them in their skins in the oven. When cooked, cut them in two lengthways and scoop out the inside carefully; put it in a bowl and mash well with a little butter, chopped parsley and stir in flakes of cooked haddock.

Fill the potato skins with this mixture well spiced, sprinkle a little grated Parmesan and put a small piece of butter on top of each. Brown quickly in the oven, or under the grill. Remnants of cold salmon can be used in the same way.

§ *Potatoes; butter; parsley; haddock or remnants of salmon; Parmesan cheese.*

CRÊPES DE POMMES DE TERRE *Potato Pancakes*

Prepare a batter for pancake in the ordinary way, but with salt in it. Let it rest two hours, then add to it about one-third of very smooth purée of potatoes. Mix thoroughly well, and see that it is properly seasoned; cook as thin pancakes, tossing as usual. Serve very hot with melted butter.

§ *Pancake batter (see pp. 10 and 213); potatoes; butter.*

POMMES DE TERRE VOSGIENNE   *Potatoes Vosgienne*

Take some potatoes (the yellow Dutch kind or the Early Rose being the best for the purpose) and cut them in thin slices. Put them in a fireproof dish which you have rubbed lightly with garlic, season them with salt and pepper, cover them with fresh cream and cook them on a moderate fire. When they are cooked add a little more cream and brown under a gas grill or in the oven.

§ *Potatoes; garlic; cream.*

CROQUETTES DE POMMES   *Potato Croquettes*
DE TERRE AU FROMAGE   *with Cheese*

Boil some floury potatoes and, once cooked, put them to dry in the oven. Press them through a sieve and season with salt and pepper. Add, little by little, a good piece of butter, and mix it thoroughly with the mashed potatoes for five minutes at least; add a little milk and whip well, then the yolks of two eggs and a tablespoonful of grated cheese. Spread the mixture on a dish, let it get cold, and leave for two hours.

Sprinkle a board with flour and flatten the potato mixture with a rolling-pin; cut it into squares (the thickness should be about one inch), put these on a buttered baking tin, and cook them in a hot oven for ten minutes. Serve at once.

You can also paint them with yolk of egg, or sprinkle them with more grated cheese if you prefer. The best grated cheese for mixing with the potatoes is half Gruyère and half Parmesan, but the Gruyère should be very finely grated; for sprinkling over the cakes Parmesan alone is better.

§ *Potatoes; butter; milk; yolk of egg; flour; Parmesan cheese; Gruyère cheese.*

POMMES DE TERRE PARISIENNE   *Potatoes Parisienne*

Peel some large potatoes and scoop out of them little balls. This is done with a special instrument in the shape of a round spoon with a very sharp edge. (The best size is about three-quarters of an inch in diameter.) Wash the little balls and put them in cold salted water.

Bring slowly to the boil, boil half a minute and drain them well. Cook them slowly in butter at the foaming stage, shaking them occasionally till they are nicely browned (about a quarter of an hour). Drain, salt and serve.

§ *Potatoes; butter.*

POMMES DE TERRE SAVOYARDE   *Potatoes Savoyarde*
Take some potatoes and cut them in very thin slices. Butter a fireproof dish, put in a layer of potatoes, salt, pepper and nutmeg, a sprinkling of grated Gruyère cheese, more potatoes, and so on till the dish is full. Do not press the potatoes down, and fill the dish with meat stock.

Bring to the boil and boil for six or seven minutes on the top of the stove; if the stock disappears add a little more, then finish, with a few pieces of butter here and there, in a moderate oven. When the stock has been absorbed the potatoes are usually ready and the top pleasantly browned. Test the potatoes with a sharp knife.

Keep it in the oven a little longer if necessary, covering the top with greased paper if it is already brown enough.

§ *Potatoes; butter; nutmeg; Gruyère cheese; meat stock.*

POMMES DE TERRE LIMOUSINE   *Potatoes Limousine*
Peel and wash some potatoes, grate them raw, and add a few small pieces of streaky bacon. Cook in fat in a frying-pan, shaking occasionally. Half-way through (you can see by the look and the feeling if they are getting cooked) turn them over and brown them on the other side.

The layer of potatoes should not be thick, otherwise the centre will not be cooked by the time the outsides are brown. The thinner and the crisper the cake is the better.

§ *Potatoes; streaky bacon.*

POMMES DE TERRE ANNA   *Potatoes Anna*
This is an attractive way of serving potatoes, not really complicated or specially difficult, and it is not necessary to have for cooking them the special utensil people advocate. All you want is a small copper pan, with a lid which fits perfectly.

The potatoes (preferably the yellow soapy kind) should be cut in thin slices, as round as possible, all more or less the same size, and no thicker than a half-crown piece. Wash them in cold water. Dry them well in a cloth, and season them with salt and pepper. Take your pan and butter it well all over; dispose the potatoes flat and in circles, so that they overlap each other slightly; more butter over this first layer of potatoes, then another layer carefully arranged, and so on till the pan is nearly full. There should be about five or six layers.

To succeed you must have butter out of which all water has been extracted (as otherwise the potatoes might catch during the cooking) which is done by pounding the butter and squeezing it well, so that when you use it it is reduced to the state of a soft ointment. See that the lid of the little saucepan fits well, and cook in a hot oven about thirty minutes.

The finished article is a kind of cake well browned outside and soft inside. It is turned out on the lid of the pan, put in the oven on the lid one minute more, cut in quarters and served at once.

§ *Potatoes; butter.*

POMMES DE TERRE SOUFLÉES   *Souffléed Potatoes*

Take some potatoes (the long Dutch kind) and cut them in thin slices (they should not be thicker than two half-crown pieces together); wipe them well. Drop them in the hot fat, not too many at the time; they must not stick together. Cook them three-quarters of the full time they ought to cook (by that time usually they come up and float on the top); then take them out. Leave the fat on the fire for two minutes more (it must reach that point when it begins to smoke); put them in again for a minute or two in a wire basket, and they will puff up at once. Make them a good colour, drain well, sprinkle with salt and serve quickly.

§ *Potatoes; fat.*

POMMES DE TERRE LYONNAISE, I   *Lyonnaise Potatoes, I*

Boil in their skins some yellow potatoes, peel them and let them get almost cold; cut them in thin slices and toss them in a pan with very hot butter; add salt and pepper. When they are beginning to colour add one or two onions finely cut and finish the cooking. The pieces of potatoes and the onions (three parts potatoes, one part onion) should have the same golden brown colour.

§ *Potatoes; butter; onions.*

POMMES DE TERRE LYONNAISE, II   *Lyonnaise Potatoes, II*

An entirely different recipe from an old book. Boil the potatoes as before and cut them in slices. Put them in a saucepan and pour over them a purée of onions. Two seconds on the fire together and serve.

§ *Potatoes; Onion purée (onions, milk, nutmeg, roux, cheese, cream).*

POMMES DE TERRE NOUVELLES　　　　　　　　　*New Potatoes*
MAÎTRE D'HÔTEL　　　　　　　　　　　　　　　　*Maître d'Hôtel*

Boil your new potatoes in their skins. Drain well. Peel them and cover with a *Maître d'Hôtel* sauce.

§ *Potatoes;* Maître d'Hôtel *sauce (parsley, butter, lemon juice).*

POMMES DE TERRE BOULANGÈRE　　　　　　　*Potatoes Boulangère*

Cut two large onions in thin slices, cook them for a few minutes only in butter. Cut your potatoes in thin slices, arrange them in a very flat dish with the onions, add a claret glass full of consommé, a good deal of pepper and salt, and brown in a moderate oven for about one hour and a half.

§ *Potatoes; onions; butter; consommé.*

POMMES DE TERRE FINES HERBES　　　　　　　*Savoury Potatoes*

Take some large potatoes of the floury kind, scrub them well with a brush under the tap, dry them and bake them in the oven. When cooked cut them in two lengthways and scoop out all the flesh, being careful not to damage the skin.

Mash it well, add a little butter, a small quantity of cream, salt and pepper, and chopped finely together, spring onions or chives, parsley and chervil. See that the mixture is smooth (and not too liquid), fill the skins and put in the oven for a few minutes, so that they are thoroughly hot, but not browned.

§ *Potatoes; butter; cream; spring onions or chives; parsley; chervil.*

PURÉE SOUBISE　　　　　　　　　　*Purée of Potatoes and Onions*

One-third floury potatoes, two-thirds onions boiled in salted water, squashed through a sieve and dried for a minute in a saucepan over the fire. Add little pieces of butter and a tablespoonful of hot milk, and grated nutmeg. Stir well and see that it is well seasoned.

§ *Potatoes; onions; butter; milk; nutmeg.*

PILAFF　　　　　　　　　　　　　　　　　　　　　　*Pilaff*

A pilaff is a very useful dish. Cook your rice according to your idea on the subject; there are several schools – some people throw it in boiling water, some put it in cold water, some stir it, others do not, others again fry it in butter as the first process. After many experiments I find that the most satisfactory way is the following: Having washed the rice, put it in a saucepan with one onion, cut in two, salt, and add just enough cold water to cover it and a little more, bring to the boil, stir lightly with a fork, add more water, a little later add for the third and last time more water in quantity sufficient for the rice to revolve freely when boiling; see that it does not catch, and do not cook it too much. When it is cooked, of course, put it under the cold tap in a colander; each grain should be separate.

Melt some butter in a frying-pan, put in your rice, salt and pepper, a teaspoonful of saffron, a pinch of curry powder, one sweet red pepper cut in small pieces, a handful of raisins (stoned and previously soaked) and whatever you have by you in the way of 'remnants' – pieces of turbot, or lobster, or veal, or chicken, slightly warmed in butter; sprinkle with paprika, add a glass of stock, a pinch of saffron, cook till the stock has disappeared; stir well and serve very hot with the sauce called in France à L'indienne, although it is only vaguely Eastern in character. For all these pilaffs and risottos the best rice to use is really Carolina rice, the Patna variety being the best for the rice served as an accompaniment to curry.

§ *Rice; onion; butter; saffron; curry powder; sweet red pepper; raisins; remains of turbot, lobster, veal or chicken; paprika; stock; Sauce à l'Indienne (roux, milk, nutmeg, curry powder).*

RISOTTO MILANESE *Risotto Milanese*

First take some thin slices of onion and fry them in butter till they are golden brown. Put the rice unwashed in the pan. Stir over a slow fire and fry it well; add a little wine and purée of tomato, then one ounce of marrow chopped finely,

The secret of the real risotto is that the grain of the rice preserves its 'entireness' although the dish as a whole, in its viscous compactness, is like cream. Chopped marrow helps a lot to that effect. Then make the whole thing yellow with a pudding-spoonful of saffron.

To prevent the rice from burning add good stock in such quantity that it is entirely absorbed by the end of the cooking. Finish by a sprinkling of cheese.

§ *Rice; onion; butter; wine; tomato purée; marrow; stock; saffron; cheese.*

PILAFF AU POULET *Pilaff of Chicken*

Having prepared a rice pilaff, or boiled it so that each grain is left separate and not too soft, toss in butter your pieces of chicken cut small, add a pinch of curry powder, one of paprika, salt and pepper; stir well, cook for one minute, then add the rice, a tablespoonful of stock (or water), a handful of seedless raisins (previously soaked). Cook, stirring, till the stock has disappeared. The dish should be at the same time well spiced and sweet,

§ *Rice; chicken pieces; curry powder; paprika; stock; seedless raisins.*

PAELLA *Paella*

This dish, also called *Arroz à la valenciana,* is delicious when properly prepared. Take some rice, the Patna kind preferably, allowing a handful for each person; shake it well to remove the dust. It should not be washed. (The Italians also, when making *Risotto Milanese,* do not wash the rice. As a famous Italian writer puts it: 'Wash your face, wash your hands, wash your conscience, but do not wash the rice; the rice is no snob...') Chop together a large onion, parsley, and a piece of garlic. Brown this in a deep pan or a *cocotte,* with two or three spoonfuls of olive oil; add the rice, and brown it lightly. Then add two or three green sweet peppers, previously grilled, and two or three tomatoes (peeled); cut all this in smallish pieces. Cook a little more, stirring with a wooden spoon, and season with salt, pepper and pounded cloves.

Meanwhile, cook in consommé or veal stock chicken, ham and pieces of fish cut in small cubes. Add them to the rice and the stock little by little, and cook slowly on a very low fire. From the moment you have begun to add the stock do not stir the rice any more, but shake the pan occasionally. There is no need to be afraid of the mixture of fish and meat, which is typical of popular Spanish cooking.

The *paella* is always cooked in an earthenware dish and served in it.

§ *Rice; onion; parsley; garlic; olive oil; sweet green peppers; tomatoes; cloves; consommé or veal stock; chicken; ham; fish.*

RIZ AUX PIMENTS *Rice with Peppers*

Boil your rice and drain it well. It should be very dry and each grain separate. Take two or three *piments* or red peppers, wash them, remove the seed, cut them in small pieces, add them to the rice with pepper and salt, a piece of butter, half a tablespoonful of consommé, and cook on a slow fire for a few minutes. You can, if you like the taste of it, add also a pinch of red saffron.

§ *Rice; green or red peppers; butter; consommé; red saffron.*

PIMENTS FARCIS *Stuffed Peppers*

Take some large sweet peppers, either red or green, cut off the top and scoop out the seeds and the white divisions inside, but without damaging the outside. Cut finely together the tops you have taken off the peppers and two or three onions; cook these together in butter and oil mixed.

Prepare a Tomato sauce with fresh tomatoes; to this you add the chopped onions and peppers and the butter in which they have cooked; this should be fairly liquid, and you use it for cooking a handful of rice. (The quantity of rice and of sauce should be according to the number of peppers you are using.)

When the rice is cooked, season it well; stuff the peppers with this mixture, moisten them with stock and with whatever is left of the sauce in which the rice has cooked. Put the stuffed peppers in a fireproof dish with butter, also a small piece of butter over each pepper, and cook first over the fire, slowly; then finish in the oven. It is indispensable to have a reserve of the tomato sauce and stock mixed, as the peppers should be basted often, otherwise they will become too dry.

§ *Sweet peppers (red or green); onions; butter; oil; Tomato sauce (tomatoes; brown roux; wine vinegar; onions; carrot; butter; stock).*

CARI *Curry*

Peel one pound and a half of onions and one pound of tomatoes. First fry the onions, cut in pieces, until well browned, in bacon fat – no other fat will produce the desired flavour – then add the tomatoes. When thoroughly cooked add salt and pepper and two or three tablespoonfuls of curry powder. Mix it all well together and add a cupful of water. Cook slowly for one hour and a half. (It is a dry curry; there should be no liquid at the end of the cooking.) Add any fruit you have, cut in slices, one or two sweet peppers if you like, and half an ounce of castor sugar. Cook quickly for ten minutes. If too dry add a little cream or milk, and just before serving break two eggs and mix well with the curry, stirring very quickly so that there is no visible sign of the eggs in the dish.

You can also add to it, pieces of fish, or mutton, or hard-boiled eggs, in fact, starting from this recipe, make many different curries, according to what you have to use up.

§ *Onions; tomatoes; bacon fat; curry powder; fruit; castor sugar; cream or milk; eggs; sweet peppers, fish, mutton or eggs can be added.*

CARI MALTAISE *Maltese Curry*

This is a dish for those who like onions, though when perfectly prepared the flavour of these is so blended with other things that the existence of the onions is almost undiscoverable. Peel one pound and a half of onions and one pound of tomatoes. First fry the onions, cut in pieces, until well browned, in bacon fat – no other fat will produce the desired flavour – then add the tomatoes. When thoroughly cooked add salt and pepper and two or three tablespoonfuls of curry powder. Mix it all well together and add a cupful of water. Cook slowly for one hour and a half. (It is a dry curry; there should be no liquid at the end of the cooking.) Add one peach, two apricots cut in slices (or apples, or bananas), one or two sweet peppers if you like, and half an ounce of castor sugar. Cook quickly for ten minutes. If too dry add a little cream or milk, and just before serving break in three or four eggs and mix well with the curry, stirring very quickly so that there is no visible sign of the eggs in the dish.

The result is a rich brown curry, at the same time hot and sweet, dry and soft and better than any curry you can get in India or anywhere else.

§ *Onions; tomatoes; bacon fat; curry powder; a peach; apricots (or apples or bananas); castor sugar; milk or cream; eggs. Sweet peppers optional.*

NOUILLES AU FOIE GRAS *Spaghetti with Foie Gras*

Boil some spaghetti and drain it well. Take a buttered dish, put a layer of spaghetti, a little purée of *foie gras,* more spaghetti, more *foie gras,* finish with a good deal of grated cheese and a few pieces of butter. Brown well in the oven. It is not necessary for this dish to use the pure *foie gras,* the purée, which is sold in small tins, will do as well, provided it is the real thing and not pig's or calf's liver masquerading as *foie gras.*

§ *Spaghetti;* foie gras; *cheese; butter.*

Salads

I must give France its due. The French, I am told, have many failings, but they can make wine, coffee and salads. It is a great deal. There is no doubt that, especially for a green salad, there is nothing better than oil made of crushed walnuts. It gives it a subtle flavour. Unfortunately, walnut oil is not now made in the farms and country houses as it used to be. There are very few places where you can buy it, even in France. The next best and more generally used is pure olive oil. No other oil except these two is any good. And malt vinegar is worse than useless; if you have no wine vinegar you had better use the juice of a lemon. Of the wine vinegars the one made of red wine is the best.

Few flowers are edible; borage, pansy, periwinkles may be mentioned; but the best is undoubtedly the nasturtium. It has a distinct peppery taste which mixes well with the lettuce and other ingredients. The flowers must be left whole, but there must be no stalk at all. Well disposed on the top of a green salad, they make a pretty show, but herbs should not be forgotten, for flowers add less to the taste of a lettuce than parsley, spring onion, tarragon and chervil.

*

ASSAISONNEMENTS DE SALADE *Salad Seasonings*

These are of three types, and can be slightly varied according to individual taste:

1. For plain green salads the French dressing, a plain seasoning of salt, pepper, vinegar (one-third) and oil (two-thirds) is the correct one. Some people add mustard and sugar, and use lemon juice instead of vinegar.

2. The Cream seasoning is made with three parts of rather thin cream, one part of vinegar or lemon juice, salt and pepper.

3. The Egg seasoning is a pleasant change; to the ordinary plain dressing you add pounded yolk of hard-boiled egg, a little mustard and

an extra quantity of oil and vinegar to make a smooth (and not too thick) sauce. Before serving, sprinkle the salad with chopped white of egg.

Mayonnaise is definitely not a salad dressing, but a sauce in itself. It should be used only for hors d'œuvre salad.

Green salads must be dressed at the last minute, otherwise the leaves will become soft and 'cooked' by the vinegar. On the other hand, vegetable salads are prepared at least one hour before, so that they are well impregnated with the seasoning.

§ French dressing: *Salt; pepper; vinegar or lemon juice; oil. Mustard and sugar optional.*

Cream dressing: *Salt; pepper; thin cream; vinegar or lemon juice.*

Egg dressing: *Salt; pepper; vinegar or lemon juice; oil; egg; mustard.*

*

GARLIC

The world is divided in two classes – those who eat garlic and those who do not, with sub-divisions: those who 'don't mind a little', those who like the taste but not the smell, and those who adore it. In any case, they all often eat it without knowing it. There is also another class, a small minority, I must say, who are haunted by the idea that French food is entirely flavoured with it, like a woman who came in sniffing at a lecture-demonstration I was giving at Liverpool, the day I had specially chosen dishes with no garlic at all: 'H'm, garlic; I thought so.' It is amusing to know that garlic became the fashion in Paris at the end of the eighteenth century. '... the femmes les plus delicates do not any more object to eating ragoûts flavoured with garlic.'

*

SALADE VERTE *Green Salad*

This is the plain salad which happens to be in season, lettuce, cos lettuce in the summer; batavia and chicory in the winter.

Some people make the mistake of keeping them in water, or wash the whole plant before even removing the bad leaves. Yet a very withered lettuce five or six days old will revive perfectly well if all the bad leaves are removed, the stalks cut and the lettuce put in cold or lukewarm water for ten to fifteen minutes. But if kept too long in water, the leaves will lose their crispness again.

Once revived, the leaves can be kept in a cloth for several hours in a cool place. They should be well dried by shaking in a wire basket or in a cloth before using.

The greatest mistake is to keep salads standing in water in order to keep them fresh; it is worse than useless. And another mistake is to wash the salad whole; you only wash the leaves chosen and already cut that you are going to eat. Also, the leaves of a salad a few days old, if kept too long in water, that is, more than fifteen minutes at the most, will become worse than ever, quite sodden and soft.

They should be dressed in a salad bowl large enough for the purpose.

They are at their best served with roasts, and not with a dish with a sauce. Chopped *fines herbes* (parsley, chervil and tarragon) go well with all green salads. To these you can add spring onion or chopped onion (with lettuce) and a little garlic (with chicory).

§ *Lettuce or batavia or chicory; French dressing.* Fines herbes, spring onion, chopped or garlic can be added.

SALADE DE CRESSON *Watercress Salad*

This is particularly good with a roast chicken, in which case it is served in the same plate as the bird, the gravy of which gives it an added attraction.

Clean the watercress well, leave only the top *bouquet* of leaves, dry thoroughly and dress, at the last second, with salt, pepper, very little vinegar (or lemon juice) and no oil.

§ *Watercress; salt; pepper; vinegar or lemon juice.*

*

And once more let us have the things that are in season. What pleasure is there in eating out of season salad artificially grown? What taste in it? And what pleasure shall we have when it comes to us, in its time, as it were, a gift from Nature, if we eat it all the year round?

We have in the winter admirable salads like curly chicory, endives, dandelion, lamb's lettuce, batavia; and in the spring and summer all the kinds of lettuce, long and round, white and brownish, and the tiny green ones, all leaves and no heart, which one sometimes finds at some small greengrocer's in the English country, and which have a delicious taste.

Ah, what better luncheon on a summer day than an omelette, cold chicken or a well-spiced home-made galantine, *a lettuce salad flavoured with* fines herbes *and spring onions and a cream cheese? It has the excellence of simplicity, and I like to think that the eggs come from our hens, the salad and the herbs from our garden, and, of course, we have made the vinegar ourselves – as it should be in every perfect household.*

*

SALADE AU LARD AVEC PISSENLIT *Bacon and Dandelion Salad*

Take some dandelion, remove outside leaves, wash the hearts well;

season them in the ordinary way, but with less oil than usual and add to it little cubes of bacon crisply fried in fresh butter. Stir quickly and serve at once. Serve on hot plates. Bacon is also good with the long kind of lettuce.

§ *Dandelions; bacon; butter; French dressing.*

SALADE DE PISSENLIT AUX BETTERAVES — *Dandelion and Beet Salad*

If you have a garden you can easily grow dandelions. In fact you cannot help their growing. Cover them with a flat stone or a tile and they will get beautifully white. Use only the hearts, add about the same quantity of beets and dress with plain oil and vinegar, salt and pepper. It is really a very good winter salad, though it is not much thought of in England.

I have the evidence in front of me; overpowering, laconical, badly printed evidence; not the evidence of scientific books or literary treatises, but that of two unbiased popular dictionaries. I have looked up the same plant in both languages, *'pissenlit'* which is in English 'dandelion'. The French dictionary, true to the racial characteristics says: *'genre de composées qui se mangent en salade'*, but the English work, sharply and scornfully brushes aside the dandelion; 'a common plant with a yellow flower'.

§ *Dandelions; beetroot; French dressing.*

SALADE D'ENDIVES ET BETTERAVES — *Endive and Beet Salad*

This is one of the best winter salads and is really a dish in itself. To three-quarters of a pound of Belgian endives, well washed and cut across in pieces about two inches long, add one medium-sized beet cut in thin slices. Add *fines herbes* (parsley, tarragon and chervil finely chopped), or at least chopped parsley, and season with salt, pepper, wine, vinegar, and olive oil: one tablespoonful of vinegar to two of oil. Dress just before serving.

§ *Endives; beetroot;* fines herbes; *French dressing.*

SALADE CARMEN — *Salad Carmen*

This is a mixture of chicory, celery and beets. The dressing should be made with very little oil, salt, pepper, or a little fresh cream and lemon juice instead of vinegar.

§ *Chicory; celery; beetroot; French dressing.*

SALADS

SALADE RUSSE *Russian Salad*

Boil carrots, beets, potatoes, string beans, peas (they should be boiled separately, as they are not all boiled in the same way). When cold, cut them in very small cubes. Add also (cut in small cubes) ham and cucumber. Season with salt and pepper, oil and vinegar. About one hour later add a mayonnaise sauce and mix well together.

§ *Carrots; beetroot; potatoes; string beans; peas; ham; cucumber; Mayonnaise sauce (eggs, vinegar, malt, pepper, oil).*

SALADE PRAIRIAL *Meadow Salad*

Take equal quantities of string beans cut in pieces, of peas and of asparagus tips, all these previously boiled and cold. Make a dressing with one-third vinegar, two-thirds olive oil, salt and pepper. Dress half an hour before serving.

§ *String beans; peas; asparagus tips; French dressing.*

SALADE DE CHOU-FLEUR *Cauliflower Salad*

When cold, remove all the hard parts of the cauliflower, break the rest in pieces. Dress with oil, vinegar, mustard, pepper and salt, one shallot and parsley chopped.

§ *Cauliflower; French dressing with mustard; shallot; parsley.*

SALADE NOUVEAU-MONDE *New World Salad*

Take the same quantity of heart of white cabbage and of red cabbage; both should be finely shredded and all hard parts removed.

The red cabbage, shredded, is seasoned with salt and pepper, then boiling vinegar is poured over it, and it is left a day to marinate before it is drained and used.

Dress the white cabbage separately with ordinary French dressing of oil, vinegar, salt and pepper.

Both cabbages are then disposed in the salad bowl neatly, according to your fancy, in two or four sections, sprinkled with finely chopped yolk of egg. The salad appears like this on the table and is mixed after it has made its effect.

It can be served also as an hors d'œuvre dish, and not mixed before serving.

§ *White cabbage; red cabbage; vinegar; yolk of egg; French dressing.*

SALADE DE LÉGUMES, I *Salad of Peppers and Cauliflower*

Take some branch celery, sweet red peppers, and cauliflower in equal quantities. Add a few slices of beetroot, half a dozen chopped gherkins, spring onions. Season with oil and vinegar, mustard, salt, and a good deal of pepper.

§ *Celery; sweet red peppers; cauliflower; beetroot; gherkins; spring onions; French dressing with added pepper.*

SALADE DE LÉGUMES, II   *Salad of Tomatoes and Beetroot*

Cut some tomatoes in slices, remove the seed; add a quarter of the quantity of beetroot. Dress with salt and pepper, mustard, oil and vinegar, chopped shallots and a teaspoonful of rum.

§ *Tomatoes; beetroot; chopped shallots; rum; French dressing.*

SALADE DE LÉGUMES, III   *Vegetable Salad*

Use boiled cold potatoes as a basis. Cut them in slices and add the same quantity of mixed vegetables – carrots, turnips and string beans – previously boiled.

Have also three hard-boiled eggs; chop the whites finely and mash the yolks in two tablespoonfuls of olive oil till it is a soft ointment.

Add then an ordinary French seasoning of salt, pepper and vinegar, and chopped parsley. Mix all well together. The salad will be all the better for being seasoned at least one hour before serving.

§ *Potatoes; carrots; turnips; string beans; eggs; parsley; French dressing.*

*

A meal worth eating must take at least an hour and a half; apart from the fact that it is not healthy to eat quickly, there is the other point of view with which we are concerned – the point of view of the pleasure of the table, to which leisure, anticipation, enjoyment contribute equally. The cook might also have something to say on the subject; indeed, some of her dishes cannot be kept waiting, while the guests intelligently can, and if our menu is, as it should be, calculated for the starring of a special dish, the entrance of this dish must be well prepared, with an effective pause, good both for our digestion and our delectation.

It appears preceded by a delicious smell; we actually see it, and we look forward to tasting its succulence. Such is the only civilized attitude in the dining-room. We must obey the rites of the cult – the cult of leisure.

*

SALADE DEMI-DEUIL   *Half-Mourning Salad*

This is a delicious salad made of celery, artichoke bottoms and truffles finely sliced in the julienne style; the dressing to be quite plain, salt, freshly ground pepper, best olive oil and red wine vinegar.

§ *Celery; artichoke bottoms; truffles; salt; peppercorns; olive oil; red wine vinegar.*

SALADS

SALADE D'HIVER *Winter Salad*

This is composed of watercress, cooked beets and celery. Use only the top *bouquet* of the watercress, so that there is as little stalk as possible, and only the white and crisp heart of the celery.

Both the celery and the beets are cut in thin strips about two inches long, and there should be about two parts of watercress and one part each of celery and beetroot.

Dress only at the last minute with olive oil (two parts), wine vinegar (one part), salt and pepper. It will be all the better if the beetroot has been baked and not boiled.

§ *Watercress; beetroot; celery; French dressing.*

SALADE FLAMANDE *Salad Flamande*

Served as a separate vegetable dish, this salad is at its best. Take some Belgian endives, and having removed the outside leaves, wash and drain them well.

Cut the endives across in pieces about one inch long, and mix with the same quantity of cold boiled potatoes (the waxy yellow kind are better for this than floury ones).

Chop together one small onion and a little parsley, and sprinkle it in the salad bowl. The dressing is the ordinary plain one as before, but with the addition of a little English mustard.

§ *Endives; potatoes; onion; parsley; French dressing with mustard.*

SALADE DE CHAMPIGNONS *Mushroom Salad*

Have some mushrooms, wash them well (if quite fresh and firm they need not be peeled), cut them in thin slices and cook them five or six minutes in a little butter; at the foaming stage, add salt, pepper and a squeeze of lemon. Shake them occasionally.

Let them get cold and season plainly with oil and vinegar. You can also add a little tomato juice.

§ *Mushrooms; butter; lemon; oil; vinegar; salt; pepper; lemon juice; tomato juice.*

SALADE DE POMMES DE
TERRE AUX ANCHOIS *Potato Salad with Anchovies*

Prepare like an ordinary potato salad, and add half a dozen fillets of anchovies cut in small pieces.

§ *Potatoes; fillets of anchovies.*

SALADE GONCOURT *Salad Goncourt*

Cook in their skins some potatoes (the yellow, waxy kind), peel them and cut them in thin slices. While still hot season them with salt, pepper and mixed spice. Add to them, chopped finely, a small onion, one truffle, very little garlic and chervil. Mix well together.

Add (for a pound of potatoes) a small glass of Madeira and one larger of Chablis. Mix well and let the potatoes soak well and absorb the wines; about one hour afterwards make your salad with a dressing composed of olive oil (two-thirds) and lemon juice (one-third). A few slices of truffle added at the last minute are an improvement both in the taste and to the appearance of the salad, which should be served as a separate dish.

§ *Potatoes; salt; pepper; mixed spice; onion; truffle; garlic; chervil; Madeira; Chablis; olive oil; lemon juice; truffle.*

SALADE DE POIREAUX   *Leek Salad*

Take some leeks, clean them well, remove the coarser leaves and cut off the green part; if they are large ones cut them in two, lengthways.

Cook them in boiling salted water till soft. Let them get cold on a plate in a slanting position so that they are well drained. Season with a plain French dressing, that is, one part vinegar, two parts oil, salt and pepper.

§ *Leeks; French dressing.*

SALADE PARISIENNE   *Parisian Salad*

Have equal quantities of good crisp eating apples, cooked white of chicken and Gruyère cheese, all these cut finely like matches.

The seasoning is of the French type – just vinegar, oil, salt and pepper, with very little cream and mayonnaise mixed, just enough to soften the mixture.

Dress one hour before in the salad bowl, and garnish at the last minute with small leaves of cos lettuce all round.

§ *Apples; cold chicken; Gruyère cheese; French dressing; cream. Mayonnaise (eggs, vinegar, salt, pepper, oil).*

SALADE DE BŒUF AUX HARENGS   *Beef Salad with Herrings*

Small pieces of beef and cut fillets of herrings in equal parts. Dress with salt, pepper, very little oil, and instead of vinegar the juice from the herrings. The kind of preserved herrings to be used for this is the kind called 'Bismarck herrings' or *harengs marinés,* not the smoked fillets of herring in oil.

§ *Beef; Bismarck herring fillets; salt; pepper; oil.*

SALADS

SALADE DE POULET *Chicken Salad*

Have some rice plainly boiled and well drained; season it, while still hot, with salt, pepper, oil and vinegar and let it get cold. Cut in small pieces the flesh of a roast chicken, and dispose it on the rice in a large bowl or deep dish, with slices of hard-boiled egg all round.

Put a little mayonnaise (with a touch of mustard in it) all over, together with chopped parsley, tarragon and chervil. Stir at the last minute only, when the dish has appeared on the table.

There should be plenty of dressing in the rice and not too much mayonnaise.

§ *Rice; salt; pepper; vinegar; cold chicken; eggs. Mayonnaise (eggs, vinegar, salt, pepper, oil); mustard; parsley; tarragon; chervil.*

SALADE DE HOMARD *Lobster Salad*

Take the flesh of a boiled lobster, cut it in pieces. Take also four fillets of anchovy in oil (cut in small pieces), six olives (stoned and cut in half) and a puddingspoonful of capers. Mix together and dress with a plain dressing of vinegar (one-third), oil (two-thirds), salt and pepper.

Add at the last minute two hard-boiled eggs cut in quarters and the leaves of two hearts of lettuce.

It is essential that the leaves of salad should be added only just before serving, otherwise they will get withered and will not be at all appetizing. The general mixing should also be done at the last minute.

Usually a mayonnaise sauce is served with the lobster salad, but it is not advisable to mix it with it; it should be served separately.

§ *Cold lobster; fillets of anchovy in oil; olives; capers; French dressing; eggs; lettuce. Mayonnaise (eggs, vinegar, salt, pepper).*

SALADE DE POISSON *Fish Salad*

Take remnants of any boiled white fish, dress with oil, vinegar, pepper, salt, a chopped shallot and parsley; a few leaves of lettuce round the dish.

§ *Leftovers of white fish; French dressing; shallot; parsley; lettuce.*

*

The classification of light dishes and mixed salads into hors d'œuvre *and* savouries *can only be an arbitrary one. In the old books* hors d'œuvres, *either hot or cold, were like the English Savouries under the heading of* entrées *or of* entremets. *Indeed they are so closely connected as to be almost indistinguishable; many of the French light luncheon entrées can be served in England as savouries and the deciding if a mixed salad is to be used as an hors d'œuvre or as a salad is entirely a question of taste.*

It will be noticed that in our week there are many salads. Personally, I would have a salad at every meal. I am told by people who know that salads are good for our health, that they contain vitamins or proteins or whatever it is. This is a poor inducement to our eating salads. The only true and human reason is that they are pleasant and useful.

*

Sweets

Sweets are a comparatively modern invention. 'Our ancestors sweetened and garnished all with Honey, of which there are some remains: In Windsor Bowls, and large simnels sent for presents from Lichfield.' In the treatise of Apicius Caelius, probably the earliest work on cookery known (and what we have of it is as apocryphal as parts of the 'Satyricon' according to Dr Lister, 'medicin Gourmand d'une reine Gourmande' and commentator of Apicius), the fifth book 'is of Pease Porridge, under which are included Frumentary, Watergruel, Milk Porridge, Flumary, Stirabout and the like', which seems a very dull collection of sweets. Though it may be said that sweets are apt to be dull unless they are of a compilation which is even worse than dullness. Puzzles are out of place at the dinner table and the choice of a sweet is conducive to extreme perplexity.

All the following are of the simplest kind, and I have purposely refrained from including in this chapter any of those dishes of unrecognizable flavour which look like an imitation of something else, and these terribly strenuous pièces montées *complicated, marvellous, awe-inspiring, jellified and crystallized, which are as difficult to make as they are to eat.*

*

POMMES FLAMBÉES *Apples Flambé*

Have some good eating apples all the same size and rather small. Peel them carefully and cook them slowly, so that they do not break, in water with sugar.

When soft, remove and drain them, keeping them hot. Add a little more sugar to the water and boil it till it has reduced to a syrup.

Dispose your apples in a metal serving-dish, pour a little syrup over each; warm some rum in a small saucepan, set it alight and pour it all over the apples.

Serve while still burning.

§ *Apples; sugar; rum.*

POMMES AU BEURRE *Apples with Butter*

Take some good eating apples all the same size. Peel them and remove the core.

Cut some round pieces of stale bread the same size as the apples and about half an inch thick. Arrange them in a buttered fireproof dish, stand one apple on each, and fill the centre of the apples with butter into which you have worked some sugar.

Bake in a slow oven, basting several times. It is necessary to have some extra sweetened butter prepared for basting, as what each apple contains would not be enough.

Serve very hot with whipped cream.

§ *Apples; stale bread; butter; sugar; cream.*

POMMES NORMANDE *Apples Normande*

Eating apples peeled, cut in quarters and cooked in butter on a moderate fire; turn them carefully one by one on the three sides. They must be flat in the pan to cook well and evenly. When ready (that is, soft but golden brown), sprinkle with sugar and a pinch of cinnamon, and just when serving pour in a glass of liqueur, which you set alight – brandy, rum, or brandy and curaçao.

§ *Apples; butter; sugar; cinnamon; brandy, rum, or brandy and curaçao.*

POMMES BALBEC *Apples Balbec*

Take some fine eating apples, peel them and cut them in quarters. Melt some good butter in a frying-pan and put in the quarters one by one and carefully. They should be turned so that they become brown on all sides, with great precaution as, when the flesh becomes soft, they might break. When they are well cooked, sprinkle them with castor sugar, shake the pan well, pour in a glass of Calvados (apple brandy), set it alight and serve at once. Serve at the same time ice-cold whipped cream.

§ *Apples; butter; castor sugar; Calvados; cream.*

POMMES À LA CRÈME *Fried Apples*

Cut the apples in quarters and brown them in butter. When cooked, sprinkle them with sugar and pour rum over them; set it alight. Add a little apricot jam to the juice. Serve with whipped cream to which you have added a little rum.

§ *Apples; butter; sugar; rum; apricot jam; cream.*

SWEETS

POMMES À LA NEIGE *Snow Apples*

Take some good eating apples, peel them, put them into a fireproof dish with sugar, a little water, and a piece of butter. Cook them in the oven until they are soft. Then add a little kirsch and let the apples cool.

Beat the whites of four eggs until very stiff, adding sugar and some whipped cream, and cover the apples with this mixture. Sprinkle with soft white sugar and serve.

§ *Apples; sugar; butter; kirsch; whites of egg; whipped cream; castor sugar.*

COMPOTE DE POMMES *Compote of Apples*

Peel and cut the apples and cook them on a slow fire, adding a tumblerful of water and sugar. When reduced to a pulp and no water left at all, add a piece of butter the size of a small egg and a teaspoonful of apricot jam. Whip the mixture well. Cook for a few minutes more, stirring all the time. Serve cold.

All fruits can be cooked en compote.

§ *Cooking apples; sugar; butter; apricot jam.*

COMPOTE DE POMMES AU CARAMEL *Compote of Apples with Caramel*

Peel and cut in quarters some cooking apples and cook them in a tumblerful of water with half a vanilla pod, and about a quarter of a pound of sugar. When they are reduced to a pulp, add a good piece of butter, a tablespoonful of apricot jam, remove the vanilla pod (which can be washed in cold water and used again several times), and let the compote cool in a dish. Melt some sugar in a small saucepan till it becomes caramel, add a little water and pour it over the apples so as to cover the whole surface. Serve very cold.

§ *Cooking apples; vanilla pod; sugar; butter; apricot jam.*

COMPOTE DE POMMES AUX MARRONS *Compote of Apples with Chestnuts*

Prepare the apples as above, and when cold add three tablespoonfuls of chestnut jam or (if this is not available) one pound of steamed chestnuts mashed through a sieve. Mix well. Whipped cream flavoured with vanilla or orange goes well with this.

§ *Cooking apples; chestnut jam or chestnuts; cream; vanilla or orange as flavouring.*

COMPOTE DE POMMES   *Compote of Apples*
À L'ANANAS   *with Pineapple*

Peel and cut your apples in quarters in the ordinary way and cook them in cold water, the proportions to be about two pounds of apples, a tumblerful of water and a handful of lump sugar (more if the apples are very sour) to four or five people. By the time they are quite soft there should be very little water left, if any; add a piece of butter the size of an egg, and cook a few minutes more. Then remove the compote from the fire, add two tablespoonfuls of pineapple jam, mix well and put the mixture in a serving-dish. Serve very cold.

§ *Apples; lump sugar; butter; pineapple jam.*

POIRES DIJONNAISE   *Pears Dijonnaise*

Peel and poach some pears and leave them to cool in the liquid. Prepare a mixture of blackcurrants and raspberries, pound them well and, if too liquid, reduce to a thin purée. Cut the pears in half. Dispose them in the serving-dish, pour over the fruit mixture, sprinkle all over a few chopped grilled almonds, serve very cold with whipped cream.

§ *Pears; blackcurrants; raspberries; almonds; cream.*

POIRES FLAMBÉES   *Pears Flambéed*

Take some sound pears, peel them carefully and, once peeled, prick them all over with a needle; stand them in water to which you add a little sugar and half a vanilla pod; the water should just cover them. Bring to the boil and finish in a moderate oven till they are fairly soft; they should remain whole and white. Remove them and keep them hot in a metal dish.

The finishing touch should really be given in the dining-room. Have some liqueur (about a liqueur-glassful to each pear) slightly warmed, it will burn more easily. Pour it over the pears, set it alight, and serve just when the flames are dying out. The best liqueur with pears is a mixture of maraschino and brandy.

§ *Pears; sugar; vanilla pod; maraschino; brandy.*

POIRES AU FOUR   *Baked Pears*

Take some fine sound pears, wash them, put them whole in a fire-proof dish – they should stand in about half an inch of sugared water, and cook them very slowly in the oven until they are quite soft. By that time they will look quite 'bloated' and just a little shrivelled after a few minutes exposure to the air.

Take also another pear, peel it, cut it in quarters, and cook it in

SWEETS

water to which you have added a sufficiency of sugar so that it becomes a thick syrup when cold. When the water is sufficiently reduced and flavoured, add a sherryglass of Cointreau or Grand Marnier and cook it a little more. Then pour the syrup through muslin over your pears, mix it well with whatever juice may be already in the dish, put back in the oven for a few minutes, and put away to cool. Serve quite cold.

It is also very pleasant to put in, instead of liqueur, a port-glassful of good claret.

§ *Pears; sugar; Cointreau or Grand Marnier or claret.*

POIRES AU CHOCOLAT *Pears with Chocolate Sauce*

Peel and cut some pears in quarters, cook them in a large saucepan with very little water, to which you add sugar and a piece of vanilla pod. When they are nearly ready remove them, also the vanilla. Put in a small saucepan two sticks of good chocolate finely grated and a drop of the water in which the pears have cooked. When thoroughly melted pour it into the large saucepan, add a little butter, the pears and more sugar if necessary. Cook slowly. When finished the pears should be quite soft and the chocolate juice the consistency of cream. Serve hot.

§ *Pears; vanilla pod; sugar; chocolate; butter.*

PÊCHES EN SIROP *Peaches in Syrup*

Take some fresh peaches, peel them and cut them in quarters. Cook them in very little water (just enough to cover them), in which you have dissolved some sugar. After two minutes they are poached enough. Remove them and reduce the juice to the consistency of thin syrup.

Put the juice and the pieces of peaches on ice for one hour and add just before serving a little brandy or kirschwasser. Serve in glasses with wafers or macaroons.

§ *Peaches; sugar; brandy or kirsch; wafers or macaroons.*

PÊCHES MARIE LOUISE *Peaches Marie Louise*

Take some peaches, remove the skin and the stone, and cut them in half. Dispose them in a serving-dish on a layer of strawberries. Sprinkle with sugar, and stand on ice for one hour. Prepare also a *sauce Sabayon* (see p. 25), but using Marsala or Moselle instead of liqueurs. Let this get cold and stand it on ice. Cover the fruit with the *Sabayon* and serve very cold.

§ *Peaches; strawberries; sugar; Sabayon sauce (see p. 25).*

PÊCHES BARBARA *Peaches Barbara*

Take some fine peaches, peel them, cut them in half, and cook them in water and sugar (and half a vanilla pod) till they are soft. The water should just cover them. When they are cooked, remove them, add a liqueur-glassful of Grand Marnier to the juice, and go on cooking it till it is reduced to the consistency of thick syrup. Then remove the vanilla pod and let the syrup get tepid.

Dispose the peaches in a hollow dish all round, and fill the centre with tomato jam, pour over the peaches the syrup, and 'drape' them with cream flavoured with *eau-de-vie de framboises* (or kirschwasser), whipped to a stiff froth, and sprinkle over the cream crushed pistachio nuts.

The whipped cream to be done in the following manner: First beat a white of egg, then add fresh cream, whip till stiff, add the flavouring, whip a little more, then, and only then, add the castor sugar; mix it in well but do not whip any more. Let the mixture rest half an hour in a cool place; dispose it over the peaches, sprinkle with the crushed nuts, and keep on ice till wanted. If you have no tomato jam (which seems incredible) you may use quince jelly. You can treat pears in the same way.

§ *Peaches; sugar; vanilla pod; Grand Marnier; tomato jam or quince jelly;* eau-de-vie de framboises *or kirsch; pistachio nuts; cream; white of egg; castor sugar.*

SALADE D'ANANAS, I *Pineapple with Grapefruit*

Get a good-sized pineapple, as ripe as possible, and scoop out the flesh with a silver knife and fork; also cut in small quarters two grapefruit, being careful there is none of the inner skin left. Sprinkle with sugar and pour over it a port-glassful of maraschino. Let it stand for at least half an hour on ice in a hollow dish. You should, of course, be careful not to waste the juice which has come out of the fruits during the initial operation.

Serve well covered with the following *crème fouettée*: fresh cream, to which you have added castor sugar and maraschino whipped to a stiff consistency. This should be served very cold and, as Brillat-Savarin says when describing a dish, *'on verra merveilles'*.

§ *Fresh pineapple; grapefruit; sugar; maraschino; cream; castor sugar.*

SALADE D'ANANAS, II *Pineapple with Fruit*

The following fruits only should be used in this salad, the great part of which lies in the blending of flavours: one medium-sized pineapple, three oranges, four bananas, the juice of half a lemon.

Scoop out the inside of the pineapple pulp with a silver fork. Peel the bananas and oranges, removing the pips and inner skins of the latter. Mash these also and mix with the pineapple. Take the kernel of a very small coconut and chop fine – do not use desiccated coconut – and stir with the fruit until all is thoroughly mixed. Add two tablespoons of castor sugar and the juice of the lemon. Stir lightly with a fork. Place in a glass dish and pack in ice for two hours before serving.

§ *Fresh pineapple; oranges; bananas; lemon juice; coconut; castor sugar.*

ANANAS GLACÉ — *Chilled Pineapple*

Take a fine ripe pineapple and cut the top off, about two inches from the little trimming of leaves; scoop out all the flesh as neatly as possible, remove the hard parts, mix it with castor sugar and a port-glassful of either kirsch or rum, or maraschino, according to taste, and put the mixture back in the pineapple, not forgetting to cut a slice off the bottom so that it can stand properly when you serve it. The pineapple should then remain about two hours, wrapped up in ice, with its top on.

§ *Fresh pineapple; castor sugar; kirsch or rum or maraschino.*

CRÈME À L'ANANAS — *Pineapple with Whipped Cream*

A very simple and pleasantly fresh sweet in the winter, when fruit is rather rare, can be made with pineapple. Take one, as ripe as possible, cut it in small cubes, and soak these for an hour in either kirsch or maraschino. Whip some fresh cream, have it very stiff, and add, when ready, castor sugar, the pieces of pineapple, and a little of the liqueur. Mix well with the cream with a spoon, but do not whip any more. Put it on ice for one hour.

§ *Fresh pineapple; kirsch or maraschino; cream; castor sugar.*

BANANES AU RHUM — *Bananas with Rum*

Cut the bananas in slices, soak them in rum for one hour, put them in a well-buttered fireproof dish, pour the rum over, sprinkle with sugar, stir lightly with a fork and bake in a moderate oven for twenty minutes. Serve hot or cold.

§ *Bananas; rum; butter; sugar.*

BANANES CRÉOLE — *Bananas Creole*

Put in half a pint of milk about eight lumps of sugar and bring to the boil; when cold stir in the yolks of two eggs. Peel six bananas and scoop out the flesh of two sweet oranges (the pith and skin having been carefully removed), mash this together, add a little castor sugar, and beat it well with a fork till foamy. Then add it to the milk, and add last, the whites whipped to froth. All this to be put in a soufflé dish, baked *au bain-marie* till set and brown, and served at once.

§ *Bananas; lump sugar; milk; eggs; sweet oranges; castor sugar.*

BANANES AUX FRAMBOISES *Bananas with Raspberries*

For this sweet, use six of the small Canary bananas, peel them, and cut each into four parts. Place them in a glass bowl and serve with the following cream poured over: Mash half a pound of raspberries into a pulp, adding sufficient castor sugar. Then whip half a pint of cream and mix with the raspberries. This sweet can also be served in the winter, when you can substitute your own home-made raspberry 'preserve' for the fruit itself.

§ *Bananas; raspberries or raspberry preserve; castor sugar; cream.*

BANANES SOUFFLÉES *Souffléed Bananas*

Take four bananas as large as possible and cut them in two lengthways (one would do for two people). Remove the flesh and squeeze it through a sieve. Put in a sauté pan a tablespoonful of flour and one of castor sugar, dilute with a tumblerful of hot milk, bring to the boil slowly and cook a little more, whipping all the time. When it has thickened, add the mashed bananas, a few pieces of butter, the yolks of two eggs and three whites whipped to a stiff froth.

Fill the banana skins with this mixture, put them on a fireproof dish and cook about six to eight minutes in a hot oven. When they are three parts cooked sprinkle icing sugar all over, which will be slightly browned when finished. Serve at once.

§ *Bananas; flour; castor sugar; milk; butter; eggs; icing sugar.*

FRAISES AU BORDEAUX *Strawberries with Wine*

Clean the strawberries, remove the stalks, sprinkle with sugar, and add a tablespoonful of good claret or white wine. Cream should not be served with this.

§ *Strawberries; sugar; claret or white wine.*

FRAISES ROMANOFF *Strawberries Romanoff*

Roll the strawberries in fine sugar, put them in a bowl, and add two tablespoonfuls of Curaçao and one of port. Shake them well and cover with fresh cream. Do this carefully and slowly, without disturbing the liqueur at the bottom. Stand on ice and stir just before serving. Serve *gaufrettes* or wafers with this.

§ *Strawberries; fine sugar; Curaçao; port; cream;* gaufrettes *or* wafers.

FRAISES CRÉOLE   *Strawberries Créole*

Cut thin slices of fresh pineapple (peeled and core removed), over which are disposed carefully peeled quarters of oranges and strawberries. Sprinkle with sugar and liqueur (preferably maraschino or kirsch), and serve very cold in a flat metal dish, with whipped cream flavoured with same liqueur.

§ *Strawberries; fresh pineapple; oranges; sugar; maraschino or kirsch; cream.*

FRAISES XENIA   *Strawberries Xenia*

Take a bottle of strawberries in brandy and also one pound of fresh strawberries; mash the latter with a fork, and put them in a dish, pouring over one half of the juice from the preserved fruit. Whip half a pint of cream with the white of an egg, add sugar and the rest of the juice, mixing lightly. Cover the mashed strawberries with this cream, and decorate it with the brandy strawberries. Place the dish on ice for two hours before it is to be eaten, and serve with *gaufrettes or wafers*.

§ *Strawberries in brandy; fresh strawberries; cream; white of egg; sugar;* gaufrettes *or* wafers.

FRAISES À LA CRÈME AU KIRSCH   *Strawberries with Whipped Cream and Kirsch*

This is the best of all the delightful ways of serving strawberries. Take a pound of strawberries, clean them and cut them in two with a silver or ivory knife (the look of the dish is not at all spoilt by this process, and the fruit gets more evenly sweetened). Also get some cream and whip it well, add sugar, a liqueur glassful of kirsch, half a dozen squashed strawberries, which will give the cream a pale pink colouring, and whip again. Sprinkle the strawberries with more sugar, and mix well with the whipped cream. Stand the dish on ice for about one hour before serving.

§ *Strawberries; cream; sugar; kirsch.*

FRAISES PRALINÉES   *Strawberries with Almonds*

Take a pound of strawberries, cut them in two, or, if very large, in four. Also take two oranges, remove very carefully with a really sharp knife skin and pith, and cut them in thin quarters. Do this over a cup so that the juice which is bound to come out is not wasted, put together in a bowl oranges and strawberries, the juice of the oranges, soft sugar, a glassful of dry white wine, and a liqueur-glassful of brandy. Shake well and put on ice for a little while. Sprinkle with chopped grilled almonds and serve very cold.

§ *Strawberries; oranges; soft sugar; dry white wine; brandy; almonds.*

FRAISES À L'ORANGE   *Strawberries with Orange Juice*

Take one pound and a half of strawberries, put aside about a pound of the best, remove the stalks, pass the other half pound through a sieve, mix the purée obtained with fine castor sugar and dilute it with the juice of two oranges. Put the purée in a serving dish, dispose the strawberries over it, sprinkle with castor sugar and serve very cold.

§ *Strawberries; castor sugar; oranges.*

COMPOTE D'ORANGES   *Compote of Oranges*

Skin the quarters of orange with a very sharp knife. Put them in a syrup made of sugar and water. Bring to the boil, remove it from the fire and repeat the operation three or four times in succession. Add a liqueur-glassful of rum; dispose the quarters of orange on creamed rice, pour the syrup over all and serve very cold. Three oranges will do for four people.

§ *Oranges; sugar; rum; creamed rice.*

SALADE D'ORANGES   *Oranges with Rum*

Oranges are peeled and cut across in thin slices, sprinkled with sugar and flavoured with rum.

§ *Oranges; sugar; rum.*

COMPOTE DE MELON   *Compote of Melon*

Cut the melon in slices, scoop out the flesh, put the pieces in a saucepan with hot water, sugar, a vanilla pod and a little lemon juice. Cook slowly about ten minutes. Remove the quarters of melon, dispose them in the serving-dish, and let the juice reduce at least by half. When cold stir in a little ginger syrup and serve very cold.

§ *Melon; sugar; vanilla pod; lemon juice; ginger syrup.*

SWEETS

MELON GLACÉ   *Iced Melon*

Cut the top of a melon so as to make an opening about four inches in diameter, remove the seeds; sprinkle the inside with soft sugar, put in two small glasses of either port wine or sherry, put back the top of the melon and stand it on ice or in a refrigerator for two or three hours. Do not serve in slices, but scoop out pieces with a spoon.

§ *Melon; soft sugar; port wine or sherry.*

MELON EN SURPRISE   *Melon Surprise*

Take a good-sized melon, cut open the top, remove all seeds, then scoop out the flesh carefully with a spoon. Prepare a mixture of fresh fruits; two peaches peeled and cut in slices, one orange in quarters carefully peeled with a sharp knife, a handful of redcurrants and the flesh of the melon cut in pieces. Add a little soft sugar and a small glass of either maraschino or kirsch. Put all this back into the melon, cover it with the piece you have cut out and put in a refrigerator or stand on ice for at least one hour. Serve in a deep dish on crushed ice.

A pineapple can be treated in the same manner.

§ *Melon; peaches; orange; redcurrants; soft sugar; maraschino or kirsch.*

FIGUES FLAMBÉES   *Fresh Figs Flambé*

A very simple sweet when fresh figs are in season, which only takes five minutes to prepare. Peel some figs, put them in a silver or bi-metal pan with a mixture of two parts of Curaçao and one part brandy over a spirit lamp. Set the liqueur alight; prick the figs with a silver fork while the liqueur burns; keep shaking the pan. By the time the figs are warm and soft, the Curaçao has reduced and the flames die out naturally. Serve at once. It should be either made in the dining-room or brought in while still alight.

§ *Fresh figs; Curaçao; brandy.*

SALADE DE FIGUES   *Fresh Figs with Cream*

Take some fresh green figs and peel them; cut them in slices. Put them in a serving-dish, standing on ice, with a glass of port wine and a drop of Curaçao and brandy mixed. Pour fresh cream over all, stir and serve at once.

§ *Fresh green figs; Curaçao; brandy; cream; port.*

FIGUES AU FOUR   *Baked Figs*

Fresh figs should be washed, but not peeled, and put in a fireproof dish with sugar and very little water. Bake slowly, pricking the figs with a fork and basting with the syrup. Serve cold in the same dish.

§ *Fresh figs; sugar.*

COMPOTE DE COING *Compote of Quince*

Take some quinces and cook them in boiling water till half done; remove them, peel and core them carefully and cut them in quarters. Put in a saucepan sugar and water, in the proportion of a quarter of a pound for a teacupful of water. Flavour with half a vanilla pod. Bring this to the boil and remove the scum. Put in the quarters of quince, which should be just covered, and cook slowly. When soft remove them and reduce the juice till it becomes a fairly thick syrup, which you pour over the quince in the serving-dish. Serve cold.

§ *Quince; sugar; vanilla pod.*

PRUNEAUX AU VIN *Stewed Prunes with Claret or Port*

Boil your prunes in water and sugar on a slow fire; put in half a vanilla pod. When the water is well reduced and the prunes about three-quarters cooked add a good glass of claret or port and simmer till the juice is the consistency of a syrup. Before serving remove the vanilla pod, wash it and dry it well; it can be used several times.

§ *Prunes; sugar; vanilla pod; claret or port.*

In the seventeenth century appetites were still enormous, and the descriptions of feasts in the memoirs of the period fill the modern man with a great deal of admiration and no little disgust. Louis XIV was a gourmand but not a gourmet. In spite of all these splendours it was not until the eighteenth century that cooking began to emerge from its complex grossness and meals to become shaped like the meals we can now conceive and appreciate.

BEIGNETS DE FRUITS *Fruit Fritters*

Cut your fruit (apples, peaches or pineapple) in slices. Soak them for a little while in rum or kirsch, dip them in the batter and fry in very hot fat. Sprinkle with sugar and serve very hot.

§ *Batter (see pp. 10 and 213); rum or kirsch; fruit; fat; sugar.*

CRÈME PÂTISSIÈRE *Cream Filling*

For a pint of milk we want four yolks and two whole eggs, also about a tablespoonful of sifted flour and a quarter of a pound of sugar. Work all these together and pour in, little by little, the boiling milk (which has been flavoured with a vanilla pod). Cook on a slow fire, whipping till the mixture is the right consistency for your purpose. You can add to the flavour by stirring in a liqueur-glassful of maraschino, rum or Curaçao, and you have then the basis for a *liqueur soufflé* instead of a *vanilla soufflé*, the adding of whipped whites being as usual.

This *crème* is very useful in the kitchen. It can be served, as it is, with biscuits; it can be used for stuffing pancakes; you can also make it quite stiff by cooking it longer. Its thickness should be regulated according to requirements; for a soufflé we want it the consistency of mayonnaise or of thick cream.

§ *Eggs; flour; sugar; milk; vanilla pod; maraschino, rum or Curaçao.*

CRÈME FRITE *Fried Cream*

Cook the *crème pâtissière* on a slow fire, whipping till the mixture has thickened (like thick custard). Remove the vanilla pod and pour the mixture on a greased marble, tin or board. When dropped it will spread slowly, and stop of its own accord, making a paste about one inch thick or a little less. When cold cut it in squares or triangles, coat these lightly with whipped egg and white breadcrumbs and fry them like any fritters till golden brown. They should be rather crisp outside and creamy inside. Serve with a hot chocolate sauce, a jam sauce, or a *sauce Sabayon* (see p. 25).

§ Crème pâtissière *(eggs, flour, sugar, milk, vanilla pod, maraschino, rum or Curaçao); white breadcrumbs; hot chocolate sauce, jam sauce or* Sabayon *sauce (see p. 25).*

CRÈME AU CAFÉ *Coffee Cream*

Take the yolks of eight eggs and stir them well in a bowl. Make two cups of very strong coffee, using twice as much coffee as you would ordinarily; boil a pint and a half of milk, add the coffee, about a quarter of a pound of sugar, and add this little by little to the yolks, stirring all the time. Pour through a fine colander in a saucepan and cook, stirring all the time and watching carefully, especially when it begins to thicken. Needless to say, it must not boil; also it must not reach the point when it might curdle. When it is about the thickness of ordinary cream it is wise to remove it from the fire and to pour it into the serving-dish. You must go on stirring occasionally and gently until it is fairly cool. Serve with it *gaufrettes* or macaroons.

§ *Eggs; coffee; sugar;* gaufrettes *or macaroons.*

*

There is another dish, the origin of which is obscure; obviously a dish of French inspiration but evolved in England, the Crème Brûlée *of Cambridge. I had this delicious sweet there many times. It was not an English custard or a French crème, being infinitely richer and thicker than either, in spite of the fact that it seemed less set.*

I tried to make it, to have it made, to have it somewhere else. It never was so good; in fact it was not right. After many unsuccessful attempts, I managed to get a recipe (the College kitchen had been obstinate on that question).

The best I ever had was at a luncheon at Trinity many years ago, and the occasion was one of some importance, for it was just before the performance of Mozart's Magic Flute, *under the admirable direction of E. J. Dent; Steuart Wilson was Pamino, and Clive Carey, Papageno; Rupert Brooke was in the chorus. Happy days. . . .*

I wrote an article on this burning subject, received many letters, including various recipes, all slightly different. Then appeared in the press, I forget where, the following letter which shows yet a different aspect of this sweet, so that the cook who fails to have the top hard, can say that it is as it should be.

'Sir, M. Hartmann, the Swiss head cook at Trinity for so many years, told me in 1896, that he had invented this dish, which was certainly known to all college kitchens as Crème Brûlée à la Trinité. . . . M. Hartmann also said that it must be semi-liquid and the caramel on the top browned to the consistency of thawing ice, capable of being shaved with a spoon into sugar again.

'In no circumstances should it be hardened into the solid varnish which so often accompanies spurious imitations of the dish. Yours, etc.

Trevor Blakemore, Savile Club, W.'

*

CRÈME BRÛLÉE, I   *Crème Brûlée, I*

1. Bring a pint of cream to the boil and pour it over the yolks of six eggs to which you have added, mixing well, five or six ounces of castor sugar. Mix well again, and bring almost to the boiling-point. Put in a shallow fireproof dish and finish in a slow oven till set.

When cold sprinkle with two ounces of castor sugar; burn it with a salamander or brown under the grill to form a kind of caramel top, which should be hard and brittle. Serve very cold.

2. Crumble six macaroons and add them, with four yolks, to the pint of cream. Cook it standing in boiling water till it thickens like custard; pour into a dish, and when cold powder very thickly with

sifted sugar. Brown as before and serve very cold. This can also be prepared without macaroons, flavoured instead with cinnamon and vanilla. For the top, mix one yolk of egg with two tablespoons of sugar and beat well. Start browning, then add more sugar on top.

§ 1. *Cream; egg yolks; castor sugar.*
2. *Macaroons or cinnamon and vanilla; egg yolks; cream; sifted sugar.*

CRÈME BRÛLÉE, II   *Crème Brûlée, II*

This is not the famous sweet from Trinity, but the eighteenth-century recipe, original theme of which the elaborate Cambridge dish is, no doubt, a variation. Prepare the caramel flavouring as explained before. Pour the boiling cream over, add the eggs, mix well, and strain. Same proportions and quantities as before. Put the strained mixture in a flat saucepan and cook slowly like French *crème* – that is, whipping till it has taken on a good creamy consistency.

§ *Castor sugar; cream; eggs.*

CRÈME DE RIZ   *Creamed Rice*

Take a breakfast cupful of Carolina rice and put it in boiling water for two or three minutes. Remove it and drain it well. Put it in a saucepan with boiling milk and a stick of vanilla. In this special case, as you want the rice very well cooked and swollen, you can put three times its volume of liquid, therefore three cups of milk. Bring to the boil and cook it for twenty to twenty-five minutes.

Then add sugar to taste, a liqueur-glassful of Grand Marnier or Curaçao, remove the vanilla pod and whip a little. Leave it to cool, and when cold add three tablespoonfuls of fresh cream, whip it well and serve very cold.

§ *Carolina rice; milk; vanilla pod; sugar; Grand Marnier or Curaçao; cream.*

DULCE DE LECHE   *Spanish Milk Pudding*

A little known and extremely good Spanish sweet. Put in a thick earthenware saucepan four pints of milk and half a pound of Demerara sugar, also half a vanilla pod. Cook on an extremely slow fire, stirring often, for at least two hours; by that time the *dulce* should be golden yellow and the consistency that of thick cream. It is ready only when it has reached that state. Serve cold in little pots or custard glasses. This sweet, put in pots, will keep for some time.

§ *Milk; Demerara sugar; vanilla pod.*

SOUFFLÉS

The principle of the soufflé is simple enough: you make your preparation, such as it is, according to recipe and when it is hot you stir in the yolks; the heat of the preparation partly cooks them. You leave the thing to cool, and then add the whipped whites, the proportion being four whites to three yolks, and so on. Cook twelve to fourteen minutes in a moderate oven.

There are a great many mistaken ideas in connexion with this delicious dish, one of them being that if you open the door of the oven it becomes flat at once; in fact, a soufflé cannot be made by exact timing, and you must watch it carefully to see if it is getting on as it should be quickly enough, yet not too quickly. Of course, you must not leave the door of the oven open or open it too much, but you must not be afraid to glance at it if necessary.

Three yolks and four whites are a good quantity for four people. Ingredients to be increased proportionately.

It is better to keep the diners waiting than the soufflé.

Soufflés can be made with all sorts of things – fish, lobster, *foie-gras,* purée of game, spinach, asparagus, cheese.

The basis of all of this is, as a rule, a rather thin *Béchamel* sauce. But if there is already a great deal of substance in the flavouring, like a purée of fish, game or vegetable, you must allow for that and work in less *Béchamel* so as not to spoil the final consistency.

SOUFFLÉS *Soufflés*

The following proportions are the basis for a soufflé for six to eight people, and should be increased or decreased according to requirements. It is always better to make two soufflés for three or four than a large one for eight.

Bring a pint of milk to the boil and keep it hot. Put in a flat saucepan two ounces of sifted flour, not quite half a pound of sugar and five yolks of egg. Mix well over the fire and add the hot milk little by little. Cook, whipping well till it reaches the consistency of thick cream. Let the mixture get cold, then add six egg whites whipped to a stiff froth. Fill the soufflé dish (lightly buttered and sprinkled with sugar) up to three-quarters and cook in a moderate oven about twelve minutes.

With this mixture you can make a vanilla soufflé by boiling a vanilla pod with the milk; or you can flavour it with any liqueurs you like.

§ *Milk; flour; sugar; eggs. Vanilla pods or liqueurs can be added.*

SWEETS

SOUFFLÉ D'ORANGE *Orange Soufflé*

Squeeze the juice out of three oranges and chop very finely the skin of one, being careful to peel it very thin, so that there is no pith at all. Take a spoonful of potato flour (or ground rice), mix it well with the orange juice and a cup of milk, add sugar, bring to the boil,stirring well till it thickens to the consistency of an ordinary *Béchamel* sauce.

Add then the chopped orange skin and the yolks of two eggs, which you stir in well with a wooden spoon over a slow fire. When it is very thick put it to cool. After that add the whites of three eggs whipped to a froth, put the mixture in a soufflé dish, buttered and sprinkled with sugar and cook like any soufflé for about twelve minutes. Five minutes before serving, sprinkle a little sugar on the soufflé in the oven.

§ *Oranges; potato flour or ground rice; sugar; milk; eggs.*

SOUFFLÉ DE POMMES *Apple Soufflé*

Peel and cut one pound of eating apples and cook them with a vanilla pod, put in sugar and very little water. When soft, mash them and dry the purée well over the fire. See that it is sweet enough, add the yolks of two eggs and cook one minute, stirring well. When almost cold add the whites of four eggs whipped to a stiff froth.

Cook in a moderate oven in a soufflé dish, standing in boiling water; two or three minutes before serving sprinkle with icing sugar, and crushed nuts (walnuts, filberts, almonds or pistachio) previously roasted.

§ *Apples; vanilla pod; sugar; eggs; icing sugar; nuts.*

SOUFFLÉ DE FRAMBOISES *Raspberry Soufflé*

Having prepared a *crème pâtissière* (see p. 206) let it get cool. Meanwhile pound through a sieve half a pound of strawberries and reduce it slowly so that it becomes thick. Add the reduced fruit juice to the crème and put it in the whites of eggs whipped to a stiff froth.

Put in a few raspberries whole, fill a soufflé dish (buttered and dusted with sugar), and cook like an ordinary soufflé.

§ Crème pâtissière *(eggs, flour, sugar, milk, vanilla pod; maraschino, rum or Curaçao); strawberries; raspberries; whites of egg.*

SOUFFLÉ AU CHOCOLAT *Chocolate Soufflé*

For this soufflé, as indeed for most soufflés, the proportion of eggs is two to each person. Chocolate soufflé is specially light, as it does not contain any flour at all.

Grate about a handful of pure cocoa, add a good deal of castor sugar (pure cocoa is very bitter), put in six yolks of eggs and melt slowly over the fire, stirring well. See that it is sweet enough and smooth. Put away to cool while you beat the six whites to a stiff froth, when they are ready add them to the chocolate mixture, put in half first and mix, then the rest and mix again. The mixing should be done with a light hand. Put the finished article in the soufflé dish, which you have previously greased with a little butter and sprinkled with sugar. Cook and serve at once.

§ *Cocoa; castor sugar; eggs; butter; sugar.*

MONT BLANC *Purée of Chestnuts with Whipped Cream*

Remove the skins of a pound of chestnuts, and boil these in milk with sugar and a vanilla pod. They should be well cooked and drained. Pound them through a sieve or press them through a potato-squeezer. They come out of these like strips of cooked vermicelli which you gather carefully to fill a mould hollow in the middle; turn out on the serving-dish and fill the well in the middle with sweetened whipped cream.

§ *Chestnuts; milk; sugar; vanilla pod; cream.*

MOUSSE AU CHOCOLAT *Chocolate Mousse*

Whip cream lightly till it is stiff enough. Add a little sugar and melted chocolate (the consistency of syrup). Let it rest half an hour before serving.

Can be flavoured with coffee, or orange instead of chocolate.

§ *Cream; chocolate; sugar.*

CRÈME DE MARRONS *Chestnut Cream*

Take some chestnuts and boil them for a few minutes; then take them out, remove both skins and put them back in the saucepan; cook till they are tender. Mash them well, flavour with vanilla, add a little sugar, and a glass of cream. Cook again on a slow fire till the mixture is quite dry, when you press it through a colander with fairly large holes directly into the serving-dish. Let it grow cold, and serve covered with whipped cream, also flavoured, if you like, with vanilla.

§ *Chestnuts; vanilla; sugar; cream.*

ŒUFS À LA REINE *Egg Custard à la Reine*

For one pint of milk take six eggs, break them, and separate the yolks from the whites. Beat up the yolks and stir in the milk, adding sufficient soft white sugar. Pour this into a well-buttered soufflé dish and bake in a very slow oven until the eggs and milk have set. Mean-

SWEETS

while, the whites should have been whisked until very stiff with a little soft sugar. Pour over the set yolks and milk a glass of good sherry, allowing a few minutes for this to soak in. Then spread over the whisked whites and brown in a quicker part of the oven.

§ *Milk; eggs; soft white sugar; sherry.*

OMELETTE AU RHUM *Sweet Omlette with Rum*

Prepare your eggs in the ordinary way and add castor sugar. Mix well, and use the mixture without delay; otherwise the omelette will be a failure. Put in the pan a little more butter than for an ordinary omelette. Fold it as usual, sprinkle with sugar and burn it with a red-hot iron. Warm some rum, pour it over the omelette and light it. It should burn for a few minutes or the flavour of rum will be too strong.

§ *Eggs; castor sugar; butter; rum.*

CRÊPES

Pancakes should be thin, dry and light. This result can be obtained if the batter is smooth and rather thin and if the pan is very hot and dry. By 'dry' I mean that there should be no liquid fat in it; it should be just shiny with grease. The best way is to grease it with a piece of pork fat or bacon (not smoked) fat, in preference to butter.

The plain French crêpes or pancakes are usually served flat, each one sprinkled with sugar as it goes to form the pile in the plate, and with lemon. They can also be rolled and stuffed with cream, custard, jam.

The Batter. There are several ways of preparing it, but the best methods are the following:

Put in a basin a half pound of flour, dig a hole in it with your finger, add a pinch of salt, a little sugar, three eggs, and a liqueur glass of rum or brandy. Mix well, and add little by little warm water and milk (in equal quantities), working the batter till it is absolutely smooth and the consistency of thin cream. Let it rest for two hours before using.

The batter can be used for all sorts of pancakes, sweet or savoury (in this case the sugar is omitted). Some people make an even plainer batter, using warm water only. Others, to make more elaborate pancakes, add cream, but it should always remain thin.

CRÊPES *French Pancakes*

The Batter: 1. A Simple Recipe – Half a pound of sifted flour, a pinch of salt, a tablespoonful of sugar; three eggs stirred in, a liqueur-glassful of rum or brandy; mix well and add, little by little, warm milk and water till the batter is the consistency of thin cream and absolutely smooth. Let it rest at least two hours before using.

2. A More Elaborate Recipe – Flour, eggs and sugar as before, but no water, milk only; leave it to rest a while, then add a glass of cream, well whipped, one pounded macaroon, a liqueur-glassful of brandy and one of *eau de fleurs d'oranger* (orange blossom water).

Making the Pancake – Have a very hot pan, rub it with lard or butter; it should be just greasy. Drop in quickly one tablespoonful of batter, swirl it round; the bottom of the pan should be just covered and the pancake extremely thin. Cook one or two seconds, toss; one or two seconds more to cook the other side, and it is ready.

§ 1. *Flour; sugar; eggs; rum or brandy; milk; lard or butter; salt.*

2. *Flour; eggs; sugar; milk; cream; macaroon; brandy; orange-blossom water; lard or butter.*

*

Who really invented Crêpes Suzette?

In his memoirs, a chef, M. Henri Charpentier, claims to have done so, at Monte Carlo in 1894, for King Edward VII, then Prince of Wales. The story is attractive and romantic, and no doubt the pancakes were delicious – though, judging by the recipe published in the book, more elaborate and of more complex flavour than they ought to be.

Being particularly interested in points of culinary history, and remembering my early days in Paris when, at the Restaurant Paillard, Crêpes Suzette were always served as a 'création de la maison', first of all I looked up books of reference; in one, the famous Prosper Montagné puts after the recipe 'création d'Escoffier'. So I had then three origins for the pancakes. In order to clear the muddle, I wrote both to M. Herbodeau and to M. Latry to have their expert opinion. Both seemed to think that the origin of the dish was somewhat obscure; probably the dish was created at Paillard during the Exhibition of 1900. M. Herbodeau very kindly wrote to Escoffier himself: that was some time ago; the letter just reached him, it was never answered, it never will be answered. . . .

I published some of these gleanings in the Evening Standard *and in* Wine and Food; *then M. Latry wrote a letter to* The Times:

'Perhaps it will interest your readers to know the true romantic history which I have just ascertained. Mlle Suzette was a star of the Comédie-Française; in 1897 she played the part of a maid, the role demanding that she should serve pancakes. These were supplied by the Restaurant Marivaux. . . . The creator was the famous Joseph, who later came to London to manage the Savoy Restaurant. His original recipe has since been much amended and elaborated,

but never improved. Its secret lies in the melted sugar and orange juice (the only permissible flavour) mixed into the butter. . . .'

Soon after, a letter reached me which seemed to help further and to be nearer still to the point:

'Dear Sir, I would like to let you know the following about Crêpes Suzette which were first made by Mons. Joseph, then the Director of Restaurant Paillard during the exhibition of 1889. He left Paris for New York, but being homesick, returned to Paris to open his Restaurant Marivaux. He was the successor of Mr Ritz at the Savoy Restaurant where I was fortunate to be under his personal supervision. Trusting this short biography might interest you, Yours,

G. VAILLANT.'

Perhaps also Crêpes Suzette, like Homer's poems, are the production of several. Who can really decide its origin, name the inventor? And since we are dealing with a pancake, we might toss for it.

And here, now, I should like to stake my claim, so to speak, to Crêpes Verlaine. These are flavoured with several liqueurs, and the final touch is given by absinthe. I chose the name for some fairly obvious and rather literary reasons. Verlaine, one of our great poets, was always fond of absinthe, and at one time schoolmaster in England. In one of the few poems he wrote during that time, he described how

> 'Le brouillard de Paris est fade
> On dirait même qu'il est clair
> A côté de cette promenade
> Que l'on appelle Leicester Square.
> Mais le brouillard de Londres est
> Savoureux comme non pas d'autres. . . .'

My first restaurant was in Leicester Square, hence the name given to the year of their birth, 1925.

*

CRÊPES SUZETTE   *Crêpes Suzette*

Having your pancakes very thin, ready on a plate, you cook them a few seconds on each side in a special butter prepared as follows: Rub some pieces of sugar on the skin of an orange so that they are well impregnated with the perfume and coated with the grated rind, moisten them with a little orange juice and Curaçao, pound them and mix them well with the same quantity (or a little more) of butter. In this you cook your pancakes.

Once you have cooked the pancakes in the specially prepared butter and folded them in the pan, sprinkle them with sugar and pour in a glass of orange liqueur (Curaçao or Grand Marnier). Set it alight and serve the moment the flames have died out. This should be done in a metal pan on a spirit-lamp in the dining-room.

You can make this sweet more elaborate still by using several liqueurs. For instance, having three pancakes for each person, and say four people to dinner, you can make three flavoured with Curaçao, three flavoured with kümmel, three with kirsch and three with Benedictine or Chartreuse.

§ *Pancakes; sugar; orange; Curaçao; butter; orange or other liqueur.*

CRÊPES VERLAINE *Crêpes Verlaine*

The liqueurs used for the flavouring are: brandy (four parts), kirsch (four parts), Mandarine (two parts), kümmel (two parts), maraschino (one part) and a very sweet liqueur called crème de cacao (two parts). The final touch is added at the last minute by a dash of absinthe. Let the mixture burn over the shaped pancakes and serve at once while still burning. There should be plenty of 'sauce'.

§ *Pancakes; brandy; kirsch; Mandarine; kümmel; maraschino; crème de cacao; absinthe.*

CRÊPES AUX NOIX *French Pancakes with Nuts*

Having your pancakes cooked on both sides, put in a mixture prepared beforehand, fold and serve.

The mixture is made with pounded walnuts and pistachio nuts mixed with warm cream.

§ *Pancakes; walnuts; pistachio nuts; cream.*

CRÊPES NORMANDE *French Pancakes Normande*

The batter being ready and having rested, take some ripe eating apples, peel them and cut them very thin – no thicker than a shilling piece. In your very hot pan, greased as usual, put a little batter as described before, and dispose immediately a few pieces of apples on the pancake. Add a little more batter, let it set, and cook two seconds more.

Do not roll this pancake, which is thicker than the ordinary one. Sprinkle with sugar and serve with cream.

§ *Pancake batter; apples; sugar; cream.*

CROÛTE AUX FRUITS *Fruit with Brioche*

This pleasant dish is easy to make and very effective. It can be simplified by buying the brioche ready made. I am, however, giving the recipe for the brioche itself.

First stew some apples in very little water, and sugar, till reduced to a pulp; also stew some pears cored and cut in halves in water flavoured with half a vanilla pod till they are soft (they should keep their shape); also chop very fine a few slices of pineapple. Mix together the chopped pineapple, the mashed apples, a tablespoonful of apricot jam, castor sugar, and add a port-glassful of good brandy. Fry slices of brioche in butter till they are nicely browned and crisp; put them standing up all round a soufflé dish; fill it half-way up with your mashed fruit; dispose the pears over it; sprinkle freely with castor sugar, add a few breadcrumbs and brown in the oven. It should be served *flambé* with brandy. It is, by the way, advisable to warm the brandy before lighting it, otherwise it may not burn – a tragic failure on the dining table.

Brioche. To make the batter for the necessary *brioche,* use, say, one pound of flour and pass it through a fine sieve, take a quarter of it and make a heap on the board; melt, in the middle, a small quantity of yeast with lukewarm water; mix it gradually with the flour, adding water if necessary, so as to make a fairly firm mixture. Put it aside in a bowl and keep it fairly warm.

Work the rest of the pound of flour with a pinch of salt, two of sugar, a quarter of a pound of butter (well worked) and six eggs. Mix and beat this well for about twenty minutes on the board. Flatten it, add the quarter of pound previously put aside, and put the whole thing away in a bowl sprinkled with flour; keep it at the same slightly warm temperature for six or seven hours; it should rise to double its original size. Then put it once more on the board, work it a little while, let it rest a few minutes, and bake your *brioche* in a very hot oven, the crown shape being the best for your purpose.

§ *Apples; sugar; peas; vanilla pod; pineapple; apricot jam; castor sugar; brandy; breadcrumbs; butter. For the* brioche: *flour; yeast; sugar; salt; butter; eggs.*

GÂTEAU PETIT DUC　　　　　　　　　　　　　*Little Duke Cake*

Whip to a stiff froth the whites of five eggs, then add successively: six ounces of fine sugar, about four ounces of potato flour, two ounces of melted butter and a tablespoonful of almonds and hazel nuts, grilled and powdered.

Put in a round mould or a soufflé dish, well buttered, and cook in a fairly slow oven till set, that is for about sixteen minutes. Turn it out if in a mould or leave it in the soufflé dish and serve with a redcurrant or blackcurrant sauce.

§ *Egg whites; sugar; potato flour; almonds; hazel nuts; redcurrant or blackcurrant sauce.*

DIPLOMATE À LA CRÈME *Diplomate with Custard*

There are two ways of preparing this simple and delicious cold sweet – with custard and candied fruit, and with fresh fruit only.

Take some sponge fingers or macaroons. Spread apricot jam over each and dispose them in layers in a buttered mould. Between each layer put in a few currants and little pieces of angelica, candied peel and glacé cherries. Dispose the layers lightly, and do not fill the mould, as the fingers will swell. Slowly pour a *crème* all over to fill the empty spaces between.

The French *crème,* or custard, is prepared with yolk of egg only and boiled milk, sweetened and almost cold (proportions: Three yolks to a pint of milk). Beat the yolks, mix them well with the milk, strain and fill the mould. Cook, standing the dish in boiling water, in a moderate oven for at least one hour.

§ *Sponge fingers or macaroons; apricot jam; butter; currants; angelica; candied peel; glacé cherries; yolks of egg; milk; sugar. Can be made with fresh, instead of candied, fruit.*

DIPLOMATE AUX FRUITS *Diplomate with Fruit*

The sponge fingers or macaroons are soaked in half water, half kirsch (or rum), and put in the mould in layers with mashed strawberries and currants or raspberries between each.

No cooking required. Leave it in the mould in the refrigerator, with a weight of about two pounds over it, till the following day, when you turn it out.

Serve it very cold, with the same *crème* as above.

§ *Kirsch or rum; sponge fingers or macaroons. Strawberries; currants; raspberries; yolks of egg; milk; sugar.*

Savouries and Cheese Dishes

Standardization is a fatal thing in cooking, as well as in anything else, and it should be not only resented but fought. How often have we tasted these sauces nearly all alike in flavour and in texture, if different in colouring; those fillets of sole hidden under a nondescript whitish covering exactly like the brownish one which adorns the following meat dish. Indeed, sometimes we cannot distinguish between a roast and a boiled chicken, or even know what we are eating.

Standardization, the worst of all modern evils, everything reduced to a common denominator. . . . Once at the end of a dinner we saw appearing a kind of cold shape. It trembled in the hands of the parlourmaid, and was garnished on the top with little red balls looking like cherries. Everybody ate it wondering. . . . Then the host, who sometimes makes rather blunt remarks, shouted across the table to his wife, 'This is not sweet enough.'

'Well,' came the unexpected answer, 'of course; it is not meant to be sweet, it is a savoury.' Apparently it was a cold cheese mousse, and what we took for cherries were bits of tomatoes.

ŒUFS DURS AUX CHAMPIGNONS *Hard-boiled Eggs with Mushrooms*

Boil the eggs quickly for at least ten minutes and then place them in cold water. When quite cold remove the shells and cut each egg in half. Take out the yolks and mash them with some cream, add salt and pepper. Then chop a little parsley and some of the small mushrooms of the 'button' variety cooked in butter and cold. Mix this with the yolks and cream and fill the whites of the eggs with the mixture, keeping a little of it to spread on little pieces of thin, crisp toast on which you serve the eggs.

§ *Eggs; cream; parsley; button mushrooms; butter; toast.*

BEIGNETS CREVETTES *Shrimp Fritters*

Toss in butter half a pound of shelled shrimps, add two ounces of flour, mix well; add hot milk little by little and cook like a *Béchamel* sauce. It should be fairly thick. Season well, stir in the yolks of two eggs; cook one minute more and let it get cold. Make small fritters with the mixture, dip them in beaten eggs, then in breadcrumbs, and fry in hot deep fat.

§ *Shrimps; flour; butter; milk; yolks of eggs; eggs; breadcrumbs; fat.*

CROÛTES AU JAMBON *Ham on Toast*

Cooked ham, finely chopped, bound with a little *Béchamel* sauce and flavoured with mustard. Sprinkle a little grated horseradish and breadcrumbs and brown lightly. Serve on Toast.

§ *Ham;* Béchamel *sauce (roux, milk, nutmeg); mustard; horseradish; breadcrumbs; toast.*

CANAPÉS DIANE *Canapés Diane*

Chicken livers, each of them wrapped up in very thin bacon, cooked two or three minutes in foaming butter and served on slices of fried bread.

§ *Chicken livers; bacon; butter; fried bread.*

CANAPÉS IVANHOE *Canapés Ivanhoe*

These are small round pieces of toast, buttered and spread with a purée of cooked smoked haddock to which a little cream is added. It should be highly seasoned with salt, pepper, red pepper and a drop of Worcester sauce. Put half a pickled walnut on top of each and brown quickly under the grill or in a hot oven.

§ *Smoked haddock; red pepper; Worcester sauce; pickled walnuts; cream; toast; butter.*

CROÛTES AUX ANCHOIS *Anchovy Fritters*

Take some salt anchovies and soak them well, remove the bones, cut them and pound them in a mortar, add very little chopped parsley, red pepper and a good pinch of curry powder. Put these in a small saucepan with butter and cook for a few minutes. Then mix with it a little grated yolk of egg, spread on crisp buttered toast; pass quickly under the grill and serve at once.

§ *Salt anchovies; parsley; red pepper; curry powder; butter; yolk of egg; toast.*

SAVOURIES AND CHEESE DISHES

CROÛTES AUX CHAMPIGNONS *Mushroom Fritters*

Take a stale loaf of white bread and cut slices as you would for toasting. Fry these quite crisp in butter. Prepare a rather stiff *Béchamel* sauce (not forgetting a little grated nutmeg), add to it two or three mushrooms cut in thin pieces and previously cooked, mix well, season with salt, pepper and a little Cayenne pepper; spread the mixture thickly on the pieces of fried bread. When these little *croûtes,* or fritters, are cold, coat them with beaten egg, sprinkle with breadcrumbs and fry in deep fat or oil. Serve very hot.

§ *Stale white bread; butter;* Béchamel *sauce (roux, milk, nutmeg); mushrooms; Cayenne; fried bread; egg; breadcrumbs; fat or oil.*

CRÈME LORRAINE *Cream Lorraine*

Fry two or three rashers of streaky bacon, and when very crisp break them into very small pieces. Take a quarter of a pound of grated cheese, Gruyère and Parmesan mixed in equal parts, and a tumblerful of cream; mix these together, add one whole egg well beaten and the bits of bacon, salt and pepper; stir well and fill with the mixture little soufflé dishes (one for each person; the quantity mentioned above would do for six or seven people); cook in a fairly hot oven. They should colour slightly and rise a little, but not as much as a soufflé.

§ *Streaky bacon; Gruyère cheese; Parmesan cheese; cream; egg.*

CROÛTE PARMESANE *Cheese and Asparagus Savoury*

Have some buttered toast or pieces of fried bread, put on each a little grated cheese (Gruyère and Parmesan mixed), a little butter, a layer of asparagus tips previously cooked, sprinkle more cheese all over, salt and pepper and brown quickly in the oven, or under the grill.

§ *Gruyère cheese; Parmesan cheese; butter; toast or fried bread; asparagus tips.*

CROQUE MONSIEUR *Croque Monsieur*

Melt a piece of butter the size of a walnut and add little by little and stirring well one heaped-up tablespoonful of flour; put in a cupful of boiling milk. Bring to the boil and let it cook and thicken for a quarter of an hour. Let it rest for ten minutes.

Add two eggs, salt and pepper, and a quarter of a pound of grated cheese. Parmesan and Gruyère mixed in equal parts. Stir well.

Cut small squares of stale bread, put on each a thin slice of lean ham and spread over some of the cheese mixture. Fry in very hot fat till golden brown without turning them, drain well, a pinch of Cayenne pepper and serve at once.

§ *Parmesan cheese; Gruyère cheese; flour; milk; butter; eggs; stale bread; lean ham; fat; cayenne.*

QUICHE *Cheese Tart*

Make your puff pastry as described on p. 11. Butter a flat mould and put in the batter. Cook it in a hot oven about twenty minutes and remove it.

Mix and beat well the following mixture: grated cheese, preferably Gruyère, not quite a quarter of a pound, one beaten egg, a tumbler of cream; put this mixture in your tart and cook about a quarter of an hour, till the cream is set and golden. You can, if you like, add a few pieces of bacon chopped fine.

§ *Puff pastry; Gruyère cheese; egg; cream; bacon.*

FONDUE *Fondue*

The necessary ingredients for this traditional Swiss dish are eggs, Gruyère and butter, though some people improve on it by adding slices of truffles, *sautées* in butter or gravy from roast fowl. The important thing is that the proportions are right: to the weight of the eggs, whatever it is, you must have a third of that weight of grated Gruyère and a sixth of good butter. First whip the whites, add one by one the yolks, then the butter in small pieces and last the grated cheese. Put this in a saucepan, add salt and a good deal of freshly ground pepper; cook, stirring well all the time till the mixture is properly thickened. It should be smooth, thick like good cream, and served at once very hot.

§ *Eggs; Gruyère cheese; butter; peppercorns. Truffles or chicken gravy can be added.*

Cakes and Jams

*'To speak then of the knowledges
which belong to our British
Housewife – I hold the principal
to be a perfect skill in Cookery.'*
(Markham's *English Housewife*)

GÂTEAU AUX AMANDES *Almond Cake*

Have half a pound of pounded almonds, mix them with half a pound of soft sugar and the skin (no pith left) of a lemon grated or very finely chopped. Add about three ounces of potato flour, four eggs and one yolk and a pinch of salt. Having well mixed all these ingredients, add the remaining white of egg whipped to a stiff froth, mix well, fill a buttered mould with the mixture and bake in a slow oven almost one hour.

§ *Almonds; soft sugar; lemon skin; potato flour; eggs; butter.*

TARTELLETTES BRETONNES *Brittany Tarts*

Line some little tins with shortcrust pastry (see p. 11), and fill them with the following mixture: about twelve small potatoes freshly boiled and well mashed, and some sugar and a little milk to bind; then bake the tartelettes in a quick oven, and when they are cool paint them all over the top with whatever jam you may have.

§ *Shortcrust pastry; potatoes; sugar; milk; jam.*

CLAFOUTIS *Cherry Cake Limousin*

The *clafoutis* is a kind of flan or cake made with batter and cherries, and special to the Limousin. The best cherries for this purpose are the soft black ones with a rather acid taste. For the batter take six ounces of flour, make a hole in the middle, put in a little salt and, one by one three eggs well beaten, then water; mix well and add more water till the batter is the right consistency (it should be a little thicker than batter for pancakes). Flavour with a puddingspoonful of either rum, brandy or kirsch. Then add half a pound of cherries and pour the mixture into a well-buttered mould. Cook for about three-quarters of an hour to one hour in a fairly hot oven. When the *clafoutis* is cooked turn it out of the mould and sprinkle with a great deal of sugar. It is usually eaten tepid or cold. The mould should be a rather shallow one, like those used for open tarts. In Limousin the cherries are not stoned and no sugar is put in the batter.

§ *Cherries; flour; eggs; rum, brandy or kirsch; butter; sugar.*

GÂTEAU DE POMMES *Apple Cake*

Make a marmalade with two pounds of eating apples, with sugar to taste, and very little water, so that at the end it is a quite dry smooth purée. Put in a pan three tablespoonfuls of breadcrumbs, a quarter of a pound of butter, and two tablespoonfuls of sugar. Mix well over the fire, cook a little while, and let it get cold.

Dress in the serving dish with alternate layers of apple and of mixture. Decorate the top with strips of redcurrant jelly and clots of whipped cream.

A few crushed dry macaroons can be added to the mixture, and it can be arranged, if preferred, with one layer of each in an open tart made of shortcrust pastry (see p. 11).

§ *Apples; sugar; breadcrumbs; butter; sugar; redcurrant jelly; cream. Macaroons can be added. Shortcrust pastry (see p. 11) optional.*

MACARONS *Macaroons*

Have half a pound of pounded almonds (also six bitter ones) and same quantity of sugar; add three whites of egg (not whipped); mix well and make little heaps on sheets of rice-paper. Bake about twenty-five minutes in a slow oven.

§ *Almonds; bitter almonds; sugar; whites of egg; rice-paper.*

LANGUES DE CHAT *Cat's Tongues*

Put in a warm bowl a quarter of a pound of butter, work it with a wooden spoon till it has become a soft ointment.

Add a quarter of a pound of soft sugar (flavoured with vanilla) and mix well for two minutes. Work in, one by one, the whites of three eggs, then a quarter of a pound of sifted flour.

CAKES AND JAMS

Put the batter in a bag and make the *langues* on a buttered baking tin. They should be about one-third of an inch wide and one inch and a half long.

Allow space for swelling. Bake six or seven minutes in a moderate oven. When the edges are coloured, they are done.

§ *Butter; soft sugar; whites of egg; flour.*

GELÉE DE POMMES   *Crab-Apple Jelly*

Get some crab-apples, wash them well and cook them whole. They should be well covered with water and boiled for at least one hour. Take a large piece of flannel, tie it to the four legs of a stool placed upside-down and pour in this straining cloth the contents of your saucepan. Leave it entirely undisturbed so as to have the juice quite clear. As it may take about twelve hours, the best plan is to do the cooking in the evening and let it strain the whole night. To each pint of the juice obtained add three-quarters of a pound of sugar, flavour with a vanilla pod and cook so that it becomes a jelly when cold – which you can find out in the usual way: that is, by putting a drop of the liquid on a cold plate; if it jellifies after a second or two, it is cooked enough.

§ *Crab-apples; sugar; vanilla pod.*

CONFITURE DE POIRES   *Pear Jam*

Peel and cut the pears in four or eight sections according to size (they should be all of the same kind) and put them in cold water with a little lemon juice. Drain them, put them in a preserving pan with sugar (one pound and a half to each two pounds of pears). Start it on a very slow fire and stir well. Cook it for about twenty-five minutes after it has reached boiling-point; the time of cooking, of course, rather depends on the kind of pears you are using. This jam can be flavoured with cinnamon or vanilla.

§ *Pears; lemon juice; sugar; cinnamon or vanilla.*

CONFITURES DE BANANES   *Banana Jam*

The ingredients required are: one pound of ripe bananas, three cups of sweet orange juice, juice of one lemon, three-quarters of a pound of white or brown sugar. Cut the bananas into slices one-quarter-inch thick, add the sugar and the juice of oranges and lemon, boil slowly till it thickens and becomes a rich red colour. Care must be taken that the mixture does not catch.

§ *Bananas; orange juice; lemon juice; sugar.*

CONFITURE DE PAMPLEMOUSSE *Grapefruit Marmalade*

Take about four or five fruit, wash them well, remove any black marks and take out the core and seeds. Do not remove the skin. Slice very thin, and to every three pounds of fruit add eight pints of water. Let it stand for twenty-four hours. Then throw off the water, add the same quantity of fresh, and boil till the chips are tender. Let it stand another twenty-four hours. Then weigh, and to every pound of juice allow one pound of granulated sugar. Boil the whole till it jellifies, and put in pots.

§ *Grapefruit; granulated sugar.*

CONFITURE DE CITROUILLE, I *Pumpkin Jam, I*

Take some pieces of pumpkin, peel and scrape them, removing the seeds; weigh the pieces. Put in a preserving pan half their weight of sugar and a glass of white wine to each six pounds of sugar. Let this rest and melt an hour or so and add the pieces of vegetable; cook two hours, stirring well. Then add one orange to each pound of sugar (skin and pips removed), and cook another hour. Fill your pots.

§ *Pumpkin; sugar; white wine; oranges.*

CONFITURE DE CITROUILLE, II *Pumpkin Jam, II*

This is another way of making pumpkin jam. Cook six good-sized apples in three pints of water; press them in a fine cloth and put the juice in a jug (there should be about two pints). Cook in a saucepan without water or sugar, on a very slow fire, two pounds of pumpkin (scraped and peeled as before) and add the apple juice little by little. It should be flavoured with either vanilla or lemon, according to taste, and cooked for at least five hours.

§ *Pumpkins; apples; vanilla or lemon as flavouring.*

CONFITURE DE COURGES *Marrow Jam*

Take some vegetable marrow, remove the skin and scrape the inside, cut it in small cubes. Put these in a pan, sprinkle with Demerara sugar (about one pound of sugar to six pounds of marrow) and let it rest a day. The following day put the water, which has oozed out, in a stewpan and add three-quarters of a pound of sugar to each pint of juice. Put also about one quarter of a pound of bruised ginger (tied in a muslin bag), one rind of lemon and two ounces of chopped candied peel. Boil all this fast for ten minutes, then add the cubes and cook slowly for three hours. Remove lemon rind and ginger before putting the jam in pots.

§ *Marrow; Demerara sugar; ginger; lemon; candied peel.*

CAKES AND JAMS

GELÉE DE COINGS *Quince Jelly*

Peel and cut the quinces in quarters (put them in water as you do so, otherwise they will get black), dry them well. Put them in a saucepan with a little water and cook them on a moderate fire till reduced to a pulp. Pass through a sieve, and add the same weight of sugar as there is of quince juice. Boil about twenty minutes, skimming well. Put in pots in the ordinary way.

§ *Quinces; sugar.*

CONFITURES DE TOMATES *Tomato Jam*

Choose some fine tomatoes, peel them, remove the seed and weigh the fruit. Take the same weight of sugar with enough water to dissolve it; boil it a few minutes, skimming well; put in the tomatoes, cook them about two hours, stirring occasionally; about half an hour before removing them put in a vanilla pod. When cooked, remove the vanilla and fill your pots, covering like any other jam. This tomato jam has a very delicate flavour.

§ *Tomatoes; sugar; vanilla pod.*

Sundries

PARTIES

Coming to London in 1904 I vainly looked for American bars as I knew them in Paris. There were no taxis, there was no income tax, no night life, no cocktails. Then the fashion spread slowly. . . . Cocktails have now come to stay.

And even the gourmet should not object to them if they are served properly; that is, a good long time before dinner, say at a cocktail party, which is almost a meal in itself.

Well and good. We'll have no dinner then, 'do a show', and have supper afterwards. But let the food be sufficient, amusing and good. A great many attractive things can be served, capable of reviving the most jaded appetite, or of tempting the most critical.

*

CANAPÉS *Canapés*

In preparing our little *croûtes*, canapés and sandwiches we must not forget that the filling is not the only thing; the bread itself, the toast, the biscuit must be carefully considered; they are part of a whole and as important as the frame of a picture.

All these bits and pieces must be varied, small, neatly served, and, above all, easy to eat. Nothing is more tiresome, for instance, than having to deal with an olive stone; so if you have olives, buy the ones where the stones are replaced either by purée of anchovy or with mashed pimentos.

Have also some very small round pieces of toast or of fried bread, so small that they are just one mouthful; dispose the trimming, whatever it is, on each, and pierce it through with a cherry stick. Do the same to each of those little Chipolata sausages that are equally good hot or cold.

Canapés can be hot or cold, and there are some particularly attractive ones:

SUNDRIES

Hot: One oyster rolled in thin cooked bacon; one oyster on a slice of French pork sausage; a slice of bacon with a filler of anchovy crowned by an olive; toasted cheese with mustard.

Cold: A slice of raw Bayonne or Parma ham; a slice of Italian salami over a thin layer of chutney; a thin slice of Gruyère cheese over well-seasoned salad leaves; a very thin slice of cold chicken over thick curry sauce.

You can also serve cheese *tartines,* little *galettes Bretonnes,* sweet or salt, and at their best advantage all the different kinds of breads: fresh English bread for rolled ham sandwich; brown bread for *tartines* of cream cheese sprinkled with chopped olives; German bread for smoked salmon with a drop of lemon juice; and Russian pancakes, the recipe for which will be found on p. 30.

WINES FOR A DINNER-PARTY

Food alone, important as it is, should not have our undivided attention, for a good meal, to be enjoyed even more, requires well-filled glasses – well-filled glasses of well-chosen wine. We must always choose our wines in relation to the food, and it is asking for disaster not to follow this rule. Our dinner-party should be as perfect as possible.

Several arrangements of wines are possible. If we have oysters and a sweet we must, of course, have a white wine. It is fatal to our palate to have a red wine with a sweet and dangerous for our health not to have a dry white wine with oysters. So we can have:

1. A dry white wine, Chablis or Pouilly, with the oysters and the soup; a claret or a red burgundy, with the roast; a glass of champagne with the pudding. This would be the typical French combination.

2. Champagne all through the meal; it solves the problem, but is an unimaginative and expensive way.

3. A simplified solution: Serve the same white wine, champagne or still wine according to our means, at the beginning and at the end of the meal, and a good glass of red wine with the bird.

Having chosen our wines in relation to our menu and our means, we must now obey the other and equally important rule: serve them correctly.

1. All white wines slightly iced.

2. Red burgundies at the temperature of the cellar, and not warmed at all.

3. Claret warmed to the temperature of the room and no more; the wine should be put in the room in the morning for the evening. That is enough; it should never be warmed either by putting near the

fire or in hot water. The heat kills the flavour of the wine and makes the alcohol it contains overpowering. Red wines in England are nearly always served too warmed and therefore spoilt.

CAFÉ *Coffee*

There is only one way of making good French coffee, and no amount of complicated utensils will improve on it. The right proportion of coffee is a heaped up tablespoonful to a cup. Put it in the filter and pour over it the boiling water little by little. As the water goes through slowly, it is advisable to stand the coffee-pot in boiling water. It is absolutely useless to make the water go through several times, as all the goodness and colour from the coffee is extracted by the very first water which goes through. It is dangerous to stand the coffee-pot on a gas ring, as the coffee might boil and all the aroma would disappear. It takes quite a quarter of an hour to make enough coffee for four people, which, I suppose, explains why so many people do not take the trouble to do it well.

The coffee must be freshly ground and not ground too finely. If too fine it will form a kind of porous cake through which the boiling water will go without being flavoured; result – a pale weak coffee.

DRIED VEGETABLES

They are always cooked in the same way. Soak them overnight, put them in a saucepan full of cold water with one onion, a *bouquet* and salt and pepper. Bring to the boil and boil for one hour; add a glass of cold water and simmer for two to three hours. You can tell by feeling them if they are soft and cooked. They are then ready to be prepared according to recipe.

§ *Dried vegetables;* bouquet; *onion.*

A WEEK'S MENU

SHOWING HOW TO USE UP EVERYTHING

Sunday

LUNCHEON	DINNER
Soft roes omelette	Vegetable soup
Grilled cutlets	Cold roast pork périgourdine
French beans	Fried potatoes
Potatoes boulangère	Salad of peppers and cauliflowers
Cheese and fruit	Compôte of apples

SUNDRIES

Monday

LUNCHEON	DINNER
Hors d'oeuvre	Pot-au-feu
Roast pork périgourdine	Risotto with peppers
Potato purée	Roast chicken
Cheese and fruit	Green salad
	Endives au jus
	Cheese tart

Tuesday

LUNCHEON	DINNER
Mackerel maître d'hotel	Sorrel soup
Hachis parmentier	Fillets of sole
Cheese and fruit	Chicken au gratin
	Vegetable salad
	Apple fritters

Wednesday

LUNCHEON	DINNER
Poached eggs béarnaise	Fish soup
Escalopes of veal	Roast mutton
Peas à la française	Soubise sauce
Cheese and fruit	Sauté potatoes
	Purée of spinach au jus
	Chocolate mousse

Thursday

LUNCHEON	DINNER
Boiled eggs with Tomato sauce	Julienne soup
Brochette of liver	Scallops
Lyonnaise potatoes	Roast beef
Cheese and fruit	Stuffed tomatoes
	Potato fritters
	Orange soufflé

Friday

LUNCHEON	DINNER
Eggs en cocotte	Tomato cream
Cold meat	Mutton Sauce Piquante
Salade russe	Potatoes maître d'hotel
Cheese and fruit	Brussels sprouts and chestnuts
	Spaghetti au foie gras

Saturday

LUNCHEON	DINNER
Turbot au gratin	St Germain soup
Sauté of beef	Sole au vin blanc
Chicory purée	Veal chop with cream sauce
Cheese and fruit	Soufflé potatoes
	Salad of tomatoes and beetroot
	Rum omelette

It will be noted that there are only three joints (pork, mutton, beef) and one chicken during the week. Now, if we look at the menus on the first day, we will see that:

The soup on Sunday evening is made with the bone out of the roast pork.

The roast pork is served again for Monday luncheon.

The hors d'oeuvre at that meal is made of the vegetable and bits of meat out of the soup, nicely arranged as a salad.

There was enough left in the tin of red peppers opened on Sunday evening for the salad to make the *risotto* for Monday dinner.

The *hachis parmentier* for Tuesday luncheon is made with the scraps of the roast pork and the boiled beef from Monday evening soup.

The main dish for Tuesday evening is made with what is left of the chicken arranged with potatoes *au gratin*.

The menus are completed by eggs, fish and small pieces of meat, according to requirements. We now reach Wednesday evening, when we have roast mutton, and Thursday, when we have roast beef. We will keep the best slices of both for a dish of mixed cold meat for Friday luncheon; the mutton will appear once more for Friday dinner,

SUNDRIES

prepared with a *Sauce piquante;* and the beef on Saturday for luncheon *sauté* with onions. So that the week, in spite of certain other dishes, the possible (or impossible) price of eggs, and the quantity of butter used to cook the dishes perfectly, will be considerably cheaper than if more meat had been used and the vegetables cooked only in water.

Descriptive Index

BASIC PREPARATIONS
Basting, 2
Batter, 10–11, 213–14
'Binding', 6
Boiling, 5
Bouquet, xi, 12
Braising, 4
Court-Bouillon, xi, 5, 8
Frying, 3
Fumet, 8–9
Gravy, 7
Grilling, 3
Liaisons, 6
Pastry, Puff, 11
Pastry, Shortcrust, 11
Roasting, 2
Roux, xi, 6, 9

SAUCES
Alsatian, 22
Béarnaise, 17
Béchamel, 9
Black Butter, 15
Bordelaise, 22
Brown, 10
Caper, 21
Celery, 19
Cranberry, 23
Curry, 17
Devil, 20
Fennel, 20
Grand Veneur, 23
Green, 19
Hollandaise, 17
Horseradish, 19
Italian, with Crushed Walnuts, 21
Landaise, 20
Maître d'Hôtel, 15
Mayonnaise, 18
Meat, 21

Mornay, 16
Mousseline, 18
Mustard, 18
Pepper, 22
Périgueux, 115
Piquante Sauce, 22
Poulette, 17
Ravigote, 24
Rémoulade, 24
Sabayon, 25
Saffron, 22
Soubise, 22
Tartar, 19
Tomato, 21
Velouté, 10
Vinaigrette, 23
White Butter, 16
White Wine, 24

HORS D'OEUVRES AND SAVOURIES
Anchovies, Grilled, 27
Anchovy Fritters, 220
Anchovy, Savoury, 27
Artichoke Hearts, Salad of, 31
Asparagus on Croûtons, 32
Cheese and Asparagus Savoury, 221
Eggs, Hard-Boiled, with Mushrooms, 219
Eggs Stuffed with Mushrooms, 32
Ham on Toast, 220
Mushroom Fritters, 221
Mussels with Saffron, 29
Pancakes, Russian, 30
Roes à la Grecque, 30
Rollmops, 28
Shrimp Fritters, 220
Shrimps, Potted, 28

SOUPS
Asparagus, Cream of, 42
Bean Soup, 38

[235]

Bouillabaisse, 44
Bourride Arcachonnaise (fish soup), 46
Cabbage Soup, 41
Carrot Soup, 39
Chestnut Soup, 39
Clear Soup, 7
Clear Soup with Vegetables and Toasted Bread, 35
Clear Tomato Soup, 42
Consommé, Cold, 35
Crab Soup, 47
Crayfish Soup, 46
Cucumber Soup, 36
Fish Bouillon, 47
Game Soup 36,
Garbure (Vegetable and Pork Soup), 40
Germiny, Soup, 36
Herb Soup without Meat, 39
Julienne Soup, 43
Leek Soup, 43
Lentil Soup, 40
Minestrone, 43
Mussel Soup, 46
Onion Soup, 44
Oyster Soup, 48
Pea Soup, 40
Polish Sorrel Soup, 37
Potato Soup, 41
Printanier, Soup, 38
Red Bean Soup, 44
Sorrel Soup, 37
Spinach Soup, 37
Tomato, Cream of, 42
Velours, Soup, 44
Vendanges, Soup, 35
Watercress Soup, 43

FISH

Carp, Stuffed, 72
Cod, Fillets of, Marinated, 72
Cod, Salt, à la Vizcaina, 72
Crayfish Bretonne, 78
Eels Bourguignonne, 74
Eels, Stewed, in Claret, 74
Fish, Grilled, 60
Fish Soufflés, Small, 75

Herrings, Devilled, 73
Herrings, Grilled, 73
Herrings Maître d'Hôtel, 73
Herrings, Marinated, 73
Lobster à l'Américaine, 76
Lobster in Cream with Brandy and Sherry, 75
Lobster Pancakes with Mushroom and Tomato Sauce, 76
Lobster Stew, 77
Lobster Thermidor, 77
Mackerel, Baked, 69
Mackerel Bretonne, 69
Mackerel Maître d'Hôtel, 69
Mussels Béchamel, 79
Mussels Marinière, 79
Mussel Pilaff, 29
Mussels Poulette, 79
Mussels Sautéed, 80
Oysters Bordelaise, 29
Oysters au Gratin, 78
Red Mullet with Cream, 71
Red Mullet with Fennel, 71
Red Mullet, Grilled, 70
Red Mullets Marseillaise, 70
Red Mullet Riviera, 70
Salmon, Baked, Horseradish Sauce, 64
Salmon Bretonne, 64
Salmon, Escallops of, Volga, 64
Salmon Papillotes, 64
Salmon, Terrine of, 65
Salmon Trout Belle-Vue, 68
Salmon Trout with Cream, 67
Scallops, 78
Smelts, Baked, 73
Soles, Baked, 63
Sole, Fillets of, Bonne Femme, 60
Sole, Fillets of, Cream Sauce, 61
Sole, Fillets of, Dorothea, 62
Sole Matelotte, 63
Sole Normande, 62
Sole in White Wine, 63
Trout à l'Auvergnate, 65
Trout Grenobloise, 66
Trout, Stuffed, Bourguignonne, 66
Trout in White Wine, 66
Turbot, Baked, 69
Turbot au Gratin, 69

INDEX

MEAT DISHES

Beef
Bœuf Bouilli Sauté (beef fried with onions), 86
Bœuf Braisé aux Petits Pois (beef braised with peas), 86
Bœuf en Daube (beef braised in slices with pork mincemeat), 85
Bœuf Farci (beef stuffed with pork mincemeat), 84
Bœuf à la Mode (beef simmered in claret), 86
Bœuf Provençale (beef braised in white wine, with olives), 84
Entrecôte Béarnaise (grilled beef steak, Béarnaise Sauce), 84
Entrecôte au Beurre d'Anchois (grilled beef steak, Anchovy Butter), 84
Entrecôte Bordelaise (grilled beef steak with marrow and sauce), 83
Entrecôte Maître d'Hotel (grilled beef steak, Maître d'Hotel Sauce), 84
Filet de Bœuf Rôti (roast beef fillet), 86
Filet de Bœuf à la Russe (fried beef fillet, cream sauce), 83
Langue à l'Italienne (beef tongue boiled in white wine and consommé), 107
Langue Savoyarde (beef tongue, salted and spiced, then boiled), 108
Petits Filets de Bœuf Grillés (grilled beef fillets, cream and horseradish sauce), 83
Ragoût de Bœuf (beef stewed with pork or bacon in wine or stock), 87
Tournedos au Foie Gras (fried beef fillet, foie gras, with White Wine Sauce), 82
Tournedos Sauce Madère (fried steak fillets, Madeira Sauce), 82
Tournedos Sautés (fried steak fillets), 81

Ham
Jambon Persillé Bourguignonne (ham simmered in white Burgundy, then boned and mashed, and covered with stock and white Burgundy with chopped parsley), 102
Mousse de Jambon (ham pounded, mixed with Béchamel Sauce, gelatine and whipped cream), 102

Lamb and Mutton
Agneau Jardinière (lamb simmered with vegetables and white wine, served with cream sauce), 98
Agneau Rôti Béarnaise (lamb roasted, served with Béarnaise sauce), 94
Agneau Rôti Gratiné (lamb roasted, coated with breadcrumbs, parsley and garlic), 95
Agneau Rôti à l'Orange (lamb roasted, gravy with orange juice), 97
Agneau Rôti Piémontaise (lamb roasted, then coated with mushrooms, cream and cheese), 96
Agneau Rôti Princesse (lamb roasted, served with asparagus tips in sauce), 96
Agneau Rôti Provençale (lamb larded with anchovy fillets, roasted, served with onion and anchovy sauce), 95
Côtelettes d'Agneau Normande (lamb cutlets fried in breadcrumbs, served with onion purée), 99
Émincés de Mouton Sauce Piquante (cold mutton warmed in butter, served with Sauce Piquante), 99
Galimafrée (pieces of lamb larded, fried and flambé, then cooked with mushrooms, and served with chestnuts and sauce), 98
Gigot d'Agneau aux Pointes d'Asperges (leg of lamb braised, sauce with asparagus tips), 97
Gigot de Mouton Rôti (leg of mutton roasted with garlic), 99
Kebabs (lamb and bacon pieces grilled on skewers), 108
Navarin Printanier (pieces of mutton or lamb simmered with potatoes and onions, tomatoes and carrots optional), 100
Rognons d'Agneau en Brochettes (lamb's kidneys grilled on skewers, served with Maître d'Hôtel Sauce), 105

Rognons d'Agneau Sautés au Vin Blanc (lamb's kidneys sliced and fried, then cooked in white wine), 105

Selle d'Agneau Farcie (saddle of lamb, served with onion and mushroom stuffing), 97

Selle d'Agneau Marinée (marinated saddle of lamb roasted, marinade reduced for sauce), 97

Pork

Cassoulet (pork cooked in tomato purée with white haricot beans, with breadcrumbs added and browned), 101

Côtelettes de Porc Nontronnaise (pork chops fried with breadcrumbs), 101

Porc Rôti Périgourdine (leg or fillet of pork, boned and rolled, baked slowly), 100

Veal

Blanquette de Veau (veal stew with sauce and mushrooms), 89

Brochettes de Veau (veal, liver and bacon pieces grilled on skewers), 108

Côtelettes de Veau à la Crème (veal chops with cream), 90

Côtelettes de Veau Gratinées (veal chops baked with cheese), 90

Côtelettes de Veau en Papillotes (veal chops grilled or baked in paper), 91

Escalopes de Veau Chasseur (veal escallops, fried, with mushrooms and tomatoes), 93

Escalopes de Veau aux Concombres (veal escallops, fried, with cream sauce and boiled cucumber), 92

Escalopes de Veau à la Crème (veal escallops fried, flambé, and baked in cream), 91

Escalopes de Veau aux Olives (veal escallops, cooked with olives), 94

Escalopes de Veau Persillées (veal escallops coated in breadcrumbs and parsley, and fried), 91

Escalopes de Veau Sautées (veal escallops fried, then simmered in gravy), 91

Escalopes de Veau Viennoise (veal escallops, fried, served with lemon and butter), 93

Escalopes de Veau Villageoise (veal escallops, fried, served on spinach with tomato sauce), 92

Foie de Veau Braisé (calf's liver larded and braised), 103

Foie de Veau Flamande (calf's liver fried then cooked in white wine), 103

Foie de Veau Sauté (calf's liver fried then baked with bacon and parsley seasoning), 103

Langue de Veau Sauce Piquante (calf's tongue braised in consommé, sliced, and served with Sauce Piquante), 107

Longe de Veau Basquaise (veal loin, with peppers, aubergines and tomatoes), 90

Ris de Veau Braisé (sweetbread braised and served with gravy or cream), 106

Rognons de Veau Flambés (veal kidney fried then sliced and flambéd, mustard and cream added), 104

Rognon de Veau Liegeoise (veal kidney fried then cooked in white wine, with juniper berries and lemon), 104

Rognons de Veau Sautés (veal kidney, fried and sliced, simmered in sauce of bacon, mushrooms, stock, tomato purée and sherry), 104

Tête de Veau Vinaigrette (calf's head boiled in court-bouillon, served with Vinaigrette Sauce), 107

Veau Bretonne (fillet veal, roasted, with grated cheese), 89

Veau Farci Braisé (veal, stuffed with sausage meat, braised), 88

Veau aux Fines Herbes (veal roasted in buttered paper, gravy with *fines herbes*), 87

Veau Niçoise (veal fillet with aubergines and tomatoes), 88

Veau Olives Provençale (veal escallops with pork stuffing, fried, then cooked in Madeira or sherry sauce), 94

Miscellaneous

Cervelles au Beurre Noir (brains boiled and served with Beurre Noir Sauce), 107

INDEX

Cervelles au Four (calf's or sheep's brains, boiled and then baked with breadcrumbs, ham and gherkins), 106
Croquettes (minced cold meat with potatoes and onions, fried), 108
Hachis Parmentier (onions and cold meat fried, then covered with potato purée and browned), 109

POULTRY AND GAME
Chicken Albufera, 117
Chicken Béarnaise, 113
Chicken Biscayenne, 113
Chicken au Gratin, 115
Chicken, Legs of, Grilled, 117
Chicken Livers, Grilled, 118
Chicken Lyonnaise, 114
Chicken Portuguese, 112
Chicken, Roast, 110
Chicken Sauté with Burgundy, 112
Chicken Sauté with Capers, 111
Chicken Sauté with Cream, 111
Chicken Sauté Marengo, 113
Chicken, Spring, Polonaise, 117
Chicken Suprême with Cream Sauce, 115
Chicken Suprêmes Smitane, 116
Chicken, Suprêmes of, Strasbourgeoise, 116
Coq-en-Pâte, Sauce Périgueux, 115
Duck, Braised, with Turnips, 122
Duck, Ragoût of, 123
Duck, Roast, with Olives, 123
Duck, Wild, with Bitter Oranges, 123
Duck, Wild, with Port, 124
Game, Ragoût of, 130
Goose, Preserved, 136
Goose, Stuffed, Landaise, 119
Hare, Fricassée of, Limousine, 132
Hare, Jugged, 131
Hare, Saddle of, Alsacienne, 132
Partridge à l'Anglaise, 125
Partridge, Fillets of, with Bitter Oranges, 126
Partridge, Poached, 125
Partridge à la Russe, 125
Pheasant with Apples, 127
Pheasant in Cream, 127
Pheasant Croquettes, 127

Pheasant, Stuffed, 126
Quail with Grapes, 128
Quail, Ragoût of, 129
Quail, Stuffed, 128
Rabbit à la Flamande, 133
Rabbit Pie, 134
Rabbit, Sautéed, 133
Rabbit, Young, Purée of, 133
Turkey Croquettes, 122
Turkey, Roast Stuffed, 119
Turkey with Truffles, 121
Venison, 130
Venison, Fillets of, Sautéed, 131
Woodcock Flambée, 129

RICE DISHES
Curry, 183
Curry, Maltese, 183
Paella, 182
Pilaff, 180
Pilaff, Mussel, 29
Rice with Peppers, 182

EGG DISHES
Belgian Eggs, 57
Eggs in Aspic, 59
Eggs with Cheese, 57
Eggs en Cocotte, 55
Eggs, Devilled, 58
Eggs, Hard-Boiled, 58
Eggs Landaise, 56
Eggs, Poached, 54
Eggs, Poached, Béarnaise, 55
Eggs, Scrambled, 55
Eggs, Scrambled, with Cheese, 56
Eggs, Scrambled, with Lobster, 56
Eggs, Scrambled, with Mushrooms, 56
Eggs, Scrambled, with Saffron, 56
Eggs, Scrambled, with Truffles, 56
Eggs, Stuffed, 59
Eggs, Stuffed, with Foie Gras, 58
Omelette, Cheese, 52
Omelette, Chicken Liver, 53
Omelette, Crab, 53
Omelette, Cream, 54
Omelette, Genoese, 55
Omelette, Ham, 51
Omelette with Mixed Herbs, 51

Omelette, Mushroom, 52
Omelette Niçoise, 53
Omelette, Onion, 51
Omelette, Potato, 52
Omelette, Salsify Flower, 52
Omelette, Sorrel, 52
Omelette, Spanish, 54
Pipérade, 57

CHEESE DISHES
Cheese Tart, 222
Cream Lorraine, 221
Croque Monsieur, 221
Fondue, 222

PÂTÉS AND PICKLED MEATS
Galantine, 137
Pâté de Foie, 138
Pâté de Foie Gras, 138
Pâté de Volaille, 137
Pork, Pickled, 135
Pork, Potted, 136, 137
Terrine de Gibier, 139

VEGETABLES
Artichokes à la Barigoule, 141
Artichoke Bottoms Florestan, 142
Artichokes à l'Italienne, 141
Artichokes Véronèse, 142
Artichokes Vinaigrette, 141
Asparagus with Cheese, 143
Asparagus Fritters, 143
Asparagus Maltaise, 143
Aubergine, Baked, 144
Aubergine Boucalaise, 146
Aubergine à l'Italienne, 145
Aubergine Napolitaine, 146
Aubergine, Souffléed, 146
Aubergine, Stuffed, 144
Aubergine à la Turque, 145
Beans, Broad, 157
Beans, Broad, with Bacon, 157
Beans, Broad, Purée of, 157
Beans, Mixed, 156
Beans, Red Haricot, Bourguignonne, 156
Beans, String, 154
Beans, String, Béarnaise, 155
Beans, String, with Cream, 155
Beans, String, à la Landaise, 155

Beans, White, 156
Beets, Fricassée of, 153
Brussels Sprouts à l'Italienne, 149
Brussels Sprouts Mornay, 150
Brussels Sprouts, Sautéed, 150

Cabbage, Green, 147
Cabbage, Green, Vendéenne, 147
Cabbage, Red, Danish, 148
Cabbage, Red, Flamande, 148
Cabbage, Red, Tyrolienne, 149
Cabbage, Stuffed, 147
Cabbage, Stuffed, à la Russe, 148
Cabbage Surprise, 147
Carrots with Cream, 152
Carrots, Fried, 153
Carrots, New, à la Poulette, 152
Carrots, Sautéed, 151
Carrots Vichy, 152
Cauliflower, Fried, 150
Cauliflower with Mint, 151
Cauliflower Polonaise, 150
Celery with Cheese, 162
Celery Croquettes, 163
Celery with Gravy, 162
Cèpes Bordelaise, 168
Cèpes à la Monselet, 169
Cèpes, Stuffed, 168
Chestnuts, Purée of, 170
Chestnuts, Steamed, 170
Chicory with Gravy, 161
Chicory, Purée of, 161
Cucumbers with Cream, 164
Cucumbers with Gravy, 163
Cucumbers, Stuffed, 164
Endive, 160
Endive Flamande, 160
Endives with Gravy, 161
Endive Meunière, 160
Endive Milanaise, 160
Endive Mornay, 160
Fennel, 159
Leeks, Chopped, 158
Lettuce, Baked, 161
Lettuce with Gravy, 161
Lettuce Mousse, 162
Marrows, Baby, with Butter, 165
Marrow, Stuffed, 164

INDEX

Mushrooms, Baked, 166
Mushrooms with Cheese, 167
Mushrooms with Cream, 165
Mushrooms, Grilled, 167
Mushrooms, Purée of, 168
Mushrooms Stuffed with Fish, 167
Mushrooms with White Wine, 165
Onions with Cream, 167
Onions, Purée of, 166
Peas with Bacon, 153
Peas à l'Étouffée, 154
Peas, French, 154
Peas, Purée of, 153
Peas and String Beans, 154
Peppers, Stuffed, 182
Potatoes Anna, 178
Potatoes Armoricaine, 176
Potatoes Boulangère, 180
Potato Cake, 176
Potatoes with Cheese, 175
Potato Croquettes with Cheese, 177
Potatoes Duchesse, 175
Potatoes, Fried, 172
Potatoes, Fried, with Artichoke Bottoms, 173
Potatoes, Fried, Paysanne, 172
Potato Fritters, 176
Potatoes, Gratin, 174
Potatoes Limousine, 178
Potatoes, Lyonnaise, 179
Potatoes, New, Maître d'Hôtel, 180
Potatoes and Onions, Purée of, 180
Potato Pancakes, 176
Potatoes Parisienne, 177
Potatoes, Purée of, 174
Potatoes, Purée of, Soufflé, 174
Potatoes Rissolées, 173
Potatoes Rissolées with Mint, 173
Potatoes, Sauté, 173
Potatoes, Savoury, 180
Potatoes Savoyarde, 178
Potatoes Sicilienne, 174
Potatoes, Souffléed, 179
Potatoes, Straw, 173
Potatoes, Stuffed, 175
Potatoes Vosgienne, 177
Pumpkin with Cheese and Bacon, 170
Pumpkin Soufflé, 171

Sorrel with Gravy, 158
Sorrel, Purée of, 158
Spinach à la Bourgeoise, 159
Spinach with Cheese, 158
Spinach Florentine, 159
Spinach with Gravy, 157
Tomatoes, Stuffed, 165
Truffles with Bacon, 170
Truffles in Sherry, 169
Turnips, Braised, 151
Turnips, Purée of, 151
Turnip Tops, 151
Vegetables, Dried, 230

SALADS

Bacon and Dandelion, 187
Beef with Herrings, 192
Carmen, 188
Cauliflower, 189
Chicken, 193
Cucumber, 31
Dandelion and Beet, 188
Egg and Potato, 31
Endive and Beet, 188
Fish, 193
Flamand, 191
Goncourt, 191
Green, 186
Half-Mourning, 190
Leek, 192
Lobster, 193
Meadow, 189
Mushroom, 191
New World, 189
Parisian, 192
Peppers and Cauliflower, 189
Potato, with Anchovies, 191
Russian, 189
Tomatoes and Beetroot, 190
Tomato and Sweet Pepper, 32
Tuna Fish and Celery, 28
Vegetable, 190
Watercress, 187
Winter, 191

SWEETS

Apples Balbec, 196
Apples with Butter, 196

Apples, Compote of, 197
Apples, Compote of, with Caramel, 197
Apples, Compote of, with Chestnuts, 197
Apples, Compote of, with Pineapple, 198
Apples Flambé, 195
Apples, Fried, 196
Apples Normande, 196
Apple Soufflé, 211
Bananas Créole, 201
Bananas with Raspberries, 202
Bananas with Rum, 201
Bananas, Souffléed, 202
Brioche, 217
Chestnut Cream, 212
Chestnuts, Purée of, with Whipped Cream, 212
Chocolate Mousse, 212
Chocolate Soufflé, 211
Coffee Cream, 207
Cream Filling, 206
Cream, Fried, 207
Creamed Rice, 209
Crème Brulée, 208
Crêpes Suzette, 215
Crêpes Verlaine, 216
Diplomate (sponge fingers with candied fruit) with Custard, 218
Diplomate with Fruit (fresh), 218
Egg Custard à la Reine, 212
Figs, Baked, 205
Figs, Fresh, with Cream, 205
Figs, Fresh, Flambé, 205
Fruit with Brioche, 216
Fruit Fritters, 206
Gâteau Petit Duc, 217
Melon, Compote of, 204
Melon, Iced, 205
Melon Surprise, 205
Omelette, Sweet, with Rum, 213
Oranges with Rum, 204
Orange Soufflé, 211
Pancakes, French, 213
Pancakes, French, Normande, 216
Pancakes, French, with Nuts, 216
Peaches Barbara, 200
Peaches Marie Louise, 199
Peaches in Syrup, 199
Pears, Baked, 198

Pears with Chocolate Sauce, 199
Pears Dijonnaise, 198
Pears Flambéed, 198
Pineapple, Chilled, 201
Pineapple with Fruit, 200
Pineapple with Grapefruit, 200
Pineapple with Whipped Cream, 201
Prunes, Stewed, with Claret or Port, 206
Quince, Compote of, 206
Raspberry Soufflé, 211
Snow Apples, 197
Spanish Milk Pudding, 209
Strawberries with Almonds, 203
Strawberries Créole, 203
Strawberries with Orange Juice, 204
Strawberries Romanoff, 202
Strawberries with Whipped Cream and Kirsch, 203
Strawberries with Wine, 202
Strawberries Xenia, 203

CAKES
Almond Cake, 223
Apple Cake, 224
Brittany Tarts, 223
Cat's Tongues, 224
Cherry Cake Limousin, 223
Macaroons, 224

JAMS
Banana Jam, 225
Crab-Apple Jelly, 225
Grapefruit Marmalade, 226
Marrow Jam, 226
Pear Jam, 225
Pumpkin Jam, 226
Quince Jelly, 227
Tomato Jam, 227

MISCELLANEOUS
Anchovy Butter, 25, 119
Black Butter, 15
Butter, Meunière, 15
Canapés, 228
Canapés Diane, 220
Canapés Ivanhoe, 220
Chestnut Stuffing, 170

INDEX

Coffee, 230
Cream Seasoning, 185
Egg Seasoning, 185
French Dressing, 185
Maître d'Hôtel Butter, 15

Sardine Butter, 29
Sausage Meat, 120
Seasonings, Salad, 185
Spaghetti with Foie Gras, 184
Wines, 229

Alphabetical Index

Agneau, Côtelettes d', Normande, 99
Agneau, Gigot d', aux Pointes d'Asperges, 97
Agneau Jardinière, 98
Agneau Rôti Béarnaise, 94
Agneau Rôti Gratiné, 95
Agneau Rôti à l'Orange, 97
Agneau Rôti Piémontaise, 96
Agneau Rôti Princesse, 96
Agneau Rôti Provençale, 95
Agneau, Selle d', Farcie, 97
Agneau, Selle d', Marinée, 97
Almond Cake, 223
Alsatian Sauce, 22
Ananas Glacé, 201
Anchoiade, 27
Anchois, Beurre d', 25
Anchois, Croûtes aux, 220
Anchovy Butter, 25, 119
Anchovy Fritters, 220
Anchovies, Grilled, 27
Anchovy, Savoury, 27
Anguilles Bourguignonnes, 74
APICIUS, CAELIUS, 195
Apples Balbec, 196
Apples with Butter, 196
Apple Cake, 224
Apples, Compote of, 197
Apples, Compote of, with Caramel, 197
Apples, Compote of, with Chestnuts, 197
Apples, Compote of, with Pineapple, 198
Apples Flambé, 195
Apples, Fried, 196
Apples Normande, 196
Apple Soufflé, 211
Artichauts à la Barigoule, 141
Artichauts à l'Italienne, 141
Artichauts Véronèse, 142
Artichaut Vinaigrette, 141
Artichokes à la Barigoule, 141
Artichoke Bottoms Florestan, 142

Artichoke Hearts, Salad of, 31
Artichokes à l'Italienne, 141
Artichokes Véronèse, 142
Artichokes Vinaigrette, 141
ASPARAGUS, 143
Asparagus with Cheese, 143
Asparagus on Croûtons, 32
Asparagus Fritters, 143
Asparagus Maltaise, 143
Asperge, Beignets d', 143
Asperges, Croûtes aux, 32
Asperges Gratinées, 143
Asperges Maltaise, 143
ASPHODELS, 143
Assaisonnements de Salade, 185
AUBERGINES, 144
Aubergine, Baked, 144
Aubergines Boucalaise, 146
Aubergines Farcies, 144
Aubergines au Four, 144
Aubergines à l'Italienne, 145
Aubergines Napolitaine, 146
Aubergines Soufflées, 146
Aubergine, Stuffed, 144
Aubergines à la Turque, 145

Bacalao à la Vizcaina, 72
Bacon and Dandelion Salad, 187
Bananas Créole, 201
Banana Jam, 225
Bananas with Raspberries, 202
Bananas with Rum, 201
Bananas, Souffléed, 202
Bananes, Confiture de, 225
Bananes Créole, 201
Bananes aux Framboises, 202
Bananes au Rhum, 201
Bananes Soufflées, 202
BASTING, 2
Batter, 10-11, 213-14

INDEX

Beans, Broad, 157
Beans, Broad, with Bacon, 157
Beans, Broad, Purée of, 157
Beans, Mixed, 156
Beans, Red Haricot, Bourguignonne, 156
Bean Soup, 38
Beans, String, 154
Beans, String, Béarnaise, 155
Beans, String, with Cream, 155
Beans, String, à la Landaise, 155
Beans, White, 156
Béarnaise Sauce, 17
Bécasse Flambée, 129
Béchamel Sauce, 9
BEEF, 2, 81–7
Beef, Braised, 85
Beef, Braised, with Green Peas, 86
Beef Braised, with White Wine and Olives, 84
Beef, Fillet of, Roast, 86
Beef, Fillet of, à la Russe, 83
Beef à la Mode, 86
Beef, Ragoût of, 87
Beef Salad with Herrings, 192
Beef, Sauté of, 86
Beef, Small Fillets of, with Foie Gras, 82
Beef, Small Fillets of, Grilled, 83
Beef, Small Fillets of, Madeira Sauce, 82
Beef, Small Fillets of, Sautéed, 81
Beef, Stuffed, 84
Beets, Fricassée of, 153
Beignets d'Asperge, 143
Beignets de Crevettes, 220
Beignets de Fruits, 206
Beignets de Pommes de Terre, 176
Belgian Eggs, 57
Beurre d'Anchois, 25
Beurre Fondu, 14
Beurre Maître d'Hôtel, 15
Beurre Meunière, 15
Beurre Noir, 15
Beurre de Sardines, 29
'BINDING', 6
Black Butter, 15
Black Butter Sauce, 15
Blanquette de Veau, 89
Bœuf Bouilli Sauté, 86
Bœuf Braisé aux Petits Pois, 86

Bœuf en Daube, 85
Bœuf Farci, 84
Bœuf, Filet de, Rôti, 86
Bœuf, Filet de, à la Russe, 83
Bœuf à la Mode, 86
Bœuf Provençale, 84
BOILING, 5
Bordelaise Sauce, 22
Bouillabaisse, 44
Bouillon de Poisson, 47
Bouquet, xi, 12
Bourride Arcachonnaise, 46
Brains, 106
Brains, Baked, 106
Braised Beef, 85
Braised Beef with Green Peas, 86
Braised Stuffed Veal, 88
BRAISING, 4
Breton Fish Soup, 45
Brioche, 217
Brittany Tarts, 223
Brochettes de Foies de Volaille, 118
Brochettes de Veau, 108
Brown Sauces, 10
Brussels Sprouts à l'Italienne, 149
Brussels Sprouts Mornay, 150
Brussels Sprouts, Sautéed, 150
Butter, Melted, 14
Butter, Meunière, 15

Cabbage, Green, 147
Cabbage, Green, Vendéenne, 147
Cabbage, Red, Danish, 148
Cabbage, Red, Flamande, 148
Cabbage, Red, Tyrolienne, 149
Cabbage Soup, 41
Cabbage, Stuffed, 147
Cabbage, Stuffed, à la Russe, 148
Cabbage Surprise, 147
Cabillaud, Filets de, Marinés, 72
Café, 230
Cailles Fourrées, 128
Cailles en Ragoût, 129
Cailles aux Raisins, 128
CAKES, 223–4
Calf's Head, 107
Calf's Liver, Braised, 103
Calf's Liver Flamande, 103

[245]

Calf's Liver Sautéed, 103
Calf's Tongue, Braised, 107
CAMBRIDGE, 208
Canapés, 228
Canapés Diane, 220
Canapés Ivanhoe, 220
Canard Braisé aux Navets, 122
Canard aux Olives, 123
Canard Sauvage aux Bigarades, 123
Canard Sauvage au Porto, 124
Caper Sauce, 21
Cari, 183
Cari Maltaise, 183
Carottes à la Crème, 152
Carottes Frites, 153
Carottes Nouvelles à la Poulette, 152
Carottes Sautées, 151
Carottes Vichy, 152
Carpe Farcie, 72
Carp, Stuffed, 72
Carrots with Cream, 152
Carrots, Fried, 153
Carrots, New, à la Poulette, 152
Carrots, Sautéed, 151
Carrot Soup, 39
Carrots Vichy, 152
Cassoulet, 101
Cat's Tongues, 224
Cauliflower, Fried, 150
Cauliflower with Mint, 151
Cauliflower Polonaise, 150
Cauliflower Salad, 189
Céleri, 162
Céleri Gratiné, 162
Céleri au Jus, 162
Celery with Cheese, 162
Celery Croquettes, 163
Celery with Gravy, 162
Celery Sauce, 19
Cèpes Bordelaise, 168
Cèpes Farcis, 168
Cèpes à la Monselet, 169
Cèpes, Stuffed, 168
Cervelles au Beurre Noir, 106
Cervelles au Four, 106
Champignons à la Crème, 165
Champignons, Croûtes aux, 221
Champignons Farcis au Poisson, 167

Champignons au Four, 166
Champignons, Gratin de, 167
Champignons Grillés, 167
Champignons, Purée de, 168
Champignons au Vin Blanc, 165
Cheese and Asparagus Savoury, 221
CHEESE DISHES, 221–2
Cheese Omelette, 52
Cheese Tart, 222
Cherry Cake Limousin, 223
CHESTNUTS, 121
Chestnut Cream, 212
Chestnuts, Purée of, 170
Chestnuts, Purée of, with Whipped Cream, 212
Chestnut Soup, 39
Chestnuts, Steamed, 170
Chestnut Stuffing, 170
Chevreuil, 130
Chevreuil, Filets de, Sautés, 131
Chicken Albufera, 117
Chicken Béarnaise, 113
Chicken Biscayenne, 113
Chicken au Gratin, 115
Chicken, Grilled Legs of, 117
Chicken Livers, Grilled, 118
Chicken Liver Omelette, 53
Chicken Lyonnaise, 114
Chicken, Pâté of, 137
Chicken Polonaise, Spring, 117
Chicken Portuguese, 112
Chicken, Roast, 110
Chicken Salad, 193
Chicken Sauté with Burgundy, 112
Chicken Sauté with Capers, 111
Chicken Sauté with Cream, 111
Chicken Sauté Marengo, 113
Chicken Suprême with Cream Sauce, 115
Chicorée au Jus, 161
Chicorée, Purée de, 161
Chicory with Gravy, 161
Chicory, Purée of, 161
CHINESE CUISINE, 68
Chocolate Mousse, 212
Chocolate Soufflé, 211
CHOICE OF DISHES, 32–3
Choux de Bruxelles à l'Italienne, 149
Choux de Bruxelles Mornay, 150

INDEX

Choux de Bruxelles Sautés, 150
Chou Farci, 147
Chou Farci à la Russe, 148
Choux-Fleurs Frits, 150
Chou-Fleur à la Menthe, 151
Chou-Fleur Polonaise, 150
Chou Rouge Danoise, 148
Chou Rouge Flamande, 148
Chou Rouge à la Tyrolienne, 149
Chou Surprise, 147
Chou Vert, 147
Chou Vert Vendéenne, 147
Ciboure, Purée de, 38
Citrouille, Confiture de, 226
Civet d'Homard, 77
Civet de Lièvre, 131
Civet de Lièvre Limousine, 132
Clafoutis, 223
CLASSIFICATION OF SALADS AND HORS D'OEUVRES, 193
Clear Soup, 7
Clear Soup with Vegetables and Toasted Bread, 35
Clear Tomato Soup, 42
COCKTAILS, 228
Cod, Marinated Fillets of, 72
Cod, Salt, à la Vizcaina, 72
Coffee, 230
Coffee Cream, 207
Compote of Apples, 197
Compote of Apples with Caramel, 197
Compote of Apples with Chestnuts, 197
Compote of Apples with Pineapple, 198
Compote de Coing, 206
Compote de Melon, 204
Compote d'Oranges, 204
Compote de Pommes, 197
Compote de Pommes à l'Ananas, 198
Compote de Pommes au Caramel, 197
Compote de Pommes au Marrons, 197
Compote of Quince, 206
Compounded Butters, 15, 25
Concombres, 163
Concombres à la Crème, 164
Concombres Farcis, 164
Concombres au Jus, 163
Confits d'Oie, 136
Confiture de Bananes, 225

Confiture de Citrouille, 226
Confiture de Courges, 226
Confiture de Pamplemousse, 226
Confiture de Poires, 225
Confiture de Tomates, 227
Consommé, xi, 7
Consommé à la Chiffonade, 35
Consommé, Cold, 35
Consommé Froid, 35
Consommé aux Huîtres, 48
Coq-en-Pâte, Sauce Périgueux, 115
Coquilles St Jacques, 78
Côtelettes d'Agneau Normande, 99
Côtelettes de Porc Nontronnaise, 101
Côtelettes de Veau à la Crème, 90
Côtelettes de Veau Gratinées, 90
Côtelettes de Veau en Papillotes, 91
Courges, Confiture de, 226
Courges Farcies, 164
Courgettes au Beurre, 165
Court-Bouillon, xi, 5, 8
Crab-Apple Jelly, 225
Crab Omelette, 53
Crab Soup, 47
Cranberry Sauce, 23
CRAYFISH, 75
Crayfish Bretonne, 78
Crayfish Soup, 46
Cream of Asparagus, 42
Cream Filling, 206
Cream, Fried, 207
Cream Lorraine, 221
Cream Omelette, 54
Creamed Rice, 209
Cream Seasoning, 185
Cream of Tomato, 42
Crème à l'Ananas, 201
Crème d'Asperges, 42
Crème Brulée, 208–9
Crème au Café, 207
Crème aux Épinards, 37
Crème Frite, 207
Crème Lorraine, 221
Crème de Marrons, 212
Crème Patissière, 206
Crème de Pois Verts, 40
Crème de Riz, 209
Crème aux Tomates, 42

CRÊPES, 213
Crêpes d'Homard, 76
Crêpes aux Noix, 216
Crêpes Normande, 216
Crêpes de Pommes de Terre, 176
Crêpes Suzette, 215
CRÊPES SUZETTE, ORIGIN OF, 214
Crêpes Verlaine, 215, 216
Crevettes, Beignets de 220
Crevettes en Terrine, 28
Croque Monsieur, 221
Croquettes, 108
Croquettes de Céleri, 163
Croquettes de Dinde, 122
Croquettes de Faisan, 127
Croquettes de Pommes de Terre au Fromage 177
Croûtes aux Anchois, 220
Croûtes aux Asperges, 32
Croûtes aux Champignons, 221
Croûte aux Fruits, 216
Croûtes au Jambon, 220
Croûte Parmesane, 221
Croûte-au-Pot, 35
CUCUMBERS, 163
Cucumbers with Cream, 164
Cucumbers with Gravy, 163
Cucumber Salad, 31
Cucumber Soup, 36
Cucumbers, Stuffed, 164
Curry, 183
Curry, Maltese, 184
Curry Sauce, 17

'DAINTINESS', 25
Dandelion and Beet Salad, 188
Devilled Eggs, 58
Devilled Herrings, 73
Devil Sauce, 20
Dinde Farcie, 119
Dinde Truffée, 121
Diplomate à la Crème, 218
Diplomate with Custard, 218
Diplomate aux Fruits, 218
Duck, Braised, with Turnips, 122
Duck, Pâté of, 137
Duck, Ragoût of, 123
Duck, Roast, with Olives, 123

Duck, Wild, with Bitter Oranges, 123
Duck, Wild, with Port, 124
Dulce de Leche, 209

Eels Bourguignonne, 74
Eels, Stewed, in Claret, 74
Egg Custard à la Reine, 212
EGG DISHES, 49–59
Eggs in Aspic, 59
Eggs with Cheese, 57
Eggs en Cocotte, 55
Eggs, Devilled, 58
Eggs, Hard-Boiled, 58
Eggs, Hard-Boiled, with Mushrooms, 219
Eggs Landaise, 56
Eggs, Poached, 54
Eggs, Poached, Béarnaise, 55
Egg and Potato Salad, 31
Eggs, Scrambled, 55
Eggs, Scrambled, with Cheese, 56
Eggs, Scrambled, with Lobster, 56
Eggs, Scrambled, with Mushrooms, 56
Eggs, Scrambled, with Saffron, 56
Eggs, Scrambled, with Truffles, 56
Egg Seasoning, 185
Eggs, Stuffed, 59
Eggs, Stuffed, with Foie Gras, 58
Eggs Stuffed with Mushrooms, 32
Émincés de Mouton Sauce Piquante, 99
Endives, 160
Endive and Beet Salad, 188
Endives Flamande, 160
Endives with Gravy, 161
Endives au Jus, 161
Endives Meunière, 160
Endives Milanaise, 160
Endives Mornay, 160
Entrecôte Béarnaise, 84
Entrecôte au Beurre d'Anchois, 84
Entrecôte Bordelaise, 83
Entrecôte Maître d'Hotel, 84
Éperlans au Four, 73
Épinards à la Bourgeoise, 159
Épinards Florentine, 159
Épinards au Gratin, 158
Épinards au Jus, 157
Escalopes de Saumon Volga, 64

INDEX

Escalopes de Veau Chasseur, 93
Escalopes de Veau aux Concombres, 92
Escalopes de Veau à la Crème, 91
Escalopes de Veau aux Olives, 94
Escalopes de Veau Persillées, 91
Escalopes de Veau Sautées, 91
Escalopes de Veau Viennoise, 93
Escalopes de Veau Villageoise, 92
EXACTNESS IN RECIPES, 12–13
EXOTIC FOOD, 110

Faisan à la Creme, 127
Faisan Farci, 126
Faisan aux Pommes, 127
Farce aux Marrons, 170
Fat for Frying, 4
Fennel, 159
Fennel Sauce, 20
Fenouil, 159
Fèves, 157
Fèves au Lard, 157
Fèves, Purée de, 157
Figs, Baked, 205
Figs, Fresh, with Cream, 205
Figs, Fresh, Flambé, 205
Figues Flambées, 205
Figues au Four, 205
Filet de Bœuf Rôti, 86
Filet de Bœuf à la Russe, 83
Filets de Cabillaud Marinés, 72
Filets de Chevreuil Sautés, 131
Filets de Perdreaux aux Bigarades, 126
Filets de Sole Bonne Femme, 60
Filets de Sole à la Crème, 61
Filets de Sole Dorothée, 62
Fillet of Beef, Roast, 86
Fillet of Beef à la Russe, 83
Fillets of Beef, Small, with Foie Gras, 82
Fillets of Beef, Small, Grilled, 83
Fillets of Beef, Small, Madeira Sauce, 82
Fillets of Beef, Small, Sautéed, 81
Fines Herbes, xi, 12
Fish Bouillon, 47
FISH, COOKING OF, 3, 4, 8, 9, 60–80
Fish, Grilled, 60
Fish Salad, 193
Fish Soufflés, Small, 75
FISH SOUPS, 45–7

FLOWERS, EDIBLE, 185
Foie de Veau Braisé, 103
Foie de Veau Flamande, 103
Foie de Veau Sauté, 103
Foies de Volaille, Brochettes de, 118
Fonds d'Artichauts Florestan, 142
Fonds d'Artichauts à l'Orientale, 31
Fondue, 222
FOWLS, 3
Fraises au Bordeaux, 202
Fraises à la Crème au Kirsch, 203
Fraises Créole, 203
Fraises à l'Orange, 204
Fraises Pralinées, 203
Fraises Romanoff, 202
Fraises Xenia, 203
French Dressing, 185
Fricassée de Betteraves, 153
Frittata alla Genovese, 55
Fritters, 4, 11
Fruits, Beignets de, 206
Fruit with Brioche, 216
Fruits, Croûte aux, 216
Fruit Fritters, 206
FRYING, 3–4
Fumet, 8–9

Galantine, 137
Game Pâté, 139
Galimafrée, 98
Gallimaufry, 98
GAME, 2, 9
GAME, COOKING OF, 124–34
Game, Ragoût of, 130
Game Soup, 36
Garbure, 40
GARLIC, 186
Gâteau aux Amandes, 223
Gâteau Petit Duc, 217
Gâteau de Pommes, 224
Gâteau de Pommes de Terre, 176
Gelée de Coings, 227
Gelée de Pommes, 225
Genoese Omelette, 55
Germiny, Soup, 36
GIDE, ANDRÉ, 14
Gigot d'Agneau aux Pointes d'Asperges, 97
Gigot de Mouton Rôti, 99

[249]

Goose Landaise, Stuffed, 119
Goose, Preserved, 136
GOURMANDISING, 206
Grand Veneur Sauce, 23
Grapefruit Marmalade, 226
Gratin de Champignons, 167
Gratin de Pommes de Terre, 174
Gravy, 7
Green Salad, 186
Green Sauce, 19
Grilled Fish, 60
Grilled Herrings, 73
Grilled Legs of Chicken, 117
Grilled Red Mullet, 70
GRILLING, 3

Hachis Parmentier, 109
Half-Mourning Salad, 190
Ham Mousse, 102
Ham Omelette, 51
Ham with Parsley and Burgundy, 102
Ham on Toast, 220
Hard-boiled Eggs, 58
Hare, Fricassée of, Limousine, 132
Hare, Jugged, 131
Hare, Saddle of, Alsacienne, 132
Harengs en Diable, 73
Harengs Grillés, 73
Harengs Maître d'Hôtel, 73
Harengs Marinés, 73
Haricots Blancs, 156
Haricots Melangés, 156
Haricots Rouges, Bourguignonne, 156
Haricots Verts, 154
Haricots Verts Béarnaise, 155
Haricots Verts à la Créme, 155
Haricots Verts à la Landaise, 155
Herb Soup without Meat, 39
Herbs, Mixed, 12
Herb Vinegar, 12
Herrings, Devilled, 73
Herrings, Grilled, 73
Herrings Maître d'Hôtel, 73
Herrings, Marinated, 73
Hollandaise Sauce, 17
HOMARD, 75
Homard à l'Américaine, 76
Homard, Civet d', 77

Homard à la Créme, 75
Homard Thermidor, 77
HORS D'OÉUVRES, 26–32, 193
Horseradish Sauce, 19
Huîtres Bordelaise, 29
Huîtres au Gratin, 78

'IDEAL' DINNER, THE, 118
Italian Sauce with Crushed Walnuts, 21

JAMAICA, FISH IN, 60
Jambes de Poulet Grillés, 117
Jambon, Croûtes au, 220
Jambon Persillé Bourguignonne, 102
JAMS, 225–7
Julienne Soup, 43
Jus, xi, 7

Kebabs, 108

Laitances à la Grecque, 30
Laitues au Four, 161
Laitues au Jus, 161
LAMB, 2, 94–9
Lamb Cutlets Normande, 99
Lamb Kidneys on Skewers, 105
Lamb Kidneys with White Wine, 105
Lamb, Marinated Saddle of, 97
Lamb, Roast, with Asparagus, 97
Lamb, Roast, Béarnaise, 94
Lamb, Roast, Gratiné, 95
Lamb, Roast, with Orange Juice, 97
Lamb, Roast, Piémontaise, 96
Lamb, Roast, Princess, 96
Lamb, Roast, Provençale, 95
Lamb, Stuffed Saddle of, 97
Lamb with Vegetables, 98
Landaise Sauce, 20
LANGOUSTE, 75
Langouste Bretonne, 78
Langues de Chat, 224
Langue à l'Italienne, 107
Langue Savoyarde, 108
Langue de Veau Sauce Piquante, 107
Lapereau, Purée de, 133
Lapin à la Flamande, 133
Lapin Sauté, 133
Leeks, Chopped, 158

INDEX

Leek Salad, 192
Leek Soup, 43
LEISURE FOR MEALS, 190
Lentil Soup, 40
Lettuce, Baked, 161
Lettuce with Gravy, 161
Lettuce Mousse, 162
LIAISONS, 6
Lièvre, Civet de, 131
Lièvre, Civet de, Limousine, 132
LITERATURE AND COOKING, 14
Little Duke Cake, 217
Liver, Calf's, Braised, 103
Liver, Calf's, Flamande, 103
Liver, Calf's, Sautéed, 103
Livers, Chicken, Grilled, 118
LOBSTERS, 75
Lobster à l'Américaine, 76
Lobster in Cream with Brandy and Sherry, 75
Lobster Pancakes with Mushroom and Tomato Sauce, 76
Lobster Salad, 193
Lobster Stew, 77
Lobster Thermidor, 77
Loin of Veal Basquaise, 90
Longe de Veau Basquaise, 90
Lyonnaise Potatoes, 179

Macarons, 224
Macaroons, 224
Mackerel, Baked, 69
Mackerel Bretonne, 69
Mackerel Maître d'Hôtel, 69
Maître d'Hôtel Butter, 15
Maître d'Hôtel Sauce, 15
Maquereau Bretonne, 69
Maquereau au Four, 69
Maquereau Maître d'Hôtel, 69
MARENGO, 113
Marrons Blanchis, 170
Marrons, Farce au, 170
Marrons, Purée de, 170
Marrows, Baby, with Butter, 165
Marrow Jam, 226
Marrow, Stuffed, 164
Matelotes d'Anguilles, 74
MAYONNAISE, 76

Mayonnaise, 18
Meadow Salad, 189
MEAT, COOKING OF, 2-5, 81-109
Meat Sauce, 21
Melon, Compote of, 204
Melon Glacé, 205
Melon, Iced, 205
Melon en Surprise, 205
MENUS, 230-33
Minestrone, 43
Mixed Herbs, 12
Mixed Spice, 12
Mont Blanc, 212
Mornay Sauce, 16
MOULES, 79
Moules Béchamel, 79
Moules Marinière, 79
Moules Poulette, 79
Moules au Safran, 29
Moules Sautées, 80
Mousse au Chocolat, 212
Mousse de Jambon, 102
Mouusse de Laitue, 162
Mousseline Sauce, 18
Mouton, Gigot de, Rôti, 99
Mushrooms, Baked, 166
Mushrooms with Cheese, 167
Mushrooms with Cream, 165
Mushroom Fritters, 221
Mushrooms, Grilled, 167
Mushroom Omelette, 52
Mushrooms, Purée of, 168
Mushroom Salad, 191
Mushrooms Stuffed with Fish, 167
Mushrooms with White Wine, 165
MUSSELS, 79
Mussels Béchamel, 79
Mussels Marinière, 79
Mussel Pilaff, 29
Mussels Poulette, 79
Mussels with Saffron, 29
Mussels Sautéed, 80
Mussel Soup, 46
Mustard Sauce, 18
MUTTON, 2, 99-100
Mutton, Roast, 99
Mutton, Sauce Piquante, 99
Mutton with Vegetables, 100

[251]

Navarin Printanier, 100
Navets Braisés, 151
Navets, Purée de, 151
NEBUCHADNEZAR, 141
New World Salad, 189
Nouilles au Foie Gras, 184

Œufs en Aspic, 59
Œufs à la Belge, 57
Œufs Brouillés, 55
Œufs Brouillés aux Champignons, 56
Œufs Brouillés au Fromage, 56
Œufs Brouillés au Homard, 56
Œufs Brouillés au Safran, 56
Œufs Brouillés aux Truffes, 56
Œufs en Cocotte, 55
Œufs à la Diable, 58
Œufs Durs, 58
Œufs Durs aux Champignons, 219
Œufs Farcis, 59
Œufs Farcis aux Champignons, 32
Œufs Gratinés, 57
Œufs Landaise, 56
Œufs Mimosa, 58
Œufs Pochés, 54
Œufs Pochés Béarnaise, 55
Œufs à la Reine, 212
Oie, Confits d', 136
Oie Farcie Landaise, 119
Oignons à la Crème, 167
Oignon, Purée d', 166
OMELETTES 49–54, 55
Omelette aux Champignons, 52
Omelette, Cheese, 52
Omelette, Chicken Liver, 53
Omelette, Crab, 53
Omelette au Crabe, 53
Omelette, Cream, 54
Omelette à la Crème, 54
Omelette à l'Espagnole, 54
Omelette aux Fines Herbes, 51
Omelette aux Fleurs de Salsifis, 52
Omelette aux Foies de Volaille, 53
Omelette au Fromage, 52
Omelette au Jambon, 51
Omelette aux Laitances, 52
Omelette with Mixed Herbs, 51

Omelette Niçoise, 53
Omelette à l'Oignon, 51
Omelette aux Pommes de Terre, 52
Omelette, Potato, 52
Omelette au Rhum, 213
Omelette, Salsify Flower, 52
Omelette, Sweet, with Rum, 213
Onions with Cream, 167
Onion Omelette, 51
Onions, Purée of, 166
Onion Soup, 44
Oranges, Compote d', 204
Oranges with Rum, 204
Orange Soufflé, 211
ORIGINAL MEALS, 48
Oseille au Jus, 158
Oseille, Purée de, 158
Oysters Bordelaise, 29
Oysters au Gratin, 78
Oyster Soup, 48

Paella, 182
PAELLA, ORIGIN OF, 110
Pamplemousse, Confiture de, 226
PANCAKES, 11, 213–14
Pancakes, French, 213
Pancakes, French, Normande, 216
Pancakes, French, with Nuts, 216
Pancakes, Potato, 176
Pancakes à la Russe, 30
Pancakes, Russian, 30
Parisian Salad, 192
Parmesane, Croûte, 221
Partridge à l'Anglaise, 125
Partridge, Fillets of, with Bitter Oranges, 126
Partridge, Poached, 125
Partridge à la Russe, 125
Pastry, Puff, 11
Pastry, Shortcrust, 11
Pâté Feuilletée, 11
Pâté de Foie, 138
Pâté de Foie Gras, 138
Pâté de Lapin, 134
Pâté de Volaille, 137
Patisserie Croquante, 11
Peaches Barbara, 200
Peaches Marie Louise, 199

INDEX

Peaches in Syrup, 199
Pears, Baked, 198
Pears with Chocolate Sauce, 199
Pears Dijonnaise, 198
Pears Flambéed, 198
Pear Jam, 225
Peas with Bacon, 153
Peas à l'Étouffée, 154
Peas, French, 154
Peas, Purée of, 153
Pea Soup, 40
Peas and String Beans, 154
Pêches Barbara, 200
Pêches Marie Louise, 199
Pêches en Sirop, 199
Peppers and Cauliflower, Salad of, 189
Pepper Sauce, 22
Peppers, Stuffed, 183
Perdreau à l'Anglaise, 125
Perdreaux, Filets de, aux Bigarades, 126
Perdreau Poché, 125
Perdreau à la Russe, 125
PÉRIGORD, 121
Petits Filets de Bœuf Grillés, 83
Petit Pois au Lard, 153
Petit Salé, 135
Petits Soufflés de Poisson, 75
Pheasant with Apples, 127
Pheasant in Cream, 127
Pheasant Croquettes, 127
Pheasant, Stuffed, 126
Pilaff, 180
Pilaff of chicken, 181
Pilaff au Moules 29,
Pilaff, Mussel 29,
Pilaff au Poulet, 181
Piments Farcis, 182
Pineapple, Chilled, 201
Pineapple with Fruit, 200
Pineapple with Whipped Cream, 201
Pipérade, 57
Piquante Sauce, 22
PITFALLS, 12–13
Poireaux en Hachis, 158
Poires, Confiture de, 225
Poires Dijonnaise, 198
Poires Flambés, 198
Poires au Four, 198

Poires au Chocolat, 199
Pois à l'Étouffée, 154
Pois à la Française, 154
Pois Mélangés, 154
Pois Verts, Purée de, 153
Poisson Grillé, 60
Polish Sorrel Soup, 37
Pommes Balbec, 196
Pommes au Beurre, 196
Pommes à la Crème, 196
Pommes, Compote de, 197
Pommes, Compote de, à l'Ananas, 198
Pommes, Compote de, au Caramel, 197
Pommes, Compote de, au Marrons, 197
Pommes Flambées, 195
Pommes Frites Paysanne, 172
Pommes à la Neige, 197
Pommes Normande, 196
Pommes, Purée de, Soufflée, 174
Pommes Rissolées, 173
Pommes Rissolées au Menthe, 173
Pommes Paille, 173
Pommes Sautées, 173
Pommes Sicilienne, 174
Pommes de Terre Anna, 178
Pommes de Terre Armoricaine, 176
Pommes de Terre, Beignets de, 176
Pommes de Terre Boulangère, 180
Pommes de Terre Duchesse, 175
Pommes de Terre Farcies, 175
Pommes de Terre Fines Herbes, 180
Pommes de Terre Frites, 172
Pommes de Terre Frites aux Fonds d'Artichaux, 173
Pommes de Terre, Gratin de, 174
Pommes de Terre Gratinées, 175
Pommes de Terre Limousine, 178
Pommes de Terre Lyonnaise, 179
Pommes de Terre Nouvelles Maître d'Hôtel, 180
Pommes de Terre Parisienne, 177
Pommes de Terre, Purée de, 174
Pommes de Terre Savoyarde, 178
Pommes de Terre Soufflées, 179
Pommes de Terre Vosgienne, 177
Porc, Côtelettes de, Nontronnaise, 101
Porc Rôti Périgourdine, 100
PORK, 2, 3, 100–1

[253]

Pork Chops Nontronnaise, 101
Pork, Pickled, 135
Pork, Potted, 136, 137
Pork, Roast, Périgourdine, 100
Potage à la Bisque, 46
Potage aux Carottes, 39
Potage au Cresson, 43
Potage Germiny, 36
Potage aux Herbes Maigres, 39
Potage Julienne, 43
Potage aux Lentilles, 40
Potage de l'Oseille, 37
Potage Parmentier, 41
Potage aux Poireaux, 43
Potage Printanier, 38
Potage à la Purée de Gibier, 36
Potage à la Purée de Marrons, 39
Potage Saint-Germain, 40
POTATOES, 171
Potatoes Anna, 178
Potatoes Armoricaine, 176
Potatoes Boulangère, 180
Potato Cake, 176
Potatoes with Cheese, 175
Potato Croquettes with Cheese, 177
Potatoes Duchesse, 175
Potatoes, Fried, 172
Potatoes, Fried, with Artichoke Bottoms, 173
Potatoes, Fried, Paysanne, 172
Potato Fritters, 176
Potatoes, Gratin, 174
Potatoes Limousine, 178
Potatoes, Lyonnaise, 179
Potatoes, New, Maître d'Hôtel, 180
Potato Omelette, 52
Potatoes and Onions, Purée of, 180
Potato Pancakes, 176
Potatoes Parisienne, 177
Potatoes, Purée of, 174
Potatoes, Purée of, Soufflé, 174
Potatoes Rissolées, 173
Potatoes Rissolées with Mint, 173
Potato Salad with Anchovies, 191
Potatoes, Sauté, 173
Potatoes, Savoury, 180
Potatoes Savoyarde, 178
Potatoes Sicilienne, 174

Potatoes, Souffléed, 179
Potato Soup, 41
Potatoes, Straw, 173
Potatoes, Stuffed, 175
Potatoes Vosgienne, 177
Potiron Gratiné au Lard, 170
Potiron, Soufflé de, 171
Pousses de Navets, 151
POULARD, MME, 49
Poularde Albufera, 117
Poulet Béarnaise, 113
Poulet Biscayenne, 113
Poulet au Gratin, 115
Poulet Lyonnaise, 114
Poulet Portugaise, 112
Poulet Rôti, 110
Poulet Sauté Bourguignonne, 112
Poulet Sauté aux Capres, 111
Poulet Sauté à la Crème, 111
Poulet Sauté Marengo, 113
Poulette Sauce, 17
POULTRY, 110–24
Poussins Polonaise, 117
PRETENTIOUSNESS, 118
Printanier, Soup, 38
Pruneaux au Vin, 206
Prunes, Stewed, with Claret or Port, 206
Puff Pastry, 11
Pumpkin with Cheese and Bacon, 170
Pumpkin Jam, 226
Pumpkin Soufflé, 171
Purée de Champignons, 168
Purée de Ciboure, 38
Purée de Fèves, 157
Purée de Lapereau, 133
Purée de Marrons, 170
Purée de Navets, 151
Purée d'Oignon, 166
Purée d'Oseille, 158
Purée de Pois Verts, 153
Purée de Pommes Soufflée, 174
Purée de Pommes de Terre, 174
Purée Soubise, 180
Purée of Young Rabbit, 133

Quail with Grapes, 128
Quail, Ragoût of, 129
Quail, Stuffed, 128

INDEX

Quiche Lorraine, 222
Quince, Compote of, 206
Quince Jelly, 227

Rabbit à la Flamande, 133
Rabbit Pie, 134
Rabbit, Sautéed, 133
Rabbit, Young, Purée of, 133
Râble de Lièvre Alsacienne, 132
Ragoût of Beef, 87
Ragoût de Bœuf, 87
Ragoût de Canard, 123
Ragoût of Duck, 123
Ragoût of Game, 130
Raspberry Soufflé, 211
Ravigote Sauce, 24
Red Bean Soup, 44
Red Cabbage, Danish, 148
Red Cabbage Flamande, 148
Red Cabbage, Tyrolienne, 149
Red Mullet with Cream, 71
Red Mullet with Fennel, 71
Red Mullet, Grilled, 70
Red Mullets Marseillaise, 70
Red Mullets Riviera, 70
Rémoulade Sauce, 24
Rice with Peppers, 182
Rillettes, 137
Rillons, 136
Ris de Veau Braisé, 105
Risotto Milanese, 181
Riz au Piments, 182
ROASTING, 2
Roes à la Grecque, 30
Rognons d'Agneau en Brochettes, 105
Rognons d'Agneau Sautés au Vin Blanc, 105
Rognons de Veau Flambés, 104
Rognon de Veau Liegeoise, 104
Rognons de Veau Sautés, 104
Rollmops, 28
Rougets à la Crème, 71
Rougets au Fenouil, 71
Rougets Grillés, 70
Rougets Marseillaise, 70
Rougets Riviera, 70
Roux, xi, 6, 9
Russian Pancakes, 30
Russian Salad, 189

Sabayon Sauce, 25
Saddle of Lamb, Marinated, 97
Saddle of Lamb, Stuffed, 97
Saffron Sauce, 22
Salade Algérienne, 32
Salade d'Ananas, 200
Salade de Bœuf aux Harengs, 192
Salade Carmen, 188
Salade de Champignons, 191
Salade de Chou-Fleur, 189
Salade de Concombre, 31
Salade de Cresson, 187
Salade Demi-Deuil, 190
Salade d'Endives et Betteraves, 188
Salade de Figues, 205
Salade Flamande, 191
Salade Goncourt, 191
Salade d'Hiver, 191
Salade de Homard, 193
Salade au Lard avec Pissenlit, 187
Salade de Légumes, 189, 190
Salade Nouveau-Monde, 189
Salade d'Oranges, 204
Salade Parisienne, 192
Salade de Pissenlit aux Betteraves, 188
Salade de Poireaux, 192
Salade de Poisson, 193
Salade de Pommes aux Œufs Durs, 31
Salade de Pommes de Terre aux Anchois, 191
Salade de Poulet, 193
Salade Prairial, 189
Salade Russe, 189
Salade de Thon au Céleri, 28
Salade Verte, 186
SALADS, 185–94
Salad, Bacon and Dandelion, 187
Salad, Green, 186
Salad Seasonings, 185
Salad, Watercress, 187
Salmis de Gibier, 130
Salmon, Baked, Horseradish Sauce, 64
Salmon Bretonne, 64
Salmon, Escallops of, Volga, 64
Salmon Papillotes, 64
Salmon, Terrine of, 65
Salmon Trout Belle-Vue, 68
Salmon Trout with Cream, 67
Salsify Flower Omelette, 52

[255]

Salt Cod à la Vizcaina, 72
Sardine Butter, 29
SAUCES, 6, 9–10, 14–25
Sauce aux Airelles, 23
Sauce Alsacienne, 22
Sauce Béarnaise, 17–18
Sauce Béchamel, 9–10
Sauce au Beurre Blanc, 16
Sauce au Beurre Noir, 15
Sauce Bordelaise, 22
Sauces Brunes, 10
Sauce au Capres, 21
Sauce de Celeri, 19
Sauce Diable, 20
Sauce de Fenouil, 20
Sauce Grand Veneur, 23
Sauce Hollandaise, 17
Sauce à l'Indienne, 17
Sauce Landaise, 20
Sauce Maître d'Hôtel, 15
Sauce Mayonnaise, 18
Sauce Mornay, 16–17
Sauce Mousseline, 18
Sauce de Moutarde, 18
Sauce au Noix, 21
Sauce Périgueux, 115
Sauce Piquante, 22
Sauce Poivrade, 22
Sauce Poulette, 17
Sauce de Raifort, 19
Sauce Ravigote, 24
Sauce Rémoulade, 24
Sauce Sabayon, 25
Sauce au Safran, 22
Sauce Soubise, 22
Sauce Tartare, 19, 24
Sauce Tomate, 21
Sauce Verte, 19
Sauce Vinaigrette, 23–4
Sauce au Vin Blanc, 24
Saumon Bretonne, 64
Saumon au Four, Sauce de Raifort, 64
Saumon en Papillotes, 64
Sausage Meat, 120
Sauté of Beef, 86
SAVOURIES, 219–22
Savoury, Cheese and Asparagus, 221
Scallops, 78

Scrambled Eggs, 55
Scrambled Eggs with Cheese, 56
Scrambled Eggs with Lobster, 56
Scrambled Eggs with Mushrooms, 56
Scrambled Eggs with Saffron, 56
Scrambled Eggs with Truffles, 56
Seasonings, Salad, 185
Selle d'Agneau Farcie, 97
Selle d'Agneau Marinée, 97
Shortcrust Pastry, 11
Shrimp Fritters, 220
Shrimps, Potted, 28
Smelts, Baked, 73
Snow Apples, 197
Soles, Baked, 63
Sole, Filets de, à la Crème, 61
Sole, Fillets of, Bonne Femme, 60
Sole, Fillets of, Cream Sauce, 61
Sole, Fillets of, Dorothea, 62
Soles au Four, 63
Sole en Matelotte, 63
Sole Normande, 62
Sole au Vin Blanc, 63
Sole in White Wine, 63
Sorrel with Gravy, 158
Sorrel Omelette, 52
Sorrel, Purée of, 158
Sorrel Soup, 37
Sorrel Soup, Polish, 37
Soubise, Purée, 180
Soubise Sauce, 22
SOUFFLÉS, 210
Soufflé au Chocolat, 211
Soufflé de Framboises, 211
Soufflé d'Orange, 211
Soufflés de Poisson, Petits, 75
Soufflé de Pommes, 211
Soufflé de Potiron, 171
SOUPS, 34–48
Soupe au Choux, 41
Soupe de Concombre, 36
Soupe de Crabe, 47
Soupe d'Haricots Rouges, 44
Soupe Marinière, 46
Soupe à l'Oignon, 44
Soupe de Poisson à la Bretonne, 45
Soupe Polonaise, 37
Soupe Velours, 44

[256]

INDEX

Soupe des Vendanges, 35
Spaghetti with Foie Gras, 184
Spanish Milk Pudding, 209
Spanish Omelette, 54
Spice, Mixed, 12
Spinach à la Bourgeoise, 159
Spinach with Cheese, 158
Spinach Florentine, 159
Spinach with Gravy, 157
Spinach Soup, 37
SPIT, USE OF, 2
STANDARDIZATION, 219
Steak with Anchovy Butter, 84
Steak Béarnaise, 84
Steak Bordelaise, 83
Steak Maître d'Hôtel, 84
Stock, Concentrated, 8
Strawberries with Almonds, 203
Strawberries Créole, 203
Strawberries with Orange Juice, 204
Strawberries, Romanoff, 202
Strawberries with Whipped Cream and Kirsch, 203
Strawberries with Wine, 202
Strawberries Xenia, 203
Straw Potatoes, 173
Stuffed Beef, 84
Stuffing, Chestnut, 170
Suprêmes of Chicken Smitane, 116
Suprêmes of Chicken Strasbourgeoise, 116
Suprêmes de Volaille Smitane, 116
Suprêmes de Volaille Strasbourgeoise, 116
Stuffed Carp, 72
Stuffed Eggs, 59
Stuffed Eggs with Foie Gras, 58
Stuffed Trout Bourguignonne, 66
Sugo, 21
Suprêmes de Volaille à la Crème, 115
Sweetbread, Braised, 105
SWEETS, 195–218

Tartar Sauce, 19
Tartellettes Bretonnes, 223
TASTING, IMPORTANCE OF, 16
Terrine de Gibier, 139
Terrine of Salmon, 65
Terrine de Saumon, 65

Tête de Veau Vinaigrette, 107
Tomates, Confiture de, 227
Tomates Farcies, 165
Tomatoes and Beetroot, Salad of, 190
Tomato Jam, 227
Tomato Sauce, 21
Tomato Soup, Clear, 42
Tomatoes, Stuffed, 165
Tomato and Sweet Pepper Salad, 32
Tongue, Calf's, Braised, 107
Tongue à l'Italienne, 107
Tongue Savoyarde, 108
Tourain aux Tomates, 42
Tournedos au Foie Gras, 82
Tournedos Sauce Madère, 82
Tournedos Sautés, 81
Trout à l'Auvergnate, 65
Trout Grenobloise, 66
Trout, Stuffed, Bourguignonne, 66
Trout in White Wine, 66
Truffes au Lard, 170
Truffes au Xérès, 169
TRUFFLES 120
Truffles with Bacon, 170
Truffles in Sherry, 169
Truites à l'Auvergnate, 65
Truites Farcies à la Bourguignonne, 66
Truites Grenobloise, 66
Truite Saumonée en Belle-Vue, 68
Truite Saumonée à la Crème, 67
Truites au Vin Blanc, 66
Tuna Fish and Celery Salad, 28
Turbot, Baked, 69
Turbot au Four, 69
Turbot au Gratin, 69
Turkey Croquettes, 122
Turkey, Roast Stuffed, 119
Turkey with Truffles, 121
Turnips, Braised, 151
Turnips, Purée of, 151
Turnip Tops, 151

VEAL, 2, 3, 87–94
Veal, Braised Stuffed, 88
Veal Bretonne, 89
Veal Chops with Cheese, 90
Veal Chops in Cream, 90
Veal Chops en Papillotes, 91

[257]

Veal Cooked with Herbs in Paper, 87
Veal, Escallops of, Chasseur, 93
Veal, Escallops of, in Cream, 91
Veal, Escallops of, with Cucumber and Cream Sauce, 92
Veal, Escallops of, with Olives, 94
Veal, Escallops of, with Parsley, 91
Veal, Escallops of, Sautéed, 91
Veal, Escallops of, Viennoise, 93
Veal, Escallops of, Villageoise, 92
Veal Kidneys Flambés, 104
Veal Kidney Liégeoise, 104
Veal Kidneys Sautéed, 104
Veal, Loin of, Basquaise, 90
VEAL, MOCK, 81
Veal Niçoise, 88
Veal Olives Provençale, 94
Veal on Skewers, 108
Veal Stew, 89
Veau, Blanquette de, 89
Veau Bretonne, 89
Veau, Brochettes de, 108
Veau, Côtelettes de, à la Crème, 90
Veau, Côtelettes de, Gratinées, 90
Veau, Côtelettes de, en Papillotes, 91
Veau, Escalopes de, Chasseur, 93
Veau, Escalopes de, aux Concombres, 92
Veau, Escalopes de, à la Crème, 91
Veau, Escalopes de, aux Olives, 94
Veau, Escalopes de, Persillées, 91
Veau, Escalopes de, Sautées, 91
Veau, Escalopes de, Viennoise, 93
Veau, Escalopes de, Villageoise, 92
Veau Farci Braisé, 88
Veau au Fines Herbes, 87
Veau, Foie de, Braisé, 103
Veau, Foie de, Flamande, 103
Veau, Foie de, Sauté, 103
Veau, Langue de, Sauce Piquante, 107
Veau Niçoise, 88
Veau Olives Provençales, 94
Veau, Ris de, Braisé, 105
VEGETABLES, 140–84
Vegetables, Dried, 230
Vegetable Salad, 190
Velours, Soup, 44
Velouté, 10
Vendanges, Soup, 35
Venison, 130
Venison, Fillets of, Sautéed, 131
Vinaigrette Sauce, 23

WASTE, 25
Watercress Salad, 187
Watercress Soup, 43
White Butter Sauce, 16
White Wine Sauce, 24
WINE IN COOKING, 61
WINES, 229–30
Winter Salad, 191
Woodcock Flambée, 129